POSTMODERN FAIRY TALES

POSTMODERN FAIRY TALES

GENDER
AND
NARRATIVE
STRATEGIES

CRISTINA BACCHILEGA

UNIVERSITY OF PENNSYLVANIA PRESS

PHILADELPHIA

10 9 8 7 6 5 4 3 2 1

Published by
University of Pennsylvania Press
Philadelphia, Pennsylvania 19104-4011

Library of Congress Cataloging-in-Publication Data

Bacchilega, Cristina, 1955–
    Postmodern fairy tales : gender and narrative strategies
/ Cristina Bacchilega.
            p.   cm.
    Includes bibliographical references and index.
    ISBN 0-8122-3392-1 (alk. paper)
    ISBN 0-8122-1683-0 (pbk.: alk paper)
    1. Fairy tales—History and criticism. 2. Symbolism in
fairy tales. 3. Sex role—Folklore. 4. Women—Folklore.
I. Title.
GR550.B33 1997
398.2—dc21   96-49318
                                                    CIP

TO THE THREE **J**'s IN MY LIFE

AND

FOR **TELLA, KRISTIN,** AND **BRUNA**

CONTENTS

PREFACE

THIS BOOK BEGAN a number of years ago (inexplicably to her, even before Bruna was conceived) and I am grateful for the many institutional, textual, and personal encounters which transformed both me and the book on my long way to writing it.

I want to acknowledge the National Endowment for the Humanities for its financial support; the *Enzyklopädie des Märchens* for the competence and generosity with which it makes folktale materials accessible; the University of Indiana for access to its collections; the University of Hawai'i for its travel grants; and the University of Hawai'i at Manoa English Department for its instructional support, research reductions, and collegiality.

I greatly benefited from reading groups, especially women's. I owe the deepening of my interest in feminist studies to long, passionate discussions within the interdisciplinary Feminist Theory Group at the University of Hawai'i in the mid-eighties. And the intensity and integrity of the group experience which Aili Nenola generated in a wonderful "Rituals and Women's Studies" seminar during the 1993 Folklore Fellows' Summer School in Turku, Finland, was inspirational. I thank her; participants Silé De Cléir, Satu Gröndahl, Marja-Liisa Keinänen, and Mwîkali Kîeti; and Barbara Babcock, visiting faculty.

Responses, challenges, and questions I encountered in my teaching were invaluable. In particular, I thank Lori Amy, Linda Middleton, Cheryl Renfroe, and Russell Shitabata, now scholars in their own right; those who participated in my "Postmodern Wonders: Gender and Narrativity" seminar for the 1991 International Summer Institute for Semiotic and Structural Studies; Honors and graduate students at the University of Hawai'i whose growing enthusiasm over the years led me further into the uncanny territory of postmodern fairy tales; and the exceptionally engaged group of graduate students in my 1996 "Folklore and Literature" seminar.

My profound thanks to those who nurtured in its *incipit* my interest in the fairy tale's relation to modern literature: Mario Materassi, Paola Cabibbo, Susan Strehle, William Spanos, and especially W.F.H. Nicolaisen, whose interdisciplinary open-mindedness, intellectual rigor, and personal warmth inspired me to stick with folkloristics. Later on, organized panels and informal discussions at the meetings of the American Folklore Society and the International Society for Folk Research provided me with the much-needed opportunity for intellectual exchange in the specific area of folklore and literature. Ruth S. Bottigheimer, Lee Haring, Galit Hasan-Rokem, Steven Swann Jones, Kathleen Manley, Ulrich Marzolph, Margaret A. Mills, Cathy Lynn Preston, Danielle Roemer, Mark Workman, and Jack Zipes have been especially challenging interlocutors over the years through correspondence, collaboration and discussion at conferences, and most of all their own scholarship.

Nell Altizer, Mieke Bal, Morgan Blair, members of the Bamboo Ridge Study Group, the late Joseph K. Chadwick, Luisa Del Giudice, Arnold Edelstein, Miriam Fuchs, Candace Fujikane, Donatella Izzo, Judith Kellogg, Glenn Man, Kristin McAndrews, Marisa Milani, Kathy Phillips, John Rieder, Susan Schultz, Ravi Palat, Stefano Tani, Valerie Wayne, Carmen Wickramagamage and Rob Wilson offered references, useful comments, and encouragement at various stages of the project. John Rieder, really, at every stage. I am particularly indebted to Craig Howes for his careful reading of a complete draft of the book and to the anonymous readers of the manuscript for their generous assessment and helpful suggestions. I also thank Patricia Smith, Alison Anderson, and Kym Silvasy at the University of Pennsylvania Press for their guidance and efficiency, so splendidly combined with caring, and the copyeditor, Christina Sharpe, for her minute attention to the text. Last but not least, Corinna Sargood for the "Little Red Riding Hood" illustration which visually embodies the transformative core of my argument in this book and also performs personal magic for me.

When I was very young, four or five, my favorite story was "Little Red Riding Hood": I would ask for it over and over again; protest when my mother would skip a detail in her retelling or change a

word; and wear my bright red coat and hat with an air of self-pos-
session. My mother and I did not know at the time that we were re-
enacting the well-known scene of storytelling, both of us
predictably and yet with unintentional effects remaking the tale. I
do not recall the ending of this fairy tale as told to me then, but
the image of the girl has stayed with me and has taken different
forms. I wish to thank my mother, Shanta, who cultivated a passion
for words and stories in me as well as the confidence that transforms life's points of arrival into adventurous departures. And my
father, Giuseppe, a man of few words and fewer stories but strong
affection and vivid dreams, who must have known that those
words, the reading and writing he recognized as my own ambition,
would take me far away (though Hawai'i came as a surprise to all),
and yet never tried to stop me. *Grazie, con affetto, a tutti e due, e sem-
pre pensando a Jenny.*

A section of "'Writing' and 'Voice': The Articulations of Gender
in Folklore and Literature" in *Folklore, Literature, and Cultural Theory: Collected Essays,* edited by Cathy Lynn Preston (New York: Garland, 1995) is reprinted in Chapter One. Chapter Two is a
substantial revision of "Cracking the Mirror: Three Re-Visions of
'Snow White'" *boundary 2* 15, 3 (Spring/Fall 1988): 1–25. And part
of the Epilogue was published as "Domestic Uses of the Fairy Tale"
in *Literature & Hawaii's Children: Stories As Bridges to Many Realms,
1992 Proceedings,* edited by Judith Kellogg and Jesse Crisler (Honolulu: Literature and Hawaii's Children, 1994), 37–44.

1

PERFORMING WONDERS:

POSTMODERN REVISIONS OF FAIRY TALES

We tell stories because, in order to cope with the present and to face the future, we have to create the past, both as time and space, through narrating it. —W.F.H. NICOLAISEN

Story demands sadism, depends on making something happen, forcing a change in another person, a battle of will and strength, victory/defeat, all occurring in a linear time with a beginning and an end.

—TERESA DE LAURETIS (revising Laura Mulvey)

ABUNDANCE, RATHER THAN LACK, motivates this study. Reproduced in a variety of discourses, fairy tales in the second half of the twentieth century have enjoyed an explosive popularity in North America and Western Europe. While many adults may not remember, and many children may not have been exposed to versions of "Snow White" or "Beauty and the Beast" other than Disney's, we nevertheless respond to stereotyped and institutionalized fragments of these narratives sufficiently for them to be good bait in jokes, commercials, songs, cartoons, and other elements of popular and consumer culture. Most visible as entertainment for children, whether in the form of bedtime-stories or of games and props marketed in conjunction with a movie or TV series, fairy tales also play a role in education. Not only are children encouraged to retell or dramatize them in schools, but college students encounter them again in across-the-curriculum readers and in courses on children's literature and folklore. This legitimizing of the genre has extended to several psychotherapeutical approaches and contexts. Bruno Bettelheim's Freudian study *The Uses of Enchantment* is still a landmark, though critically revisited; professional storytellers have been instrumental in helping abused children move beyond a burdened-by-guilt stage; and Jungian popularizers, as Gertrud Mueller Nelson in her hopeful *Here All Dwell Free* and Robert Bly in his mythifying *Iron John: A Book About Men*, have enlisted fairy tales in their best-seller projects of healing the wounded feminine *and* masculine.[1] Creative writers seem equally inspired by the fairy tale, which provides them with well-known material pliable to political, erotic, or narrative manipulation. Belittled, yet pervasive and institutionalized, fairy tales are thus produced and consumed to accomplish a variety of social functions in multiple contexts and in more or less explicitly ideological ways.

Thinking of the fairy tale predominantly as children's literature, or even as "literature of childhood," cannot accommodate this proliferation of uses and meanings. The fairy tale "cannot be defined one-dimensionally," and in any case, "adults have always read, censored, approved, and distributed the so-called fairy tales for children" (Zipes, "Changing Function" 28 and 23). While keeping in mind the history of the fairy tale as literature for children, it is within the adjacent realms of folklore and literature that I intend to seek a clearer understanding of contemporary transformations of fairy tales. Though not the only legitimate mode of inquiry, this approach is historically and generically sound. Why? Because the "classic" fairy tale is a *literary* appropriation of the older folk tale, an appropriation which nevertheless continues to exhibit and reproduce some *folkloric* features. As a "borderline" or transitional genre, it bears the traces of orality, folkloric tradition, and socio-cultural performance, even when it is edited as literature for children or it is marketed with little respect for its history and materiality. And conversely, even when it claims to be folklore, the fairy tale is shaped by literary traditions with different social uses and users.

The context of folklore and literature, and more specifically the more limited field of folk and literary narrative, is also especially productive to the analysis of those transformations found in the privileged, though not isolated, concern of this book—postmodern literary texts for adults.[2] Throughout the nineteenth and twentieth centuries, literary authors have exploited the fairy tale in a variety of ways. To cite only a few of the most prominent examples, the fairy tale serves as structuring device for Charlotte Brontë in *Jane Eyre* and William Faulkner in *Absalom, Absalom!* as an explicitly ideological theme for Charles Dickens in *Hard Times* and Anne Sexton in *Transformations,* or as an expectation-setting allusion for Henry James in *What Maisie Knew* and for Italo Calvino in his early works, starting with *Il sentiero dei nidi di ragno.* Literary authors such as Johann Wolfgang von Goethe in "The Fairy Tale" or George MacDonald in "The Day Boy and the Night Girl" have also written their own "original" fairy tales or *Kunstmärchen*, not necessarily for children. In works like Anatole France's "The Seven Wives of Bluebeard," they have rewritten specific classic fairy tales to advance individual interpretations of them. And modern feminist writers from Olga Broumas to Fay Weldon have engaged the "inherited" tradition of fairy tales to "refuse to obey their authority by revising and appropriating them" (Walker 83).[3] Recent studies like *Theorizing Folklore: Toward New Perspectives on the Politics of Culture* (*Western Folklore*'s 1993 special issue edited by Charles Briggs and Amy Shuman) and *Folklore, Literature, and Cultural Theory: Collected Essays* (edited by Cathy Lynn Preston, 1995) have provided theoretical frameworks for folklorists to rethink not only the multiple roles of tradition within culture today, but to view transformations within an interdisciplinary context which does not necessarily require a defense of the integrity and autonomy of scholarly fields.[4] An informed knowledge of both folklore *and* literature can help us to question and redefine their borders, to articulate how narrative rules are (re)produced; such an approach also has wide-ranging implications for an understanding of literary texts within a broader cultural dynamics—an understanding which I would define as semiotic.

Literary and non-literary contemporary narratives which rewrite and revise "classic" fairy tales are the specific objects of this study, whether Margaret Atwood's "Bluebeard's Egg" or the TV-series *Beauty and the Beast.* When reading these texts I want to address—within a critically semiotic understanding of folklore and literature, and culture in general—several problems related to how fairy tale materials are selected, appropriated, and transformed. Three questions direct my efforts. What kinds of images of *woman* and *story* do these rewritings/ revisions project? What narrative mechanisms support these images? And finally which ideologies of the subject underlie these images? In short, this book explores the production of gender, in relation to narrativity and subjectivity, in classic fairy tales as re-envisioned in late twentieth-century literature and media for adults.

To pursue this feminist and narratological project, I will have to struggle at times with still larger questions. How can we distinguish among the many ideological and narrative manipulations these transformations operate? How are the objectives and functions of contemporary transformations different, if at all, from earlier ones? And can we establish a typology of contemporary fairy tale transformations which would move towards a critical systematizing of their proliferation and yet resist closed classification? Since this interdisciplinary perspective draws on the study of the fairy tale, folklore and literature, and of feminism and postmodernism, the rest of this chapter will outline my perspective on these fields and their debates, thus supplying a frame for my ensuing discussion of contemporary tales of magic. In the process, I will also explain how I am using such terms as "tale of magic" or "fairy tale"; narrativity, performance, and performativity; and subjectivity and postmodernism.

THE TALE OF MAGIC AND ITS MIRRORS

So it is my turn to tell stories—stories about stories, or "theories," as we call them. And since nobody, from psychologists and historians to parents and artists, feels any qualms about defining and discussing fairy tales, I will follow tradition here and tell my own version of the "fairy tale" story.

The fairy tale's magic fulfills multiple desires. As literature for children, fairy tales offer symbolically powerful scenarios and options, in which seemingly unpromising heroes succeed in solving some problems for modern children. These narratives set the socially acceptable boundaries for such scenarios and options, thus serving, more often than not, the civilizing aspirations of adults. *Dulce et utile*: fiction at its most successful, at the height of its magic. As a hybrid or transitional genre, the fairy tale also magically grants writers/tellers and readers/listeners access to the collective, if fictionalized past of social communing, an access that allows for an apparently limitless, highly idiosyncratic re-creation of that "once there was." Though it calls up old-time wisdom, the fairy tale grants individuals the freedom to play with this gift, to dismiss it as children's fantasy. And for girls and women, in particular, the fairy tale's magic has assumed the contradictory form of being both a spiritual enclave supported by old wives' wisdom and an exquisitely glittery feminine kingdom. Regardless of the group, though, the fairy tale still proves to be everyone's story, making magic for all.[5]

Jack Zipes, Ruth B. Bottigheimer, Maria Tatar, and other critics have taught us the value of breaking this magic spell. Looking with Dorothy behind the curtain at Oz to investigate the mechanisms of enchantment, their research has revealed how the workings of this magic, however benevolent, rely on privilege and repression. Clever and industrious boys, dependent and hard-working girls, and well-behaved "normal" children in general—such products demonstrate how the fairy tale's magic act requires not only social violence and appropriation but a careful balance of threats and rewards.[6] My own thinking about this critical disenchantment has taken two directions: an attempt to place this double-edged magic more firmly within a folklore and literature frame; and a study of the fairy tale's narrative construction of magic as "natural," with an emphasis on the gendered implications for women.

From *Breaking the Magic Spell* (1979) to *Spells of Enchantment* (1992) and, most recently, in *Fairy Tale as Myth/Myth as Fairy Tale* (1994), Jack Zipes has relentlessly focused our critical attention on the changing social functions of fairy tales in Europe and the United States, identifying the ideologically narrow and repressive uses the fairy tale has been put to, but also stressing its emancipatory impulses. I have no quarrels with Zipes's much needed genealogy or social history of the European fairy tale; however, I would like to take his discussion of the relationship between folk and fairy tales in a somewhat different direction. In *Breaking the Magic Spell*, where Zipes affirms the continuity between folk and fairy tales, he complains that the two are often confused nowadays. This is not a contradiction, but an historically grounded distinction which demands that narrative be understood within specific social contexts. A tale told by peasants in Medieval Europe simply does not express the same desires or values as the "same" tale written by a Romantic German poet, and since narratives often symbolize different needs and aspirations for different social groups, Zipes follows in August Nitschke's steps, by arguing that, at different times and in different contexts, the "same" fairy tales support dominant ideologies or articulate a desire for change. In his more recent "The Changing Function of the Fairy Tale" (1988), Zipes focuses more closely on the continuity between the "wonder folk

tale, often called the *Zaubermärchen* or the magic tale" (7) and the
fairy tale, to reveal their multiple and elaborate ideological functions. While both genres "awaken our regard for the miraculous
condition of life" (11), both have also served conservative and
emancipatory purposes.

Yes, folk and fairy tales are ideologically variable desire machines.[7] And certainly Zipes's social history provides the necessary
backdrop for my own inquiry. When I reflect on the continuity between the "wonder folk tale" and the fairy tale, I find I want to emphasize the ideological paradox or "trick" which in its multiple
performances informs both: that magic which seeks to conceal the
struggling interests which produce it. Zipes's social history of the
fairy tale contains a somewhat devolutionary premise, arising at
least in part from his strong sympathy for the needs of the socially
oppressed. In the middle ages, folk tales served *more* of an emancipatory function because they expressed the problems and desires
of the underprivileged; in modern times, the fairy tale has more
often than not been "instrumentalized" to support bourgeois
and/or conservative interests. My point is that the tale of magic
within a folk context was not and cannot be simply liberatory because within its specific community it would also, to some degree,
rely on and reinforce social norms. In describing this process,
Zipes rightly points out that the printing and privatization of the
fairy tale "violated the communal aspects of the folk tale" (*Fairy
Tales as Myth* 13), since in an oral context "the voice of the narrator was known. The tale came directly from common experiences
and beliefs. Told in person, directly, face to face, [tales] were altered as the beliefs and behaviors of the members of a particular
group changed" (10). Even such face to face, community-cen-
tered interaction, however, can hardly be imagined as operating
outside of established hierarchies, systems of authority, or common assumptions. Though we may not think of them as folkloric
"preliminary censorship," tradition and consensus go together,
and it is their dynamic interaction with an "innovative" or subversive impulse that constitutes folk narratives. As folk and fairy tale,
the tale of magic produces wonder precisely through its seduc-
tively concealed exploitation of the conflict between its *normative*
function, which capitalizes on the comforts of consensus, and its
subversive wonder, which magnifies the powers of transformation.[8]

What interests me, then, is how the narrative construction and manipulation of the tale of magic contribute to making different ideological effects possible within specific historical and social contexts.

Of course, most narratives seek to resolve their contradictions. Even those literary narratives which celebrate paradox in the name of the avantgarde still rely on some norms and reproduce some minimal consensus simply to be intelligible. What distinguishes the tale of magic or fairy tale as a genre, however, is its effort to conceal its "work" systematically—to naturalize its artifice, to make everything so clear that it works magic, no questions asked. As Jack Zipes notes, the fairy tale operates as "myth" par excellence.[9] This quality itself provokes different responses. Max Lüthi's stylistic portrait of the European fairy tale describes its magic precisely in these terms, but from within an essentialist framework that projects a set of unchangeable humanistic values onto these narratives. Lüthi's celebration of the fairy tale's enchantment as an artistic achievement is, however, precisely the spell that Zipes and others have, in an anti-universalizing and historicizing move, struggled to break. My own wish is to make visible the narrative construction of this magic through a *narratological* effort to name its paradoxes and articulate its variable ideological effects. To break the magic spell, we must learn to recognize it as a spell that can be unmade.

Adults and children, rich and poor, storytellers and literary artists, boys and girls, social groups and individuals. . . . If the fairy tale seduces all even as it articulates or represses their conflicting interests, how does it do so? And in name of whose desire? As Teresa de Lauretis notes, "the object of narrative theory," semiotically speaking, "is not . . . narrative but narrativity; not so much the structure of narrative . . . as its works and effects." For feminist theory, this turn to narrativity means examining the relationship of narrative to desire, and "rereading . . . sacred texts against the passionate urging of a different question, a different practice, and a different desire" (*Alice Doesn't* 107). What happens, then, if we articulate what Max Lüthi calls the "one-dimensionality" and the "universal interconnection" of the fairy tale with "a different desire"? We know that in folk and fairy tales the hero is neither frightened nor surprised when encountering the otherworld, receiving magic gifts, holding conversations with animals, or experiencing miraculous transformations.[10] The numinous is artfully made to appear natural. Similarly, isolation from a specific community allows the hero to form "all-encompassing interrelationships" (Lüthi, *European Folktale* 54), and the narrative to exercise its stylistic unity. What would require explaining in a culturally-grounded legend, for instance, is not mysterious or accidental, but natural in the tale of magic. These and other features of abstract style produce that "effortlessness" which Mircea Eliade notes when defining the folktale as "a lighthearted doublet of myth and initiation rite" (Lüthi, *European Folktale* 116).[11] Since consenting to the rules of one's community is represented as a natural process, the stylistic and thematic projects of the tale of magic, then, are the same: to disguise its artifice and its social project.[12]

This disguise, however, seems doubly persuasive and dangerous when assumed by tales centering upon the experiences of women. That long tradition of representing woman both as nature and as concealed artifice contributes to the success and power of such images in the tale of magic. As much anthropological and historical research has shown, women are commonly "identified as being closer to nature than to culture," which in a patriarchal system makes them "symbolic of an inferior, intermediate order of being" (Lerner 25). Simone de Beauvoir wrote that as man represents her, woman incarnates his dream: "she is the wished-for intermediary between nature, the stranger to man, and the fellow being who is too closely identical" and therefore competitive and possibly hostile (de Beauvoir 172). This association of woman with nature paradoxically produces the artifice of "femininity," both as naturalizing make-up and as representations of womanly "essence." To take an extreme case, when Snow White is presented as a "natural" woman, the artful construction of her image encourages thinking of her and other stereotypical heroines in pre-cultural, unchangeable terms. By showcasing "women" and making them disappear at the same time, the fairy tale thus transforms us/them into man-made constructs of "Woman."

Considering that questioning the fairy tale's magic has been a feminist project for several decades at least, with its own several phases and problematics, we fortunately do not need to reject fairy tales as inherently sexist narratives which offer "narrow and damaging role-models for young readers" (Stone 229).[13] Feminists can view the fairy tale as a powerful discourse which produces representations of gender—a "technology of gender," for de Lauretis; and studying the mechanisms of such a production can highlight the dynamic differences and complex interdependence between "Woman" in fairy tales and "women" storytellers/writers and listeners/readers. Marina Warner's 1994 *From the Beast to the Blonde*, for instance, takes up this challenge by focusing on "images" of women in classic fairy tales, especially the symbols of beauty and blondeness, "in the light of the tellers' position and interests" as these "practitioners"—and so many have been women—negotiate the strategies of gossip and silence within their specific historical and social contexts (xxiv). Within a feminist frame that critically recognizes the power of "magic," fairy tales are sites of competing, historically and socially framed desires. These narratives continue to play a privileged role in the production of gender, and as such are deconstructed and reconstructed in a variety of ways which this book seeks to analyze.

In its multiple retellings, the fairy tale is that variable and "in-between" image where folklore and literature, community and individual, consensus and enterprise, children and adults, Woman and women, face and reflect (on) each other. As I see it, the tale of magic's controlling metaphor is the *magic mirror*, because it conflates mimesis (reflection), refraction (varying desires), and framing (artifice).[14] My readings of postmodern tales of magic will focus on how they reproduce these mirror images while at the same time they make the mirroring visible to the point of transforming its effects. Each chapter will address a specific narratological aspect of this doubling strategy: narrative frame for "Snow White," voice in "Little Red Riding Hood," focalization for "Beauty and the Beast," and agency in "Bluebeard."

Given my way of telling this story, it is no accident that in post-Lacanian theories the mirror is the site for the production of the "subject."[15]

FOLKLORE, SEMIOTICS, AND THE SUBJECT

Richard Bauman's 1982 essay, "Conceptions of Folklore in the Development of Literary Semiotics," presents itself as a "critical evaluation by an American folklorist of the folkloric foundation" of studies central to the development of semiotic theory—specifically the works of Vladimir Propp, Petr Bogatyrëv, Roman Jakobson, and Mikhail Bakhtin. "What about their work in *folklore* is likely to be productive for folklorists (and others) currently turning to them as semioticians?" Bauman asks (1), and then goes on to examine how their remarks on folklore articulate with what folklorists believe today. He finds much of value: Propp's articulation of the fabula/story relationship; Bogatyrëv's and Jakobson's understanding of folklore as a system; Bogatyrëv's focus on "function" as a dynamic variable affected by improvisation as well as tradition; and Bakhtin's truly ethnographic approach in *Rabelais and His World*. For Bauman, the work of Bogatyrëv, Jakobson, and Bakhtin in fact converges with the contemporary approach to folklore he identifies with: the ethnography of performance, which builds on the ethnography of speaking to study the conventions of performance as *parole* in a specific cultural system.

Bauman concludes by suggesting "some of the ways in which the work of current folklorists goes beyond the work of the founders . . . , charting directions that should be of interest to students of the semiotics of literature both oral *and* written" (13). Bogatyrëv and Jakobson, for instance, emphasized the conservative function of folklore as shaped by tradition and communal censorship. However, ethnographers of performance who study folklore within specific social situations see folklore texts as "emergent, the product of the complex interplay of expressive resources, social goals, individual competence, community ground rules for performance, and culturally defined event structures" (Bauman, "Conceptions of Folklore" 13–14). This event-centered perspective not only moves beyond earlier abstract conceptualizations of censorship in folklore, but also makes possible the study of how performers manipulate available communicative functions to achieve specific and varying social ends, and reinforces an intertextual interpretation of oral and written texts as well. Or as Bauman puts this last point, "to identify a particular oral text as traditional is to highlight its place in a web of intertextuality that, far from placing it apart from written literature, unites it with written literature still more firmly" (16).

The implications of the theoretical itinerary traced by Bauman are wide-ranging (and I am not evaluating here the trajectory that his own research has taken more recently). To begin with, semioticians and folklorists no longer contrast folklore and literature by invoking the Saussurian distinction of *langue* and *parole*, they choose instead to examine the socially situated dynamics of tradition and creativity or performance in both.[16] Viewed in this light, individual performers deserve the same attention as artists that individual authors already receive. Second, an event-centered perspective on folklore runs parallel to the triadic sign-event first conceptualized by Charles Peirce and later by Umberto Eco and Thomas Sebeok, all of whom emphasize the materiality and the socially-variable functions of a sign. Third, studying verbal art in both folklore and literature raises questions about the text's relationship to other texts, the strategies adopted when communicating with specific audiences within given generic and social parameters, and the social functions or ideological effects of these strategies. And finally, Bauman's account suggests that the study of folklore *in* literature has become an integral part of the study of folklore *and* literature, simply because these two artistic forms of communication systematically interact and transform each other.[17]

Semiotics and folkloristics, folklore and literature. I am tempted here to say "and they lived happily ever after," but not so long as nagging questions remain. Is communication the *primary* function of verbal art and of language in general? And do a performer's or author's strategies necessarily represent a unified, immediate expression of that individual's ideology or social practice? Something is lacking: that sustained concern with the subject, as socially and symbolically constituted in ways that question the primacy of consciousness and experience, which informs much contemporary criticism. By stretching its own post-structuralism or "post-Saussurianism"[18] to accommodate the problematics of postmodernity, semiotics has generated polymorphous intellectuals like Roland Barthes and Julia Kristeva, and also produced the related but distinct species of grammatologists. Optimistically satisfied with the fullness of presence projected by actual events, performers, and audiences, however, many folklorists have resisted reflecting on the subject, preferring to go on celebrating the creative individual.[19] More than a decade after Bauman's essay appeared, I find myself posing a qualified version of his question: if my interest in oral and written narrative extends to the issue of subjectivity, is there still something to be gained in connecting semiotics with folklore and literature?

I believe there still is, but only if the semiotic emphasis on the communicative functions of language can be modified by reflecting on its symbolic functions, and if semiotic tools can be employed critically rather than descriptively. The methodological framework of this book is therefore informed by a compositely deconstructive approach to language, which draws on Jacques Derrida and Hélène Cixous; my framework is also informed by Mieke Bal's critical narratology of semiotic descent. Deconstruction displaces the speech-centeredness of folkloric and generally verbal signs, a shift I find theoretically enabling when reaching for problems of ideology and gender. As for narratology, it establishes itself as an analytical tool precisely by prioritizing the study of "narrative subjectivity," which Bal defines as a network rather than an unquestionable identity.[20]

Appropriating Derrida's notion of writing or *écriture* allows me to situate the tradition/performance opposition differently. As already noted, performance-oriented folklorists have strengthened the ties between folklore and literature by treating the speaking subject as an individual artist, the center of a communicative and social network. Yet, while privileging an event or performance might even lead to a reversal of the elitist opposition of written and oral literature,[21] structurally a hierarchy is left intact.[22] Displacing this hierarchy will require reconsidering more fully that the spoken word, always in an intra-subjective form, is not unmediated, even though the signifier's evanescence in speech and the speaker's physical presence may contribute to an impression of the direct presence of thought. As conceptualized by Derrida, "writing" locates the continuity of the written and the oral in *mediated* meanings and *absence*—features traditionally identified with writing to brand it as a poor substitute for the direct fullness of speech.[23] Communication is inevitably distorted representation, and the symbolic function of speech, its supplemental materiality, is made intelligible as a symptom of already mediated signification and absence. Thus, the speaker or tale-teller cannot be considered the immediate or unified source of meaning, and the subject both *of* language and *in* language cannot simply be viewed as an active situational variable, but as problematic.

Redefining "writing" along these lines shifts attention from communication to representation, and deconstructs the independent subject who speaks his own words and gives them meaning through his presence. Hélène Cixous exposes this subject as a specifically patriarchal one which privileges speech not only over writing, but over "voice" as well. Like Derrida, she challenges the primacy of speech over writing, but by affirming a feminine "voice" Cixous also confronts patriarchal deconstruction. As I read Cixous, this "voice" is neither the essentializing expression of what it is to be a woman, nor is it something a woman can "find" and recognize as her "own" in some purely liberatory explosion of authenticity. As Cixous describes it, the feminine "voice" claims a complex affinity with writing and a material connection with the body, without returning us to the unified subject. "Writing," she chants, is "the passageway, the entrance, the exit, the dwelling of the other in me"; this "peopling gives neither rest nor security, always disturbs the relationship to 'reality,' produces an uncertainty that gets in the way of the subject's socialization" (*The Newly Born Woman* 85–86). Working analogously, the marginalized feminine "voice" turns into privileged access to such writing: "Listen to woman speak in a gathering (if she is not painfully out of breath): she doesn't 'speak,' she throws her trembling body in the air. . . . She exposes herself. . . . She inscribes what she is saying because she does not deny unconscious drives the unmanageable part they play in speech" (92). Both "writing" and "voice" are thus "the experience of not-me within me" (85), and represent a different subjectivity, which since it is not *propre* (as both "own" and "proper") does not rely on the authority of presence.

But both "writing" and "voice" are also material processes: here, the emphasis is on the body, the involvement of its materiality. For "voice," in particular, this involvement translates into listening for and producing song, making sounds reverberate as such in what we otherwise hear as speech, and playing out metaphors to release the "living word" which "can be felt full of flesh."[24] In this way, Cixous explicitly brings the question of gender to bear on the relationship between writing and orality,[25] furthering a deconstructive project, yet seeking to voice the perspective of women. By affirming the reciprocal implication of "writing" and "voice" (which are not identical to these terms in their common usage), she exposes speech as a patriarchal illusion of self-presence and self-sameness from which women should free themselves, especially since we/they have experienced this fiction only vicariously through men or in fragments. A plurality of variously empowered and disempowered voices now displaces (rather than opposes) the masculine speaker and constitutes the practice of "writing."

This continuity between writing and voice is not, however, free of struggle. Many of the more ideologically powerful voices in "writing" reinforce patriarchal structures, just as much writing, literary or otherwise, models itself on the "self-same" fiction of speech, preferring not to "admit there is another." Cixous offers a way into the struggle. By privileging "voice," she peoples language, thus making Derrida's "writing" less overbearing and more diversified from the perspective of those who are othered by it. In the specific analysis of a folk or literary narrative, when the objective is not to explain in a generally philosophical framework how all narratives partake of "writing" as polyvalence and absence, Cixous's peopling of language helps us articulate the ideological and semantic struggles at work in the narrative. And finally, the displacement of speech through "voice" emphasizes the material, bodily aspect of language—a questioning of the patriarchal body/mind split with important repercussions for the study of women's/feminine verbal narratives in particular, since it encourages a reading *and* writing of the body. Writing, then, is holding a mirror to our bodies (and subjectivities) so as to transform into symbols those bodily symptoms which want to speak but which on their own are iconic rather than verbal signs.[26]

To clarify the interplay between paradigms I've been discussing, the table in Figure 1 represents "tradition" and "performance" in relation to the structuralist *langue* and *parole* and to the deconstructive "writing" and "voice." These paradigms do not simply replace one another in an evolutionary narrative; rather, as they interrogate one another, their function changes without being nullified. For instance, "tradition and performance" does not impose a conservative distinction between folklore and literature, but seeks to articulate variables within both, while "writing" and "voice" bring to the forefront of that articulation the problematics of an ideologically-constructed, symbolically-produced, and gendered subjectivity. I am not, therefore, replacing the long-estab-

lished paradigm of "tradition and performance" with imported
non-folkloristic concepts,[27] but I am making visible the ideological
implications of this couple, contesting and thereby transforming it
by naming what it represses—first, symbolic representation, of
which the subject is a product rather than the source; and second,
the gendered pluralization of voice as an intra-subjective site of
struggle.

This ideological framing of "tradition and performance" informs my understanding of folklore and literature, and explains

Figure 1.

Approach to Folklore & Literature	Opposition	Key Variable
Structuralism	*langue/parole*	censoring system
Functionalism	tradition/innovation norm/creativity (Saussure, Propp, Jakobson and Bogatyrëv)	function
Semiotics and Ethnography	tradition and performance (Peirce, Bakhtin, Bauman)	event
Deconstruction	writing and speech (Derrida, Workman)	independent speaking subject as product of a metaphysics of presence
Deconstruction *féminine*	writing and voice (Cixous)	"peopling" (as articulation of power/gender struggles)

my broader use of "performance" to include written texts. It also qualifies my use of critical narratology in this book. As presented by Mieke Bal, the objective of "critical narratology" is to limn "ideology at work in narrative subjectivity" (*On Story-Telling* 47). Following an Althusserian definition of "ideology," Bal emphasizes its naturalizing power, its discursive production of a seemingly coherent subject, and its discriminating— that is, hierarchical—shaping of a society's representations and a subject's positions. When ideology succeeds, a subject occupies one or more positions as if they were natural, in an it-goes-without-saying fashion. "Described in this way, ideologies contribute to the legitimization and the maintenance of social institutions and practices, to the unequal distribution of power, and therefore to the possibility of satisfying conscious and unconscious needs and desires, and, finally, to the masking of contradictions" (46). The primary task of a critical narratology then, is to make visible a narrative's *im*position by unfolding its strategic *pro*position of meaning—its subjectivity. Achieving this task involves tracing the network of subject roles, positions, and actions within a text, and then measuring this specific ideologically produced subjectivity against narrative and social norms. Shying away from the humanistic link between "subject" and "individual human being," Bal identifies a "subjectival network" which articulates narration (who speaks?), focalization (who sees?), and agency (who does?). Distinguishing among these aspects of the text's subjectivity breaks up the text's apparent coherence, and allows its features and symptoms to be interpreted in relationship with the social.[28]

Though Bal's various books contain a wealth of critical implements, I have found certain tools especially useful when analyzing postmodern transformations of the tale of magic. First, the seemingly obvious statement that the narrator exists only in the first person allows us to assign narrative and ideological responsibility to the so-called "third-person" narrator who, thanks to the naturalizing "once upon a time" fairy tale frame, is usually considered to be objective. Second, Gérard Genette's important distinction between narration and focalization becomes even more valuable when Bal uses it to pose questions about the *articulation* of voice and vision in a text. Does in short the perspective through which we see match or conflict with the words of the narrator? Third, by demonstrating that focalization includes selection and gaze along with the purely visual, and extends to what is seen (the focalized) as well as who sees (the focalizer), Bal supplies a fuller apparatus for making explicit the "vision" or ideology transmitted by a text's words. Fourth, her emphasis on "self-reflection" as a "socially indispensable critical function" insists on the inevitable narrative tie between the ideological and the critical, identification and alienation (*On Story-Telling* 31).

How does Bal's project connect with semiotics, deconstructive practices, and feminine/feminist interests as I have represented them in relation to the study of folklore and literature? Explicitly with Peirce's semiotics and implicitly with folkloristic applications of semiotics, Bal's project shares an attentiveness to signs in relation to their users and in socially-variable situations. Her analytical approach to narrative's multi-layered production does not hierarchically distinguish between written and oral texts, since in both cases "interpretation" requires listening for lack (what is omitted or denied) and repetition (which can emphasize or displace).

Finally, Bal's philosophical aligning of her narratology with "critical sciences" signals her recognition of the history of semiotics. This "scientific" yearning for comprehensiveness and clarity distinguishes Bal's approach to narrative from deconstruction, while her critical focus on the text's subjectivity marks their affinity. By attempting to fill in gaps, to interpret symptoms and violations of norms, Bal's narratology seeks to bring about an awareness of the text's unconscious—an analytic translation of it—but also brings into relief the untied threads and tacit interests that unmake the coherence of both textual production and interpretation.[29]

Perhaps the most powerful point of condensation between these distinct lines of inquiry—semiotics, deconstruction, feminist studies, and critical narratology—is their keen attention to the "performative" as constituting the link between verbal signs and their users (senders and receivers), that is, to the social uses of an utterance or a narrative performance. As studied by speech-act theorists, however, the performative force of an utterance—that it does what it states—ultimately depends on the subject's conscious intention (is she or he serious in promising, ordering, parodying?), which, somewhat like the ethnography of performance, again makes the self-present and ever-conscious subject the center of a contextually-bound performance. Within deconstruction, many feminisms, and critical narratology, while the meaning of a (sign-)event still depends on its performative force, its context-bound performance, that context can be framed and reframed, resulting in different meanings which no one subject can master. And without discounting the significance of agency, the effect of this shift is to resituate responsibility not within individual intention, but in the network of ideologies articulated in a performance as interpreted within multiple frames.

There it is, then, a happy ending to my meta-narrative. I do believe, after all, in the compatibility of critical narratology and deconstruction, just as I wish to enlist both to unmask naturalizing gender-constructions. And yet, more than a point of arrival, this theoretical frame is a willfully constituted starting point. The critical practices I bring into play serve distinct interests, and I must therefore recognize their differences and their struggles.[30] For struggle there is, within and between the frameworks I have drawn, and within and between my own positions in these frameworks.[31]

POSTMODERN FAIRY TALES AND THE PERFORMATIVE

Why and how do I want to refer to "postmodernism"? Whether we like it or not, postmodernism has affected many of today's configurations of Western culture and its hierarchical distinctions among disciplines and genres, especially literature, popular culture, and folklore. Though conflicting interpretations of postmodernism have almost succeeded in theorizing it out of existence, several of its versions still attest to its vitality. Most significantly, postmodern studies have advocated anti-humanistic conceptualizations of the subject, played with multiplicity and performance in narrative, and struggled with the sexual and gender ramifications of problematizing identities and differences.[32]

The working definition of postmodern narratives I have adopted here rejects a purely stylistic understanding of the postmodern, does not celebrate or condemn its subject, and wishes to encourage distinctions among performative uses of postmodernism. Though I agree with Margaret Ferguson that "postmodernism" is "the best umbrella term for the cultural, social, and theoretical dimensions of our period" ("Feminism and Postmodernism" 3), I would also like to make some distinctions among the poetics and politics of such a diversified cultural landscape. Linda Hutcheon's approach to postmodernism has its appeal. She reads postmodern fiction as a primarily European and American "cultural enterprise" which distinguishes itself from other contemporary practices through its self-conscious contradictions, parodic intertextuality, and conflictual dialogue with historicity ("Beginning to Theorize Postmodernism" 10). Since they rhetorically and literally "incorporate that which they aim to contest"—modernism, history, the humanistic subject, other narrative texts and genre—Hutcheon sees postmodern fictions as "'borderline' enquiries" practicing "writing-as-experience-of-limits" (16–17), crossing borders between genres, and challenging "a definition of subjectivity and creativity that has ignored the role of history in art and thought" (21–22). From the perspective of these proliferating and contradictory narratives, History, like the other "master narratives," to use Lyotard's term, is de-naturalized and re-evaluated in the present as another made-up story.[33] Complicity and challenge, "writing" and "voice"—postmodernism self-consciously activates this informing paradox of narrative.

A fairy-tale related example might be helpful at this point. Italo Calvino's framework for the collection *Italian Folktales* (1956; English trans. 1980), I would argue, is not postmodern. Angela Carter's project in the collection *The Virago Book of Fairy Tales* (1990) is. In his journey into folklore, Calvino discovered not only that "folktales are real" in their abstract logic as a "general explanation of life," but also that he could identify and value certain Italian characteristics—as opposed to the French or the German characteristics of the tale (xviii). Like the Grimms', Calvino's approach thus supports a humanistic and nation-building project. Carter, on the other hand, assumes that fairy tales transmit unofficial, cross-culturally varied, and entertaining knowledge. Similarly, though for both writers the folk/fairy tale is clearly tied to the struggles and labor of the ordinary people, for Calvino the genre embodies human destiny in narrative, while for Carter it documents the resourcefulness and diversity of people's—especially women's—hard work. For Calvino, the fairy tale's appeal lies in the "joyous logic and precise rhythm" of transformation (*Italian Folktales* xxix); for Carter, in its active and varied responses to the "same common predicament—being alive" (*The Virago Book* xiv). It is Carter's focus on subjectivity as constructed in social and narrative contexts that makes hers a postmodern approach.

Though they both work with the folk tradition in a text-mediated way—Calvino in archives and with earlier published collections, Carter with all published works—as editors they also locate themselves differently in relation to the storytelling tradition they seek to represent in their collections. When Calvino wishes to become a "link in the anonymous chain" of transmission by modifying tales as all tellers do, his goal is to embellish the tale according to clearly literary standards of narrative style. Carter overtly participates in the chain of transmission by explicitly marking her selection of tales on the basis of specific class and gender considerations. Having made her choices, however, she re-presents a variety of styles and voices without making any textual changes herself. If Calvino's collection presents a somewhat essentialized metaphoric Italian fairy tale, animated by "a continuous quiver of love," then Carter's book precipitates a conversation with and among different kinds of tales and female protagonists—jokes as well as romantic and moral tales; "sillies," clever women, brave and good ones. In spite of his well-documented notes, Calvino's shaping of the tales remains in the background. Carter's positioning is there, tongue-in-cheek, in the chapter headings and in the two titles of the collection (*The Virago Book of Fairy Tales* in England and *The Old Wives' Fairy Tale Book* in the United States) but not evident in the tales themselves—a strategy designed to maximize the entertaining dialogue among fairy tales and to multiply the performative effects of their "domestic art." In this sense above all, Carter's editing project is postmodern while Calvino's is not.

But what is this "performative," and how does it relate to gender? In linguistics, performative speech has exceptional force because in a ritual of display it constitutes what it names, "man and wife" in a marriage ceremony, for instance. As I understand it, Judith Butler's distinction between "performance" and "performative" relies on their intimate relation. Through repeated performances, the power of the performative is both actualized and parodied. Butler makes two significant moves here. First, she views gender itself as performative discourse which involves "the repeated stylization of the body, a set of repeated acts within a highly regulatory frame that congeal in time to produce the appearance of substance, of a natural sort of being" (*Gender Trouble* 33). The seeming statement of recognition "It's a girl!" is thus an interpellation which initiates the process of "girling," an assignment never to be fully completed because "femininity" is "the forcible citation of a norm" and not a pre-existing reality. Second, like Derrida, Butler locates the source of authority for these pronouncements in citationality or reiteration while, at the same time, emphasizing the provisionality of such power, since "reiterations are never simply replicas of the same" (*Bodies* 226). Gender is performative. The authority of the performative depends on repetition, which requires multiple performances. In certain hyperbolic cases, however, this authority produces twisted effects which expose the norm as fantasy and compulsion.[34] In such instances, the "resignification of norms is thus a function of their *inefficacy*, and so the question of subversion, of *working the weakness in the norm*, becomes a matter of inhabiting the practices of its rearticulation" (*Bodies* 237). As such, performance is always already implicated in the citation of a norm, whether it be gender, subjectivity or narrativity, but can re-articulate this norm by way of exposing its constructedness.

As I read postmodern transformations of the fairy tale, I want to argue that they are doubling and double: both affirmative and questioning, without necessarily being recuperative or politically subversive. As literary texts, cartoons, movies, musicals, or soap operas, postmodern fairy tales reactivate the wonder tale's "magic" or mythopoeic qualities by providing new readings of it, thereby generating unexploited or forgotten possibilities from its repetition. As "borderline enquiries," postmodern re-visions of traditional narratives do more than alter our reading of those narratives. Like meta-folklore, they constitute an ideological test for previous interpretations, and in doing so, postmodern fairy tales exhibit an awareness of how the folktale, which modern humans relegate to the nursery, almost vindictively patterns our unconscious and "secretly lives on in the story" (Benjamin 102). Semiotically speaking, the anti-tale is implicit in the tale, since this well-made artifice produces the receiver's desire to repeat the tale anew: repetition functions as reassurance within the tale, but this very same compulsion to repeat the tale explodes its coherence as well-made artifice. Finally, and perhaps most simply, the postmodern fairy tale's dissemination of multiple possible versions is strangely powerful—all re-tellings, re-interpretations, and re-visions may appear to be equally authorized as well as unauthorized.

Though these "parodic" texts—in Linda Hutcheon's sense of the word—self-consciously exploit the articulation of "writing" and "voice," they are not performatively the same. As Nancy A. Walker suggests, re-vision "is not merely an artistic but a social action, suggesting in narrative practice the possibility of cultural transformation," but only those rewritings which "expose or upset the paradigms of authority inherent in the texts they appropriate" are "disobedient" (6–7). Depending on the degree to which one category reflects on the others and to which specific desires intersect as the texts are produced and consumed, the ways postmodern fairy tales produce subjectivity, narrativity, and gender can differ greatly. Multiple permutations produce postmodern transformations of fairy tales because their simultaneously affirming and questioning strategies re-double in a variety of critically self-reflexive moves. As my readings will show, some postmodern revisions may question and remake the classic fairy tale's production of gender only to re-inscribe it within some unquestioned model of subjectivity or narrativity. Other postmodern tales expose the fairy tale's complicity with the "exhausted" forms and ideologies of traditional Western narrative, rewriting the tale of magic in order to question and re-create the rules of narrative production, especially as such rules contribute to naturalizing subjectivity and gender. Still other tales re-place or relocate the fairy tale to multiply its performance potential and denaturalize its institutionalized power. In every case, though, these postmodern transformations do not exploit the fairy tale's magic simply to make the spell work, but rather to unmake some of its workings.

Postmodern fictions, then, hold mirrors to the magic mirror of the fairy tale, playing with its framed images out of a desire to multiply its refractions and to expose its artifices. Frames and images may vary, but gender is almost inevitably the privileged place for articulating these de-naturalizing strategies. And while this play of reflection, refraction, and framing might produce ideologically "destructive," "constructive" and "subversive" effects, the self-reflexive mirrors themselves are themselves questioned and transformed.

FRAMING MAGIC

As for myself, perhaps I could tell the tale of these complex and inter-woven narratives this way: "In the beginning, were stories— or better, people would tell enchanting stories. These stories might seem old and worthless, but performing their magic's many tricks once more unleashes new powers which, in turn, can expose the magic as trickery and thus unmake its spells." This revised magic, which Zipes calls "antimythic,"[35] is the play of re-tellings, re-evaluations, and re-figurings or re-visions which I see as constituting postmodern transformations of fairy tales. Postmodern fairy tales are wonders in performance, and as such perform varying wonders.

The folklorist W.F.H. Nicolaisen has recently posed the seemingly innocent question "Why Tell Stories?" then answered it by showing how the etymology of *story* carries us down to narrative's shared roots with history, knowledge, and wisdom (6). Nicolaisen's discussion of "storying" as an "essential component of our intellectual survival kit" also reminds us that "we continually invent ourselves," because the stories we tell produce and find us in the past, and enable us to live through the present's uncertainties by projecting us into the future. We encounter stories "not only as narration from knowledge and wisdom but also as a narrative given shape through ideas and relevance through vision" (6). This apparently simple definition thus ties story to history (knowledge), values (ideas), and figuration (vision); implicitly, it also signals that mastery of such narrative ingredients produces power, as both privilege *and* empowerment.

As I work with the multiple versions, conflicting interests, and articulations of verbal and visual, I will seek to show how the magic of postmodern fairy tales retells history, values, and gendered figurations. For each text, this uncovering takes place at the crossroads where the postmodern fairy tale's telling marks meet—its dialogue with the history of the tale of magic, and with its own place in a postmodern market; its replay of tradition and performance, or "writing" and "voice"; its scripted desires and performative effects; and, most tellingly, the specific configurations of gender, narrativity, and subjectivity that it performs. Chapter Two examines the strategies by which postmodern texts for adults expose the construction of "Snow White"'s narrative frame and its complicity with an essentializing ideology of gender. Though all popular fairy tales do not inscribe static and "natural" beauties like Snow White, the voices, gazes, and actions of female fairy-tale heroines inevitably find themselves measured against such a normative frame. To qualify this negative assessment of the fairy tale's narrative and gender construction further, Chapter Three explores the historicizing and performance-oriented side of the postmodern project of self-reflection by developing an intertextual reading of "Red Riding Hood" in folk versions and literary retellings. With the double vision of postmodern fairy tales already established, Chapter Four proceeds to differentiate, along the lines of gender and subjectivity, among the narrative strategies and ideological projects that selected contemporary revisions of "Beauty and the Beast" perform. Finally, Chapter Five focuses on specifically feminist manipulations of the "Bluebeard" plot to powerful but varied effects.

2
THE
FRAMING OF
"SNOW WHITE"
NARRATIVE AND
GENDER
(RE)PRODUCTION

THE FAIRY TALE'S MAGIC depends on our suspension of disbelief: we do not expect the tale's events to be realistic. Even more, though, magic is invoked through the tale's matter-of-fact, artfully simple narrative that relies on dialogue and single strokes of color to produce a feeling of familiarity and wonder at the same time. Wolves, eagles, ants, even the fish talk, and we understand. Flowers and jewels fall from the heroine's lips. A queen gives birth to a pig or to a bush of rosemary; a dead girl revives when her poisoned shoes are removed. The magic is not that such things happen in fairy tales, but that they are immediately recognizable as "true" in Bettelheim's terms, or in some abstract way as part of our own experience—"a general explanation of life" as Calvino put it (*Italian Folktales* xviii). Not the actual events, but the wonder itself is recognized in the images, in their symbolic resonance, in their logic. Like a magic mirror, the fairy tale reflects and conforms to the way things "truly" are, the way our lives are "truly" lived.

As with all mirrors, though, refraction and the shaping presence of a frame mediate the fairy tale's reflection. As it images our potential for transformation, the fairy tale refracts what we wish or fear to become. Human—and thus changeable—ideas, desires, and practices frame the tale's images. Further, if we see more of the mirror rather than its images, questions rather than answers emerge. Who is holding the mirror and whose desires does it represent and contain? Or, more pointedly, how is the fairy tale's magic produced narratively?

In this chapter, I will show how several mirroring or mimetic strategies—externalization, nature metaphors, the invisible external narrator, mirrors themselves—sustain the fairy tale's wonder by unobtrusively easing us into recognizing correspondences between the natural world and the psycho-social human world. As my reading of "Snow White" will emphasize, this mirroring, or highly-distilled mimesis, is no value-free or essential distillation of human destiny, but a "special effect" of ideological expectations and unspoken norms—a naturalizing technology that works hard at, among other things, re-producing "Woman" as the mirror image of masculine desire. Within the fairy tale's narrative frame, Snow White is the crystallized image of the "natural" woman. Examining the construction of such a frame can at the very least contribute to unmaking the power of that crystal.

All popular fairy tales do not of course inscribe such static beauties. I choose "Snow White" as my example because, even among the "innocent persecuted heroine" fairy tales, it is a particularly "fixed" and mimetic narrative. By analyzing the mirroring strategy in "Snow White" as it re-produces the passively beautiful female character with very limited options, I seek to magnify norms at work in the fairy tale, the narrative frame which measures the voices, gazes, and actions of all the genre's female heroines.

* * *

Best known nowadays in its Disney movie version and the Grimms' nineteenth-century printed text, the immensely popular "Snow White" (AT709) has hundreds of oral versions, collected primarily in Europe, but also in Asia Minor, Africa, and the Americas (Jones 14).[1] When preparing their *Kinder- und Hausmärchen*, the Brothers Grimm themselves collected several German versions, and the tale they selected for publication has in turn influenced the oral tradition. As one would expect, "Snow White" versions vary greatly in details or allomotifs. The (step)mother attacks Snow White in a variety of ways; the girl finds refuge with robbers, assassins, giants, fairies, instead of with dwarves. The narrative structure and thematic interpretation have however been comparatively homogeneous, fixing "Snow White" more firmly than most fairy tales in our imaginations.[2]

Giambattista Basile published an early literary retelling, "La schiavetta" or "The Young Slave" (Second Day, Eighth Tale), in *Lo Cunto de li Cunti* or *The Pentameron* in 1634–36. Lilla, the baron's young sister, swallows a rose petal to win a bet and finds herself pregnant; the fairies help her conceal her condition, and then bestow gifts on baby Lisa. On her way to bless the child, one of the fairies trips and curses her instead, declaring that when Lisa turns seven her mother will leave a comb in the girl's hair and she will die. After Lisa does die, her mother entrusts the child's body, contained in seven glass coffins, to her brother and then dies of grief.[3] After some time, the baron's wife discovers the girl, who has kept growing as the glass coffins lengthen. Thinking this beautiful young girl might be her husband's lover, the baroness pulls Lisa's hair: the comb falls out, and the girl awakens. Filled with jealousy, the baroness beats the girl, cuts her hair, and treats her like a slave. Pitying the young girl, after having asked everyone else in the household, the baron asks her what she would like when he returns from a trip. Shortly after she receives the doll, the knife, and the piece of pumice she wanted, the baron overhears Lisa telling the doll her story and promising to kill herself with the knife she has already sharpened if she gets no answer from the doll. Recognizing her to be his niece, the baron sends his evil wife away and marries Lisa to a good husband.

In the Grimms' "Sneewittchen," translated as "Little Snow White" or "Snow Drop," a queen wishes for a child as white as snow, as red as blood, and as black as ebony. She then dies in childbirth. Seven years later, the child's beautiful and proud stepmother consults a magic mirror, which, instead of stating as usual that "You, my queen, are the fairest of all," declares the child to be the most beautiful instead (Zipes, *Grimms* 196). Envious and angry, the queen orders a huntsman to kill Snow White and then eats what he presents to her as the girl's lungs and liver. In fact, struck by Snow White's beauty, he has taken pity on her and set her free. Wandering in the forest, she comes upon a small house, where seven dwarves offer to take care of her in exchange for housework. The queen, upon learning from the mirror that Snow White is still alive and as beautiful as ever, plots to kill her. Three times the disguised queen attacks the girl—with lace, a comb, and finally a poisonous apple. Twice the dwarves revive her; the third time, Snow White remains dead. Having placed her in a glass coffin, the dwarves continue to admire and honor her beauty. When a passing prince falls in love with her, out of pity the dwarves eventually give him the coffin. One of his servants trips while carrying it, the piece of apple is dislodged from her throat, and Snow White wakes up and marries the prince. The queen is forced to dance in red-hot shoes until she falls down dead.

While Basile's tale differs in many ways from the Grimms', they share as basic plot ingredients the heroine's wondrous origin, her innocence, her persecution at the hands of a jealous older woman, her apparent death, and her accidental resuscitation. These tales also share a narrative structure: the "Innocent Persecuted Heroine" dramatic sequence first identified by Ilana Dan and then analyzed in detail by Steve Swann Jones.[4] Oral versions are similarly uniform. Though the heroine's name might be Bianca, Blanca Rosa, Bella Venezia, Myrsina, or Snow Bella, and she might be attacked with food, flowers, shoes, or dress, the overall narrative development is unvaried.[5]

It is no surprise, then, that different interpretations of "Snow White" tend to agree that its basic themes are female development and female jealousy. For Bruno Bettelheim, "Snow White" represents the daughter's successful resolution of the oedipal conflict. N.J. Girardot focuses on the ritual and sacrificial pattern of initiation Snow White must undergo in order to rejoin her society as an adult. Sandra Gilbert and Susan Gubar emphasize the constraints that patriarchal images such as the "angel-woman" (Snow White) and the "monster-woman" (the Queen) place on female characters' and women readers' potential. In a balanced synthesis based on extensive comparative analysis, Steve Swann Jones concludes that "Snow White" is "a metaphoric representation of the types of problems a young woman is likely to encounter" (Jones, *Western Folklore* 39), while Shuli Barzilai reads "Snow White" as the story of "a mother who cannot grow up and a daughter who must" (534).[6]

Within this narrative of female development, jealousy seems a necessary ill.[7] Though Paola, the teller of Basile's "La schiavetta," warns her listeners that nothing good will come of jealousy, Lisa comes back to life when the baroness, out of jealousy, pulls her hair. That the heroine's exceptional beauty sets in motion the drama of jealousy may help to explain why critics have focused on the magic mirror so insistently that it has become a metaphor for "Snow White" itself. What tends to get shortchanged, however, is the mirror's *magic*—the makings of its power. What I propose to

examine, then, is how mirroring—and not simply the mirror—
works within the tale of "Snow White" and what the gender implications of this activity are for the character Snow White, and for
"her" narrative.[8]

In the Grimms' text, Snow White's wondrous birth is itself a
complex instance of mirroring:

> Once upon a time, in the middle of winter, when snow flakes were
> falling like feathers from the sky, a queen was sitting and sewing at a win-
> dow with a black ebony frame. And as she was sewing and looking out the
> window, she pricked her finger with the needle and three drops of blood
> fell on the snow. The red looked so beautiful on the white snow that she
> thought to herself, If only I had a child as white as snow, as red as blood,
> and as black as the wood of the window frame!
>
> Soon after she gave birth to a little daughter who was as white as snow,
> as red as blood, and her hair as black as ebony. Accordingly, the child was
> called Snow White, and right after she was born, the queen died. (Zipes,
> *Grimms* 196)[9]

Other versions of Snow White's conception do not present such
an artfully framed portrait of her mother, but they enact a similar
aesthetic translation of the external, natural world into the inner
mind or body of the mother-to-be. Assimilating the attractive red-
and-white contrast out there, or the beauty of a fruit or flower, she
then gives new life to it in the form of a girl-child.[10]

What are the effects of this mirroring process? First, motherhood and feminine beauty appear as "natural" because the mother's wish, the child's conception, and the child herself are
represented as imitating nature.[11] Second, because the tale's language openly seeks to reproduce "natural" beauty and to perform
"natural" wishes, the aesthetics themselves are naturalized. Snow
White's birth as a character and the narrative that produces her
are both legitimized through mirroring, the "magic" of which is to
image their mimetic relationship to a cultural world as natural. Finally, while Snow White is apparently born out of her mother's
wish, the spilling of blood calls forth an image of beauty that does
not necessarily imply the mother's desire. Could the motifs of
bleeding and eating seeds or fruits, which often accompany the
conflation of wish and conception in fairy tales, be not only "suggestive of the actual sexual act of procreation" (Jones 40), but also
symbolic of "immasculation," the assimilation of patriarchal ideals

of femininity? After all, when Snow White's mother gives birth to
the image of woman she has internalized, what appears in the
heroine are the beauty and purity of white, the transformative
powers of red or gold, the ritual—and sexual—death of black.[12]
These symbolic ingredients suggest that the "good" mother actually gives birth to the absent King's wish, as a German version of
the tale makes explicit:

> A count and a countess drove by three mounds of white snow which
> made the count say, "I wish I had a girl as white as this snow." A short
> while later they came to three holes full of red blood, at which he said: "I
> wish I had a girl with cheeks as red as this blood." Finally, three black
> ravens flew by, at which moment he desired a girl "with hair as black as
> these ravens." As they drove on, they encountered a girl as white as snow,
> as red as blood, and with hair as black as the raven; and she was Snow
> White. (Bettelheim's translation from Bolte and Polívka 200)[13]

Of course, the mirroring is overt when the (step)mother interrogates her magic glass and the beautiful Snow White appears before her instead of her own waning beauty. On one level, in typical
fairy-tale style the mirror simply externalizes the natural process of
life and change. (Some versions feature the sun or a wise animal
in the role of the sentencing mirror.[14]) On another level, though,
the tale's magic trick is to conflate once again the natural with the
ideological, thus presenting the mirror's judgment as unquestion-
ably authoritative. Whose voice do we hear when the mirror says
"You, my queen, may have a beauty quite rare, / but Snow White is
a thousand times more fair" (Zipes, *Grimms* 197)? "The daughter's," suggests Bettelheim, for whom the tale reflects the girl's
projections of jealousy onto her mother. "The voice of truth,"
states Girardot, since the mirror is a site of self-reflection. "The
mother's," answers Barzilai, for the mirror "images the mother's
wound" of separation from her growing child (530).[15] "The father's," propose Gilbert and Gubar, since the tale reinforces patriarchal definitions and prescriptions. "Both the young woman's
and 'society's,'" mediates Jones. But no matter whose voice we
hear, its judgment has power and credibility because "seeing is believing": we forget that the mirror's reflected or refracted image is
framed.

In a few versions, though, the patriarchal frame becomes visible.

In the Italian version "Bella Venezia," for example, a beautiful innkeeper asks traveling men if they've ever seen anyone lovelier than herself. When one names her daughter, Bella Venezia promises to marry the kitchen boy if he will kill the young girl (Calvino 395–98).[16] In "Snow Bella" from Louisiana, a male vendor, "a hunched and wrinkled old man, wearing thick glasses over his tiny eyes" (Edwards 592), provides the stepmother first with the clairvoyant mirror, then with the poisonous comb and apple. Within that version, the stepmother actually disguises herself as a man when making her final attack on Snow Bella.[17] Whether speaking with the women's collusive voice or the men's, it is a patriarchal frame that takes the two women's beauty as the measure of their (self)worth, and thus defines their relationship as a rivalry.[18] Snow White is just as framed as her (step)mother, and the positive or negative value we ascribe to Snow White's development as a character depends on how we understand mirroring in the tale.

What in "Snow White" conceals this frame and naturalizes the plenitude of the feminine image in the mirror? That very simple but powerful narrative strategy that stands as one of the narrative rules for fairy-tale production: an external or impersonal narrator whose straightforward statements carry no explicit mark of human perspective—gender, class, or individuality. Though in an oral context the teller of "Snow White" is often a woman, the genre's conventions require her to narrate in what is awkwardly called the "third person," a form of ventriloquism that highly complicates the issue of narrative accountability.[19] When the Grimms' version introduces us to the queen framed by the window, this portrait is ostensibly there to be viewed and understood as an uninflected "fact." "There was," "there are," "she was"—such statements present the narrative's vision as the only possible one. Like the mirror, the narrator knows all, telling—or even better, showing—things as they are. But there is no pure mimesis in narration, only its illusion; language necessarily mediates "showing" through a "telling," which cannot be innocent, because whether through a voice, or on the page, a narrator exists only in the first-person.[20] Narrative cannot be a mirror, but by engaging in mimeticism to the utmost extent, it can, as it so often does in fairy tales, function as a magic mirror.

As a mimetic narrative, "Snow White" claims to tell us the truth about the world: the human world mirrors nature.[21] More specifically, by silently assuming a set of social conventions, the narrative strategy of mirroring sustains among many other social norms the re-production of gender construction.[22] Such mirroring frames and freezes Snow White as an image of beauty and suffering—the "innocent persecuted heroine." Actually in some versions, when the prince's mother or sisters discover the girl's body in his room, they wonder how he can love a "doll" or a "dead body."[23] "Snow White rarely has a voice of her own, and when she does speak, she merely accepts things as they are. In several Italian versions, she declares herself willing to be killed to honor her mother's wish, and ready to carry out the wishes of others ("Yes . . . with all my heart," she answers when the dwarves ask her to do a long list of household chores). Though she is more vocal in Basile's early literary version, asking the baron to bring her specific gifts and telling the doll of her tribulations, here, too, her words break through the external narrator's only at extreme moments of desperation. Otherwise, in an indirectly silencing move, her speech is reported and summarized.[24] It is as a silent image that she arouses the Prince's love, as the Chilean version, "Blanca Rosa and the Forty Thieves," bears out. When accidentally resuscitated by the prince, the girl becomes quite "distraught" at seeing herself "alone with this man she had never met, and totally nude." Since she "would not be calmed and insisted on leaving," the prince responds simply by driving the needle back into her head, thus quieting her down, and getting a chance to think "what he could possibly do with the lovely maiden" (Edwards 617). Whether "written" by the narrator's words, author(iz)ed by masculine desire, or imaged by the mirror, Snow White is a constructed child-woman whose snow-white features and attitudes are assumed to conform to nature in a powerfully metaphoric way.

Postmodern re-visions of "Snow White" acknowledge the power that such a metaphor has had. Rather than simply renewing and updating that power, however, they name and question its ideological nature. If the fairy tale symbolically seeks to represent some unquestionable natural state of being, postmodern fairy tales seek to expose this state's generic and gendered "lie" or artifice. Assuming that a frame always selects, shapes, (dis)places, limits, and (de)centers the image in the mirror, postmodern retellings focus precisely on this frame to unmake the mimetic fiction. These retellings make the implicit link between narrative and gender (re)production in "Snow White" apparent, and narrative and psychological claims to truth can be questioned. Each of the metafictions I will discuss explores different narrative possibilities, and in the process of re-vision exposes and challenges the authority of the mirror.

Although no mirror appears in Angela Carter's "The Snow Child," published in *The Bloody Chamber* (1979), the story itself mimics the logic and strategies of mirroring to expose the intertwined re-production of narrative and gender in "Snow White." Carter's own essays mock myth and "mythic versions of women" as "consolatory nonsenses," dealing "in false universals, to dull the pain of particular circumstances." In her fictions, Carter consistently engages not only "the mythic schema of all relations between men and women" but also the imagination that authorizes them (*The Sadeian Woman* 5).

Mirroring the beginning of "Snow White" but with a difference, the first words of the two-page long "The Snow Child"—"Midwinter—invincible, immaculate" (91)—immediately play with mimesis. Apparently descriptive, and objectively so, this phrase seems to rely like the fairy tale on abstractly symbolic elements of nature. The "transitional period in the cosmic round of the year" (Girardot, "Initiation and Meaning" 286), midwinter ritually marks the end of a cycle and the beginning of another, thus externalizing and generalizing a specific event from "Snow White": the Queen must die for Snow White to be born. By setting her tale in midwinter, Carter invokes this strong symbolic resonance, but her narrative will soon question how "immaculate" and "invincible" this mythic winter actually is in terms of human practice. Like pornography and myth, the landscape of "The Snow Child" does not "encompass the possibility for change, . . . as if sexual relations were not necessarily an expression of social relations, as if sex itself were an external fact, one *as immutable as the weather*, creating human practice but never a part of it" (Carter, *The Sadeian Woman* 3–4, my emphasis).

Carter's hall of symbolic mirrors superimposes sexual, social, and economic relations to lay bare their naturalization as a constrictive, repressive fiction. The version of "Snow White" she retells—one the Grimms collected, but not one they chose to pub-lish—presents the heroine's birth as the direct outcome of her fa-ther's desire.[25] The Count's three wishes mirror his surroundings: the whole world is white; a hole in the snow is filled with blood; a raven is perched on a leafless bough. Mirroring in reverse what we have come to think of as Snow White's legitimate origin—the mother's wish—the Count's appetite for this "child of his desire" is instantly satisfied, mimetically and aesthetically. "As soon as he completed her description, there she stood, beside the road, white skin, red mouth, black hair and stark naked." Clearly, the Snow Child is a masculine fantasy, an image of "woman."

Through the Countess, however, Carter exposes the naturalized human dynamics presented in "Snow White" as not-so-white lies covering the inequity of patriarchal social relations. With her black fox furs and "high, black, shining boots with scarlet heels, and spurs," she rides beside the count through the snow-covered countryside with which she seems to share no whiteness at all. When the desired girl appears, "the Countess hated her" instinc-tively as a rival. Mirroring the plot of the folk version, the Countess drops her glove in the snow and demands that the girl pick it up—the goal is to abandon the child, who traditionally then wanders off and finds refuge in the dwarves' home. The Count, however, prevents this course of action by stating: "'I'll buy you new gloves,'" and "at that, the furs sprang off the Countess's shoulders and twined round the naked girl." Another attempt on the girl's life by the Countess leaves the older woman as "bare as a bone and the girl furred and booted." And now the Count suddenly feels "sorry for his wife." Any shift in the Count's affections is immedi-ately reflected in the relationship of the two women, whose socio-economic fortunes mirror each other in reverse—as the one gains, the other loses—and depend entirely on the Count's words.

Carter's tale places on top of this pattern a highly concentrated and parodic version of the traditional fairy-tale heroine's initia-tion. When the Countess wishes for the girl to pick her a rose, the Count consents. Mirroring the traditional "innocent persecuted heroine," the Snow Child is thus given a task and, in a way, she completes it. By plucking the rose, the "eternal" symbol of femi-ninity in both its sexual and its mystically sacrificial connotations, she comes of age—she bleeds—and then fulfills her function as passive object of the Count's desire. In this case, however, the shallowness of this initiation which amounts to her death, rape, and fetishizing becomes painfully visible. Like Sleeping Beauty, another "innocent persecuted heroine," the Snow Child pricks her finger and falls; like Basile's Sleeping Beauty (*Pentameron*, Day 5, tale 5), she is subjected to sexual intercourse while asleep/dead. But this rape brings no re-birth. As the Count satisfies his desire, the girl, whose living flesh never really was, melts back into her post-initiation symbolic ingredients—no snow, but a (black) feather, a bloodstain, and a rose.[26]

In this way, Carter's tale "bites" its readers by exploiting our sentimental familiarity with "Snow White"'s scenarios and symbols to expose the sterility of both the Count's mimetic desire, and the narrative it sets in motion. No child—no flesh and blood, no life—is produced by the Count's wish. Only an imaginary being. And yet, when the Count offers the rose to the fully reclothed Countess, she must drop the flower, crying out "It bites!" Here the *vagina dentata* motif resonates not as a "false universal," but with "the pain of particular circumstances" (*Sadeian Woman* 5). In this snow-covered landscape, the only relationship possible between women is one that re-produces itself as rivalry, as struggle to survive at the other woman's expense. Within this initiatory and narrative cycle no possibility for human growth and transformation exists.[27]

As my own signposts—"mirrors," "exposes," "shows," "makes visible"—indicate, "The Snow Child" achieves these de-naturalizing effects by playing with mimesis, by adapting the fairy tale's mirroring strategies to make us question the immutability and invincibility of the mirror. As we would expect, Carter's characters are flat, her protagonist is silent and passive, her Countess's jealousy is sufficient motive for wanting to kill the rival, and her Count's words and acts have a logic all their own. And yet, by mirroring these familiar stylistic features Carter woos us into the comfortable plot even as she makes visible its implausibility and de-humanizing assumptions.

Other postmodern writers have rewritten "Snow White" by rejecting the external, invisible narrator, the strategy that sustains the mirror's authority. In "The Dead Queen" (1973), Robert Coover unmakes the intertwined re-production of gender and narrative mirroring in "Snow White" by adopting an inquisitive, first-person narrator. Through flashbacks, the prince—wed to Snow White the day before, and now gazing speculatively at her dead stepmother in the glass coffin which so recently contained his wife—retells the traditional story with more than a twist.[28] Not only does his narrative begin after the wedding—the point where many fairy tales end—but even more unusually, the opening scene is actually a funeral. Speaking in the past tense and in a quasi-existentialist and reflective mode that lends itself to comic effects, the prince adds details to the tale as we know it from his magic wedding night as well as a new episode at the stepmother's grave with himself as protagonist. Puzzled first by Snow White's passionate and anything but innocent lovemaking, and then by the realization that, whatever happens, her hymen cannot be broken, the prince comes to believe that the evil queen has plotted the whole story to free herself from the mirror and to lead him—her true love, from the prince's self-centered viewpoint—"away from the merely visible to vision, from the image to the imaged, from reflections to the projecting miracle itself, the heart, the pure snow white" (312–13). Now hoping to resuscitate the dead queen, he kisses her rubbery and cold lips twice. When nothing happens he leaves, wounded in his pride and as nauseated as his spectators are. Coover's story closes on this princely reflection: "If this is the price of beauty, it's too high. I was glad she was dead" (313).

This prince (Charming, as I shall refer to him from now on) is not the flat, one-dimensional fairy-tale figure who fulfills his role and mission unquestioningly. He has an inquiring mind, and as self-conscious speculations replace the traditional hero's feats, the familiar tale of action becomes one of words. At the wedding, for instance, what troubles him among other things is his bride's "taste for luxury and collapse." His questions about Snow White and "the true meaning" of her name (307–8) challenge the developmental growth many associate with the "innocent persecuted heroine"'s initiation, and destabilize the metaphor around which her tale is built.

As is usually the case in fairy tales, marriage is certainly a moment of revelation in "The Dead Queen," but not as a symbolic resolution of psycho-social conflicts. Instead, marriage intensifies differences and magnifies the "frozen" and ideologically framed construction of Snow White. "Thrice around the world we'd gone in a bucking frenzy of love and lubricity," Charming recalls of their wedding night, "seven times we'd died in each other, and . . . at last, in a state of delicious annihilation, I'd lost consciousness." But the following morning he awakens to find "the bed unmussed and unbloodied, her hymen intact" (312). As the prince senses before entering the nuptial chamber, Snow White is a proper name, an anthropomorphism like Narcissus or Daphne, "a frozen void named Snow White" (309). If however she is her name and that is her substance, she cannot possibly experience any transformation.[29] For Coover, who significantly does not give his story her name, Snow White is thus an empty signifier—abused, but not marked, by time. The Prince soon realizes that Snow White has "suffered no losses, in fact that's just the trouble, that hymen can never be broken . . . this is her gift and essence" (305). To conform to the paradigmatic image of beauty and innocence she represents, Snow White can only be a heartless, fleshless, unconscious child who cannot change. She is as "dead" as the dead queen.

Charming's questions about the narrative he is a part of also denaturalize and unsettle the well-ordered fictional universe of the "Snow White" fairy tale. Thinking back to his first encounter with Snow White, the prince is troubled by "the compulsions that had led me to the mountain, the birdshit on the glass coffin when I'd found her." Chance and contingency often lie outside the fairy tale's field of vision to the extent that this narrative genre often provides its protagonists with an answer or a magic object before they even have a question or a problem.[30] Resisting this script, Charming wonders "why did things happen as though they were necessary?" (308). The prince realizes that his success was guaranteed in advance at the same time that his discomfort points to the highly manipulative, restrictive logic of the tale. Because he is attentive to these narrative mechanisms, the prince translates the conflict between the Queen and Snow White into aesthetic terms. The Queen plots not simply because she is jealous, but because she is an artist. Snow White is "innocent" not because she is morally superior, but because she "doesn't even know there is a mirror on the wall" (305). Her squealing and applauding at her stepmother's macabre shoe-driven dance disturbs the prince, as it suggests to him that Snow White had "become the very evil she'd been saved from" (304). The Queen, in short, has lived and died in full awareness of the power of the mirror, while Snow White has been unconsciously framed by it.

Charming thus recognizes the role the mirror plays in the rivalry between the two female characters, but he does not see how mirroring works more generally within the tale. By identifying the Queen as its narrative motor, the prince strives to change "Snow White," but inevitably fails. "The old Queen had a grin on her face when we buried her in the mountain," Charming notes as the story opens, "and I knew then that it was she who had composed this scene, as all before, she who had led us, revelers and initiates, to this cold and windy grave site, hers the design, ours the enactment, and I felt like the first man, destined to rise and fall, rise and fall, to the end of time" (304). While this reading of "Snow White" certainly acknowledges the Queen's creative energy, the prince fails to see that the Queen's actions and plots do not break away from the mimetic conventions and imagination of the "innocent persecuted heroine" fairy tale. Internalizing the cultural and narrative norms that sustain this genre, the Queen seeks to use them to her advantage in her struggle with the 'innocent' Snow White. Therefore, in contrast to Charming's view of her, the Queen has no real transformative power. Though she goes against the mirror's verdict, she compulsively returns to it in order to establish the "truth": "Mirror, mirror, on the wall, / who in this realm is the fairest of all?" (Zipes, *Grimms* 196). In her fight to free herself, she had "used the mirror as a door, tried to" (312), thus remaining within a narrative logic that demands her death.

Charming himself falls victim to a mimetic imagination when his desire for other plots and solutions leads him to kiss the dead Queen. Simply as the reflection of other princely disenchanting kisses, this comes "naturally" to him: he acts within the established norms of princely behavior in fairy tales. He had missed his chance with Snow White, whose resuscitation was, as is often the case, "accidental." "Why hadn't I been allowed to disenchant her with a kiss like everybody else?" he complains, still longing for a more romantic role in the heroine's rescue. Precisely when he is attempting to break away from the narrative and social norms he is dissatisfied with, Charming does so in the most conventional way possible. As he kisses the dead Queen, his earlier thought resonates more fully than he realizes: "It was the mirror that had fucked her, fucked us all" (305). So when his rather egocentric interpretation of the Queen's plotmaking proves wrong—she was not waiting for him to awaken her!—he abandons his desire for a different Beauty/beauty.

Coover's "The Dead Queen" works relentlessly to make us aware of how mirroring limits the options of both female and male characters in "Snow White." By featuring a questioning but unfulfilled narrator, Donald Barthelme's novel *Snow White* (1967) seeks to escape the frame by explicitly inviting readers to become more aware and wary of our narrative expectations. He breaks down the narrative's transparent unity in a number of ways. *Snow White* has three parts, a structure which perhaps re-produces on a narrative level Snow White's three-fold nature and three-part initiation process (separation, liminality, and aggregation). Otherwise, most of the novel's features are provocatively un-fairy-tale-like. The narrative and mimetic unity of "Snow White" is dismembered into several voices which rarely communicate. In spite of Bill's and Paul's sacrificial deaths, there is no happy ending—actually, there is no recognizable ending. Barthelme greatly amplifies one episode in the traditional tale—the heroine's stay with the dwarves—and the relationship is explicitly and primarily sexual. Finding a narrative or psychological development is difficult; nothing much happens. Instead, the language of comic books, politics, technology, street talk, and so on unleashes images and replaces the narrative of action.

Nor does a summary of the novel's plot tell us much. Snow White wants something different and does not find it, but in the end she might be transformed into a floating signifier. The alienated bourgeois dwarves (Clem, Dan, and the others) work in the city, washing buildings and making Chinese baby food. Paul, the poet and prince figure, acts out of a fateful misunderstanding when he drinks the poisoned vodka Gibson that Jane, Snow White's rival, had meant for her. Part I culminates in a self-parodying questionnaire which shakes readers out of passivity but offers no direction:

2. Does Snow White resemble the Snow White you remember?
   Yes (   )   No (   )

. . .

9. Has the work, for you, a metaphysical dimension?
   Yes (   )   No (   )
10. What is it (twenty-five words or less)?

. . .

14. Do you stand up when you read? (   ) Lie down? (   )
    Sit? (   )
15. In your opinion, should human beings have more shoulders?
    (   ) Two sets of shoulders? (   ) Three? (   )

Part II "concludes" with Snow White still hanging her beautiful hair out the window, just as she did at the section's beginning. "No one has come to climb up," she laments. "That says it all. This time is the wrong time for me. . . . There is something wrong with . . . the very world itself, for not being able to supply a prince. For not being able to at least be civilized enough to supply the correct ending to the story" (131–32). Part III's inconclusive list of possible endings mocks any expectations of a denouement (181):

> THE FAILURE OF SNOW WHITE'S ARSE
> REVIRGINIZATION OF SNOW WHITE
> APOTHEOSIS OF SNOW WHITE
> SNOW WHITE RISES TO THE SKY
> THE HEROES DEPART IN SEARCH OF
> A NEW PRINCIPLE
> HEIGH-HO

This *Snow White* systematically refuses to provide a linear narrative with a meaning that develops and an ending that satisfies: it refuses to fulfill our expectations of what the fairy tale as a well-made narrative ought to do. When Barthelme does employ stylistic features of the classic fairy tale, such as externalization, it is with parodic effect. For instance, though the height of Snow

White's seven dwarfed companions reflects their moral and aesthetic stature (they have no potential for growth, individually or as a group), their job—washing buildings—is ironically associated with "the idea that man is perfectible" (8). Similarly, Snow White's beauty, which in the fairy tale mirrors her inner qualities, is described so literally that any symbolism fades away:

SHE is a tall dark beauty containing a great many beauty spots: one above the breast, one above the belly, one above the knee, one above the ankle, one above the buttock, one on the back of the neck. All of these are on the left side, more or less in a row, as you go up and down. (3)

Her black hair and moles are identified as landmarks of her beauty, and a schematically visual representation of those beauty spots follows on the same page. But when "you go up and down" her body as if it were a space or object, those very human spots actually de-humanize her.

As Barthelme's plot and style resist the narrative re-production of "Snow White," he re-inscribes the representation of Snow White as aesthetic object to challenge it with a new framework. The dwarves' reification of Snow White for example parallels the one traditionally enacted by the mirror. In the words of dwarf Dan:

Now, what do we apprehend when we apprehend Snow White? We apprehend, first, two three-quarter-scale breasts floating towards us wrapped, typically, in a red towel. Or, if we are apprehending her from the other direction, we apprehend a beautiful snow-white arse floating away from us in a red towel. Now I ask you: What, in these two quite distinct apprehensions, is the constant? The factor that remains the same? Why, quite simply, the red towel. I submit that, rightly understood, the problem of Snow White has to do at its center with nothing else but *red towels.* . . . We can easily dispense with the slippery and untrustworthy and expensive effluvia that is Snow White, and cleave instead to the towel. (100–101)

In this parody of the metonymic identification of Red Riding Hood, Dan reduces Snow White to a red towel which can be possessed and used as an unproblematic point of reference. Chang responds with a more familiar form of sexual reification: "I don't want a ratty old towel. *I want the beautiful snow-white arse itself!*" (101). In the mind of yet another dwarf, she is a shower, for in that space their sexual encounters take place. Clearly, Snow White is a fetishized object. She is not framed by the magic mirror in these scenes, but because she is a sexual object in the dwarves' imagination she is just as lifeless as the traditional Snow White.

Barthelme's text tries to escape this objectification of Snow White by giving her a voice as one of the novel's several narrators, a strategy which to some extent disrupts both narrative and gender re-production. Significantly, Snow White's dissatisfaction with language sets Barthelme's fragmentary plot in motion: "Oh I wish there were some words in the world that were not the words I always hear" (6). Faced with the limits of the script she has been handed, Snow White decides to write her own: a poem which begins "'bandaged and wounded'" ("'run together'" as one word, she insists) and explores the theme of loss (59). Though not allowed to see it, the dwarves describe it as "a dirty great poem four pages long," while Snow White defines it as "'free, . . . free, free, free'" (10, 59). As a deferred presence that affects the relationship, for the dwarves the poem means that "'something was certainly wrong,'" while for Snow White it is a sign that her own "imagination is stirring" (59). Both readings work. Snow White finds out that she does not like the world of the dwarves, that she is "tired of being a horsewife [sic]" (43), and that she is angry at "male domination of the physical world" and of language. The reproduction of gender in language and its pseudo-mimetic logic especially infuriate her: "Oh if only I could get my hands on the man who dubbed those electrical connections male and female! He thought he was so worldly. And if I could just get my hands on the man who called that piece of pipe a nipple! He thought he was so urbane" (131).

The no-longer-muted Snow White extends her criticism beyond words and language to heterosexuality as procreation, which she contrasts with a different kind of pleasure. Referring to one of her shower rendezvous with the dwarves, Snow White decides to herself: "Everything in life is interesting except Clem's idea of sexual congress, his Western confusion between the concept, 'pleasure,' and the concept, 'increasing the size of the herd'" (34). By insisting that all sexual activities with the dwarves take place in the shower, Snow White tries to minimize her dissatisfaction with her role as textual and sexual object, or as she puts it: "the water on my back is interesting. It is more than interesting. Marvelous is the word for it" (34). As Alan Wilde suggests, "marvelous," may here be opposed to "extraordinary," as a strategy for disenchanting our (narrative and sexual) fictions, as a strategy for arousing our imaginations to wonder/wander, to speculate curiously, without freezing or excluding the ordinary.[31] In the flow of the water, in its "thousand points of perturbation," Snow White finds the same kind of pleasure and freedom she experiences when writing her own poem.

But she still tries to enact her traditional role as an "innocent persecuted heroine." She lets down her ebony hair from the window—mirroring the symbolic gesture of another of her imprisoned sisters, Rapunzel—and, like the Disney character, she exclaims: "'Someday my prince will come.' Snow White announces here that she lives her own being as incomplete, pending the arrival of one who will 'complete' her" (70). She does also realize that "'waiting as a mode of existence is . . . a darksome mode'" (77), and cries out: "'O Jerusalem, Jerusalem! Thy daughters are burning with torpor and a sense of immense wasted potential, like one of those pipes you see in the oil fields, burning off the natural gas that it isn't economically rational to ship elsewhere!'" (102). And yet Snow White's consciousness of being imprisoned in her own fiction does not enable her to produce a new narrative or sexual subjectivity for herself. Incapable of playing her assigned role convincingly, she is nevertheless bound to try to sustain it. There is no viable alternative: after experimenting with words and action, she finds herself as powerless as she was to start with, more afraid of "being out" than "being home" (117). At the height of her confusion, she surrenders her new beginnings to the mirror and reproduction, knowingly letting herself be kept in a tower under surveillance by Paul—the prince figure—through a system of mirrors and trained dogs. Reverting to the status of a "long-sleeping stock certificate" (59), Snow White's imagination after Paul's accidental death is reduced to pure aestheticism: "Snow White continues to cast chrysanthemums on Paul's grave, although there is nothing in it for her, in that grave" (180). Though she knows there is nothing for her in a world where female characters mirror masculine expectations, Snow White knows how difficult it is to imagine a different world.[32]

* * *

Does this surrender imply a failure in women's imagination? Does it mirror women's lack? I think not, for in Barthelme's narrative Snow White is still, however unwillingly, the image of Woman within a patriarchal script which she can disrupt but not change. Like all Snow Whites, she is what writer Ursule Molinaro describes as "The Contest Winner"—"void of course," a motherless "fantasy of helpless purity/pure helplessness that is obscuring the desirability of real women," and "almost without a voice":

> The most assertive sound to come out of her is the choked gurgle as she upchucks the poisoned piece of apple. —Whose red cheek is coated with her saliva, mirroring hundreds of tiny snow white lies. (*A Full Moon of Women* 147-48, 149)

If in this fiction, "the ultimate judge is the mirror," then as Molinaro's word-portrait concludes, "mirrors should reflect more deeply." Apollinaire made a similar demand when he said he expected "to see his poetry instead of his face" (149). Since "his" image of our faces often constitutes "his" poetry, and leaves "us" out of the picture, women's demands need to be even higher.

While Coover's tale articulates the prince's dissatisfaction with his own mimetic imagination which objectifies beauty and women, Carter's tale reflects that frozen-like stillness back to its generator and judge. But recognizing the flatness of such limited reflection is not the end of the story. Both Coover and Carter have continued over the years to pursue the project of undoing the strategies of the magic mirror, demanding more, but from distinctly gendered perspectives. Coover's explorations of the stifling effects of women's objectification on women and especially men, at least those whose homo-social bonds are weak and whose imaginations would enjoy a life-giving and reciprocal partnership, have proliferated in order to precipitate patriarchal awareness into de-construction. In particular, sexuality and its politically framed power games have played a central role in Coover's self-consciously interruptive and hypertextual re-awakening of dormant metaphors in fairy tales (see *Pricksongs & Descants* and most recently "Briar Rose").[33] Carter's re-vision of the sexual politics of fairy tales has more definitely been woman-centered, even in its intimate closeup of Bluebeard's imagination. Because women have more consistently and en masse worked to re-flesh the fairy tale, the bulk of this book amplifies and glosses women's voices, looks, and actions in postmodern narratives by women.

3
NOT
RE(A)D ONCE
AND FOR ALL
"LITTLE RED RIDING HOOD"'S VOICES IN PERFORMANCE

*The lines of an
imaginary are inscribed on the
social flesh by the knifepoint of history.*
— CHARLES BERNSTEIN, "Of Time and the Line"

REREADING IS THE MAGIC KEY to rewriting: re-viewing a narrative like "Snow White," as Barthelme, Coover, Carter, and Molinaro have done, raises questions that demand revising its
naturalized artifice. As we have seen, this rewriting need not be
simply a stylistic or ideological updating to make the tale more appealing to late twentieth-century adult audiences. In the above
cases, it involves substantive though diverse questioning of both
narrative construction and assumptions about gender. Nor is such
a narrative and ideological critique necessarily one-sided or negative. Postmodern revision is often two-fold, seeking to expose,
make visible, the fairy tale's complicity with "exhausted" narrative
and gender ideologies, and, by working from the fairy tales' multiple versions, seeking to expose, bring out, what the institutional-
ization of such tales for children has forgotten or left unexploited.[1] This kind of rereading does more than interpret anew or
shake the genre's ground rules. It listens for the many "voices" of
fairy tales as well, as part of a historicizing and performance-oriented project.

Though she has listened with a particularly keen ear to these
voices, readers of Angela Carter have at times found her engagement with fairy tales restrictive, especially for women. In "Re-Imagining the Fairy Tale: Angela Carter's Bloody Chambers," Patricia
Duncker applauds Carter's ambition to rearrange "the bricks of
our inner worlds" (3), but faults her for "re-writing the tales within
the strait-jacket of their original structures" (6). According to
Duncker, the tale, and "especially the fairy tale, is the vessel of
false knowledge, or more bluntly, interested propaganda" (3–4).
Its imagery, which derives from the unconscious, can only reflect
the power relations of patriarchy. Its rigid sexual patterns teach

fear and masochism as tenets of femininity, and its symbolic inver-
sions do not undermine established hierarchies. By amplifying
these images, conflicts, and transformations, Carter's revisions
simply confirm sado-masochistic arrangements instead of conceiv-
ing of "women's sexuality as autonomous desire" (7).

Avis Lewallen and Robert Clark also take issue with the erotic
and political dynamics in Carter's stories. "Sex is always and everywhere heterosexual," Lewallen complains. She further notes that
Carter's own analysis in *The Sadeian Woman* of the socio-political
constructedness of desire seems to have been left out of her own
tales (156). Robert Clark's interest in ideology and its narrative
staging in "Angela Carter's Desire Machine" leads him to con-
clude that her fictions generally "offer their readers a knowledge
of patriarchy" yet reinscribe "patriarchal attitudes":

> [H]er writing is often a feminism in male chauvinistic drag, a transvestite
> style, and this may be because her primary allegiance is to a postmodern
> aesthetics that emphasizes the non-referential emptiness of definitions.
> Such a commitment precludes an affirmative feminism founded in refer-
> ential commitment to women's historical and organic being. (158)

What these critics share is a profound mistrust of Carter's handling of the fairy tale in *The Bloody Chamber*. Duncker calls Carter's
"lavish and ornate" style her "great strength" (12), presumably because of its potentially subversive excess which should be allowed
to flourish in an extended narrative. The fairy tale's imagery and
short form, however, can only restrict this excess of style and desire. Lewallen warns women readers about the sexy, tricky "surface
gloss and shimmer" (144) of Carter's writing. Such irony and play-
fulness can manipulate us into sympathizing with masochism or
choosing "between rape and death" (154). Clark laments Carter's
"self-pleasing concern with textual style" (159) because it com-
modifies and blunts her ideological critique of patriarchy. Her
postmodern commitment is not the only problem; the symbolism
of the fairy tale, what Clark more generally calls "allegory," is itself
a trap.[2]

All three critics see style as a transformative strategy which
Carter directs upon the fixed ideological and sexual dynamics of
the fairy tale. But this magic re-clothing does not work for them
because, like the wolf in grandmother's night clothes, heterosex-

ual sadomasochism eventually shows its teeth. The fairy tale's brevity, imagery, and symbolism cause it inexorably to reproduce a conservative ideology. Duncker states this problem explicitly when she argues that Carter's heroines remain inside "the infernal trap inherent in the fairy tale, which carries its ideology in its own form" (6):

> Carter chooses to inhabit a tiny room of her own in the house of fiction. For women, that space has always been paralysingly, cripplingly small. I think we need the "multiplying ambiguities of an extended narrative." . . . We cannot fit neatly into patterns or models as Cinderellas, ugly sisters, wicked step-mothers, fairy god-mothers, and still acknowledge our several existences, experienced or imagined. We need the space to carve out our own erotic identities, as free women. ("Re-Imagining the Fairy Tale" 12)

All well and good, as far as it goes. But as Carter herself notes in *The Sadeian Woman*, "a free woman in an unfree society will be a monster" and her sexuality, even if based on personal privilege, will be like that of men, "a mirror of their [relationships'] inhumanity, a magnified relation of the ambivalence of the word 'to fuck', in its twinned meanings of sexual intercourse and despoliation: 'a fuck up', 'to fuck something up', 'he's fucked'" (27). Neither the struggle for freedom or a belief in change should be abandoned; but to actually transform desire, an action both Carter and Duncker advocate, may require acknowledging and confronting, rather than simply rejecting, the fairy tale's "several existences" as a genre in history, as well as its stylized configurations of "woman."[3]

To counter such negative political assessments of both fairy tales and Angela Carter's recourse to them, I will discuss her revisions of "Little Red Riding Hood" in fiction and other media—first to foreground their layered, genealogical construction, and then to argue that this plural self-reflexivity can (re)produce empowering possibilities for women and narrative. Specific questions about Duncker's rhetoric of confinement lead me to explore this gen(de)red "bloody chamber." Does Carter's narrative chamber of choice—the fairy tale—have a prison-like lock? Do Carter's heroines remain definitively shut in this tiny room? And does the text's closure inevitably make the lock click? As I discuss the play of narrative closure and representational enclosure or captivity, I will show how Carter explodes the stereotype of the fairy tale as a static and "closed system" by mobilizing the multiple and contradictory refractions of sexualized imagery and symbolism which the tale's very fusion of "sign and sense," its concentration of meaning, generates as the tale is performed in different social contexts.[4] In the process, I will also be implicitly qualifying the kind of critical reading of narrative and gender symbolism I conducted in Chapter Two, a reading that focused primarily on the tale's authoritative framing as prescriptive "writing" to the exclusion of the tale's multiple "voices."

* * *

Published in 1697, Charles Perrault's tale, "Le petit chaperon rouge," marks an important moment in the history of "The Glutton" or "Red Riding Hood" (AT333).[5] While taking goodies to her granny, a little country girl, "the prettiest that had ever been seen" and named after the red hood her doting grandmother made for her, meets "old neighbor wolf." Not knowing that it is "dangerous to stop and listen to a wolf," Red Riding Hood explains where she is going and he proposes a "race," as each takes a different path to the grandmother's house. Arriving first, the wolf knocks, "toc, toc." Pretending to be the little girl, he lets himself in, and then, "for it had been more than three days since he had last eaten," devours the "good woman." Lying in the grandmother's bed, he waits for the little girl. "Toc, toc": she lets herself in hesitantly and obeys the grandmother/wolf: "Put the biscuits and the pot of butter on the bin and come lie down beside me." After undressing, the girl is in bed with the grandmother/wolf. There, "astonished" at how the grandmother looks in "dés-habillé," Red Riding Hood recites the familiar litany—arms, legs, ears, eyes, all so big. When however she exclaims "'What big teeth you have, grandmother!,'" the wicked wolf replies, "'The better to eat you,'" and does. The customary moral in verse follows this uniquely unhappy ending in Perrault's *Histoires ou contes du temps passé*, warning all children, and "pretty, well-brought up, and gentle" girls especially, that "all wolves / Are not of the same kind," and that those appearing "tame, good-natured, and pleasant" might be "most dangerous of all" (Zipes, *Trials and Tribulations* 91–93).[6]

As the very first printed version of "Red Riding Hood," Perrault's text shaped the ensuing literary tradition, and powerfully affected oral retellings as well. "Little Red Riding Hood" began to circulate in the British literary and folkloric context only after Robert Samber's 1729 translation of Perrault. In Germany, the tale was not well known until the Grimms collected their "Little Red Cap" from a teller familiar with Perrault, and in France itself many subsequently collected oral tales derive such significant details as the red hood and the moral from Perrault's text. By studying oral tales collected primarily in the nineteenth century, and in a specific area—the basin of the Loire in France, Tirol and northern Italy, where "Red Riding Hood" possibly originated and certainly was popular—folklorists have however reconstructed pre-Perrault versions which he presumably modified to suit his own narrative and ideological purposes when constructing a fairly atypical but authoritative text.[7]

In this localized European oral tradition of the late middle ages, a peasant girl would, on her way to visit her grandmother, meet a werewolf (*loup-garou*) or wolf. One then takes the "path of the needles," while the other takes the "path of the pins." Having devoured the grandmother, the wolf in disguise waits for the girl and welcomes her with something to eat and drink: some of the grandmother's flesh and blood, presented as sliced meat or local specialties and wine. In most versions, the girl accepts. Then she strips, one item of clothing at a time, and following a formulaic question-and-answer sequence, she burns her clothes in the fire and joins the wolf in bed. Finally, after the ritual exchange which reveals the wolf's intentions ("The better to eat you, my child!"), the wolf gobbles the girl up *or* the girl escapes by pretending she needs to go outside to answer the call of nature.[8]

Debate over the closure of "Red Riding Hood" has been intense and significant to the interpretation of the tale as a whole. For historian Robert Darnton the death of the protagonist exemplifies the dangers and miseries of peasant life in eighteenth-century France, while Marianne Rumpf sees the unhappy ending as the definite mark of the warning tale tradition to which "Red Riding

Hood" belongs. Jack Zipes, however, contends that the authentic and most typical folkloric ending is the happy one, and Steven Swann Jones points to the heroine's escape and its scatological humor as authentic components of the oral tradition. Both endings appear in the 1885 sample of oral tales studied by Paul Delarue,[9] and Marc Soriano concluded from Delarue's findings that both traditions were alive before Perrault (432-33). I too will take this co-existence of variants as the starting point of my own genealogy: first, because the pre-Perrault "oral text" is necessarily reconstructed and therefore not strictly "authentic"; second, because choosing one variant over the other here limits the social functions of warning and initiation performed through this story's telling; and third, because the popularity of both endings in a literary and folkloristic context attests to their value and vitality. But even when we acknowledge the dual folkloric tradition, Perrault's text differs dramatically from the oral "Conte de la mère-grand" or "The Story of Grandmother." Perrault offers no pins or needles choice, no cannibalistic motif, no sexual or bodily elements such as drawn-out stripteases, hairy bodies, and defecation, and absolutely no happy ending, inserting instead a metonymic naming of the protagonist (the red hood) which was not typical of the oral versions. How do the omitted episodes function and what do they mean? And similarly how do Perrault's changes operate?

Historians and anthropologists have helped scholars of folklore and children's literature to answer these questions. As a warning tale, or *Warnmärchen*, in the folkloric tradition, "Red Riding Hood" took on specific and "real" objects of fear. During the winter in the French, Tirolian, and Italian Alps, wolves were an actual danger to peasants, and their children especially.[10] The story's unhappy ending thus fits within the tradition of cautionary tales—this, boys and girls, could happen to you. The belief in werewolves was also particularly strong in these mountain areas. Trials, treatises, and customs referring to werewolves can be documented well into the sixteenth and seventeenth centuries. As etymology tells us, the werewolf or "manwolf" embodied the proverbial peasant distrust of human nature. Any neighbor or relative could be such a shape-shifter and turn dangerous when called upon by the Familiar or the moon.

But what could the devil want from little children? Easy victims, apparently. In many trials "werewolves" were accused of, and occasionally even confessed to, having killed and eaten children (Otten 49–97, Röhrich 114). While scary stories about strangers and wild creatures might not be pedagogically respectful, we still tell them today. And finally, when the victim is a female—which in most versions of "Red Riding Hood" she is[11]—the medieval werewolf/devil association has specifically sexual connotations[12] which Perrault both foregrounds and sanitizes. Though his tale is undeniably cautionary, its warning is more clearly gendered—"Pretty girls, beware of smooth-tongued seducers"—yet less eroticized. Although the girl still climbs into bed with the wolf, it is no longer a *man*wolf, and her elaborate strip-tease is reduced to the simple statement that she "undressed." For Perrault, then, while still the devil's doing, seduction relies on words and manners. The flesh remains concealed or repressed.[13]

As an initiatory tale in the oral tradition, "Red Riding Hood" did more than symbolize the child's ability to defeat danger and evil by resorting to cunning: it also demonstrated the importance of women's knowledge to survival.[14] In most general terms, the oral message focuses on the girl's relation to her (grand)mother. Just as the protagonist must enter and exit the older woman's house successfully, she must also negotiate the older woman's changing nature and death. Yvonne Verdier has argued that the crucial exchange in the French peasant tradition is between the grandmother, whom the title used to identify as the central character, and the girl. By eating the flesh and drinking the blood, the young girl incorporates the grandmother's knowledge and takes her place. This involuntary and sympathetic cannibalism requires the older woman's sacrifice—in all known versions, either the grandmother or the mother "dies"—but brings about the re-birth of the younger woman. The wolf is merely a mediator or the symbolic representation of an aged woman (Verdier).[15] That the girl is often required to cook what the wolf eats raw merely stresses the cultural nature of this consummation, and, though much of this knowledge (sewing, cooking, giving birth) points to the domestication of women, simply representing this cultural (grand) mother-girl assimilation speaks for some form of woman-centered genealogy.[16]

Though Perrault's tale also has an initiatory function, the focus is strictly heterosexual. He foregrounds the dynamics between the wolf and the girl, and justifies the tale's violent outcome by pointing to the devil-associated red garment as evidence of the victim's complicity.[17] Perrault thus narrows down the oral tale to a heterosexual scenario in which girls are "naturally" both victims and seducers. Furthermore, because his fairy tales were written for the aristocracy, with a style designed to satisfy the highly cultivated adult reader, and morals meant to educate the young in civilized behavior, Perrault's "Red Riding Hood" bans the flesh and the body from the scene of seduction. No partaking of flesh as vital exchange, no hairy grandmother-wolf, no defecation or urination: the flesh can only be the mark of damnation and the body of impropriety.[18]

The effects of such narrative tailoring are still apparent when the Brothers Grimm bring the "happy ending" tradition to the literary history of "Red Riding Hood." In their 1812 German text, influenced by both Perrault and Tieck, a "sweet little maiden" always wears the "red velvet cap" made by her grandmother who loves her the most, so "Little Red Cap" (*Rotkäppchen*) becomes her name. Her mother warns her "not to stray from the path" when the little girl leaves for the woods with a basket of goodies to visit her sick grandmother, and Red Cap promises to obey. When she meets and begins talking with the wolf, she is not afraid of him because she does not know he is "wicked," and eventually takes his advice to enjoy the beauty of the woods and indulge herself in picking flowers. The wolf goes straight to grandmother's house, "swallows" her up, and puts on her nightcap to disguise himself. When Little Red Cap arrives, the frightened girl wonders out loud about the "strange appearance" of her grandmother's ears, hands, eyes, mouth. The wolf leaps on her and swallows her up too. A hunter passing by investigates the loud snoring he hears coming from the frail old woman's house, and discovers the wolf lying asleep and full in her bed. "Perhaps she can still be saved. I won't shoot, thought the hunter," so he slits the wolf's belly open instead, and the girl and her grandmother jump out, happy to see the light again. Little Red Cap fills the wolf's body with heavy stones. When he wakes up, he falls "down dead," which pleases the other three characters. The hunter skins the wolf, the grandmother eats and drinks her goodies, and the girl thinks to herself: "Never again in your life will you stray by yourself into the woods when your mother has forbidden it." An addendum follows: when the girl meets another wolf, she and her grandmother trick him by appealing to his uncontrollable gluttony and he falls to his death (Zipes, *Trials and Tribulations* 135–37).

Though this "Rotkäppchen" seems quite different from Perrault's "Le petit chaperon rouge," their gender ideology and their sexual politics are remarkably similar. Little Red Cap survives, but, unlike the shrewd girl of the oral tradition, at least the first time around she requires a savior—the hunter.[19] The Grimms' tale softens Perrault's pedagogy and yet remains cautionary. The girl has learned her lesson: obey your mother and don't give in to errant desires. Furthermore, in the Grimms' version, all bodies must be regulated, contained, or rendered as unfeeling and sterile as the wolf's stone-filled belly.[20] The girl never undresses, never lies in bed with the wolf, and never eats anything—though in later retellings she enjoys the goodies with grandmother and the hunter in a "happy-family" scene. Even the wolf's devouring of the two females is a punishment with no blood-spilling, no crunching of bones, thus allowing the bodies to emerge intact from the wolf's belly precisely because their consumption is not an experience of the flesh. In the two most popular literary versions of "Red Riding Hood," then, the wolf is either a "smooth-tongued" seducer, covertly associated with the devil, or the natural instrument of lawful punishment; the girl is either too naive to survive or so unreliable that she must be saved from herself; and the grandmother is simply an appetizer.[21] The traditional lore of wolves and werewolves is suppressed, the girl is stripped of her wits and courage, the grandmother's knowledge and body are robbed of their nurturing possibilities, and the flesh is deprived of its life and blood.

The *literary* tradition of "Red Riding Hood" therefore does lock the protagonist into a gendered and constricting chamber. Whether she survives her journey into the outer world or not, the girl is *inside* when the tale ends—inside the wolf's belly for Perrault, or her grandmother's home for the Grimms. Devoured or domesticated, charged with sin or in charge of the feminine hearth, in the literary fairy-tale tradition Red Riding Hood is subjected to the laws of one deliberative masculine body. When the wolf punishes the girl's curiosity, and when the hunter saves her and the grandmother, males determine feminine limits. Or as Hélène Cixous suggests, because they partake of the same masculine or "immasculated" order ("Castration and Decapitation"), the wolf and the grandmother are one.

This is the fairy tale as "institution," that confining narrative which "educates" upper- and middle-class girls in the propriety of keeping to their place as "angels of the home," and thus never to be mistaken for demonic sexual beings. But "Red Riding Hood" cannot be confined to this script. The tale has other wonders to perform, and I want to argue that Angela Carter's postmodern rewritings are acts of fairy-tale archeology that release this story's many other voices. As an enthusiastic listener/reader of both folk and fairy tales, and as a writer who draws from many versions, oral and literary, Carter tells tales that reactivate lost traditions, trace violently contradictory genealogies, and flesh out the complex and vital workings of desire and narrative. I will focus on two strategies in "The Werewolf," "The Company of Wolves," and "Wolf-Alice," Carter's three "women-in-the-company-of-wolves" stories (*The Bloody Chamber*). First, her dialogue with the folkloric traditions and social history of "Red Riding Hood"; second, her own invocation of plural versions, to explore performance as a social and textual practice that variedly negotiates between norms and departures from them in the company of its audiences/readers. These strategies transform the commonly accepted and fixed representation of gender and sexuality in fairy tales by revaluing both economically and narratively (female) blood, and in the screen play for "The Company of Wolves," by voicing the protagonist's self-reflecting desires and narratives.

As in "The Snow Child," winter is the setting for "The Werewolf"—but a winter neither invincible nor immaculate, since it is sullied by "wild beasts in the forest," graveyard "picnics," and ritual murders. In addition, the narrator's foregrounding of the historical and ideological distance separates her and her audience/reader from the fictional world: "To these upland woodsmen, the Devil is as real as you or I. More so; they have not seen us nor even know that we exist" (108). These northern people lead "harsh, brief, poor lives." Food, or more accurately the scarcity of it in cold weather, dominates their existence. They also fear those who feed

on them—the bears, but the witches and vampires as well—and
these anxious people kill to gain some control over what they do
not understand:

> some old woman whose cheeses ripen when her neighbours' do not, an-
> other old woman whose black cat, oh sinister! follows her about all the
> time, they strip the crone, search for her marks, for the supernumerary
> nipple her familiar sucks. They soon find it. Then they stone her to death.
> (108)

As a result, the immediately familiar words of mother to daughter come almost as shock: "Go and visit grandmother, who has
been sick. Take her the oatcakes I've baked for her on the hearth-
stone and a little pot of butter" (109). This cold and violent context, a quasi-ethnographic sketch of early modern upland peasant
life and its "popular sentences" or naturalized beliefs, resembles
the French peasant world of the seventeenth century as historian
Darnton would have it. A time-worn warning and initiatory tale
thus emerges from a specific economic and social situation. We
cannot help but hear the story anew.

Danger is real and ordinary. The mother bids the "good girl"
not to leave the path "because of the bears, the wild boar, the
starving wolves" and to take her father's hunting knife: "you know
how to use it." When the girl, in "a scabby coat of sheepskin," is attacked by a huge wolf, she behaves like the "mountaineer's child"
that she is, and slashes off "its right forepaw" (109). She then treks
through the snow, carrying the oatcakes, knife, and beastly paw in
her basket to her grandmother's. The old woman is really sick,
with a high fever. An explanation—offered by the external narrator with no comments—quickly follows: what was the wolf's paw is
now "a hand toughened with work and freckled with old age." Recognizing a wart on the index finger to be her grandmother's, the
girl struggles with the old woman to see the "stump where her
right hand should have been."[22] Because the girl *knows* that the
werewolf is a creature of the devil, she crosses herself and immediately calls for help. Because the neighbors *know* that the wart is a
witch's mark, they take the old woman out into the snow, then
beat and stone her to death. The narrator concludes emphatically:
"Now the child lived in her grandmother's house; she prospered"
(110).

While the mother's warning and the happy ending for the girl with help from the woodsmen indicate that the Grimms' version is in the background, the shape-shifting devils, witches, and werewolves of the folkloric tradition have not only repopulated the tale but also unmade the girl, wolf, and granny as we know them from the Grimms or Perrault. In the name of historical accuracy? Hardly. Carter's archeology is of the genealogical kind, which exposes the struggles of one story's attempt to devour another story, as each teller tries to become "the" teller, and each ideology represents itself as the truth.[23] Thanks to the contrasting voices represented in Carter's tale, the werewolf's reappearance brings with it contradictory warnings. In this cold forest a girl clearly "must always be on her guard" (109) to survive. No matter what appearances might be, she must recognize the devil. The girl's success confirms the belief system that supports her actions, and the community's as well, as they righteously defeat "evil." "Any one will tell you that" (108)—such matter-of-fact, impersonally harsh popular wisdom prevails.

And yet, though her lamb-like purity is rewarded, this girl only wears "a scabby coat of sheepskin." Is she too in disguise? Economics after all can turn sheep into wolves—the grandmother into a witch, the young girl into a killer. And economics, which the narrator juxtaposes from the beginning against the moral dichotomies of popular sentencing, are also at issue when the girl "prospers" after taking over her grandmother's house. Though grandmother and wolf are one here, the confusion has a different valency than it does in the tales by Perrault and the Grimms. In Carter's tale, while the starving wolf is a deadly danger to the struggling and poor community, the wolf-witch serves as that same community's scapegoat. Carter's version of initiation works in disturbingly shifting ways. Instead of drinking her ancestor's blood to reinforce family/female ties, the girl spills that blood in a scapegoating ritual that ensures her own livelihood. She replaces the old woman, not by assimilation but through a violent severance that reproduces the wolf's ferocity. As the narrative comes to a close, the ambiguous implications of the girl's possession of her grandmother's house allow for no easy moral judgment or unmediated explanation. Has she defeated the witch? Turned into one herself? Both or neither? Violence is our "familiar" here, implicating all parties including the audience/reader, and implying that the devil is only the institutionalized projection of our fears and desires.

"The Company of Wolves," a counterpoint to "The Werewolf," continues Carter's critical dialogue with folkloric and literary voices within the "Red Riding Hood" tradition. Like "The Werewolf," this short story begins with popular beliefs, proscriptions and exhortations; like "The Werewolf," these warnings end with the single injunction: "Fear and flee the wolf" (111). But the audience here is addressed as "you": like the child who was told cautionary tales in the Alps centuries ago, "you" must listen to the reasons humans have for fearing the wolf, and since "you are always in danger in the forest, where no people are," you must also identify with the potential victim (111). As in "The Werewolf," you learn that the wolf is "carnivore incarnate," "cunning," and "ferocious." Howling with sequin-like eyes, he is the worst of "all the teeming perils of the night . . . for he cannot listen to reason" (110–11). As some werewolf anecdotes bear out, you also are aware that this dangerous prowler lurks in the forest where you might unwisely wander, and "at your own hearthside" as well, for "the wolf may be more than he seems" (111). By drawing on other strands of lore, however, Carter reminds us that werewolves are not simply devilish creatures devoted to witchcraft and cannibalism, but also sad creatures, whose "canticles" hold "a vast melancholy."[24] These tormented beings cannot redeem themselves, for "grace could not come to the wolf from his own despair, only through some external mediator, so that, sometimes, the beast will look as if he half welcomes the knife that dispatches him" (112).[25] Fear and sympathy are common and traditional attitudes toward the damned.[26]

Also in counterpoint to "The Werewolf," "The Company of Wolves" works from and against Perrault's seduction-filled version to foreground the heterosexual, rather than familial, plot. Male and strangely attractive, the werewolf playfully tries to impress the girl with his up-to-date "magic object," a compass. When she ignores her mother's warning and she leaves for her grandmother's house in midwinter (113), like the child-protagonist of "The Werewolf," the girl is unafraid. But for different reasons: "too much loved ever to feel scared," her "thick shawl" has her "dressed and ready" for kisses (146–47).²⁷ Though she too has a knife, and a red shawl with "the ominous if brilliant look of blood on snow," it is not certain just whose blood will be spilled, or why (147). When she meets a "fine fellow" dressed in green in the forest,²⁸ she wagers this hunter a kiss if, guided only by his compass, he can reach her grandmother's house first. Though she stays on the path, she wishes to lose the bet. As for granny, this "aged and frail," ever so "pious" woman, almost ready to succumb to mortality, proves an easy victim for the young hunter/wolfman (115). When the girl realizes that not only has she lost her bet, but her grandmother is gone, she cannot reach for her knife, too far in the basket she let him carry, and her scarlet shawl no longer protects her from fear. Will she now turn from "rustic" seductress into a rape or murder victim—like her granny and her Perrault predecessor?

She probably would—except that she can hear the sadness of the wolves' "concert" outside in the cold, can see their eyes, reflecting "the light from the kitchen," shining "like a hundred candles" (117). The warning handed down to her cannot restrict the perceptions of "this strong-minded child" (113). Open to other, equally traditional rituals, instead she does away with her fear, and plays an old game with a twist. As in earlier folkloric versions, she takes her shawl off and throws it in the fire, continuing the ritual strip-tease until her naked body, "dazzling" as "firelight," gleams "as if snow had invaded the room" (117–18). The outside and the inside, cold and warmth, the wild and the hearth are no longer separate. This "wise child" recognizes that simply because he has been on the outside the hunter/wolfman need not have deadly appetites:

> What big teeth you have! . . .
> All the better to eat you with.
> The girl burst out laughing; she knew she was nobody's meat. She laughed at him full in the face, she ripped off his shirt and flung it into the fire. (118)

Both will be naked, wearing only their flesh and hair: a fiery sabbath, some would see; inevitable violence, others would say.²⁹ But by acting out her desires—sexual, not just for life—the girl offers herself as flesh, not meat. The "carnivorous" nature of their encounter is transformed, and "See! Sweet and sound she sleeps in granny's bed, between the paws of the tender wolf" (118).[30] Playing on the shifting nature of orality, the pun in "tender" is also a trace of that sympathetic, life-giving cannibalism which in older versions joins the girl with granny. Both carnivores incarnate, these two young heterosexual beings satiate their hunger not for dead meat, but flesh, while at the same time embodying it.[31] Inside her grandmother's house, between the paws of the wolf, she (girl and wolf?) is no longer a "closed system" (114). Just as the girl has slipped out of her overdetermined and victimizing propriety, so now is the wolf, that excluded and demonized other, allowed to slip in. And, as "the door of the solstice stands wide open" (118), life is once again celebrated.[32]

"One must howl with the wolves." Carter dramatizes this ambiguous old saying, as in "The Werewolf" one heroine preys on her grandmother in order to survive, and in "The Company of Wolves" another fearlessly lives out her sexuality. In "Wolf-Alice," Carter's third "women-with-wolves" story, a girl who quite literally howls embodies yet another dimension of the wolf-human association. Found "in the wolf's den beside the bullet-riddled corpse of her foster mother" (119–20), with this girl "nothing about her is human except that she is *not* a wolf; it is as if the fur she thought she wore had melted into her skin and become part of it, although it does not exist" (119, my emphasis). Taken to a convent, where she learns some hygiene but rejects the ritual of grateful prayer, she eventually becomes the servant of an outcast werewolfish Duke. Living in his "Mycenaean tomb," the Duke has "ceased to cast an image in the mirror" (120), and preys on dead bodies at night.[33] Exiled from the company of both wolves and humans, she begins to "invent" her own subjectivity—perhaps as a new Eve or as a Blakean "bud of flesh in the kind lion's mouth," or even as an unexpected Man Friday. Whatever the choice, though, the narrator suggests that "she might prove to be the wise child who leads them all and her silence and her howling a language as authentic as any language of nature" (121). In the Duke's gloomy mansion, where the moon and the mirror are her only sources of (self)reflection, she experiences menarche and thus enters time. When an avenging silver bullet wounds the Duke, Wolf-Alice runs to the rescue wearing a dead woman's wedding dress. Back in his chamber, she tenderly cleans the fiend's gun-produced wound since wolves—unlike humans—took care of her because of her imperfection, and so Wolf-Alice turns to her "gaunt grey" as a role-model, tending to that wounded parody of both wolves and humans, the Duke.

Less overtly, but no less significantly, Carter's "Wolf-Alice" revives other silenced voices in the complex, contradictory "Red Riding Hood" and (were)wolf traditions.[34] As in "De puella a lupellis seruata" ("About a Girl Saved from Wolf Cubs"), a seldom mentioned medieval "Red Riding Hood" analog that Jan M. Ziolkowski notes "should be registered somewhere on the family tree" (575), we discover the female protagonist not in her granny's home, but unexpectedly safe in the lair of the wolf.[35] In the medieval poem, the girl tames the wolves thanks to her red tunic, which represents the redemptive power of baptism; while actively overturning this christianizing message, "Wolf-Alice" also celebrates the redeeming powers of a blood-marked girl "in the wolf's den" (119).

"Suckled by wolves"—this girl is both a feral child, much like the inarticulate, intractable "wolf children" studied by twentieth-century scientists, and a hero, marked like Romulus and Remus or Beowulf by association with the ancestral wolf.[36] Though humans believe they have rescued Wolf-Alice, she proves to be the savior. "We" have language, but her "gentle tongue" has other powers. "We" judge and spill blood, while her brave acceptance of difference revalues life.

> The lucidity of the moonlight lit the mirror propped against the red wall; the rational glass, the master of the visible, impartially recorded the crooning girl.
> As she continued her ministrations, . . . little by little, there appeared within [the glass], . . . as if brought into being by her soft, moist, gentle tongue, finally, the face of the Duke. (126)

This closure paradoxically gives birth, *peopling* the bloody chamber, re-envisioning it from within by redefining what "human" is, as these differently wounded beings inaugurate new reflections and songs.[37]

Together, then, these three radically different "women-in-the-

company-of-wolves" scripts bring into being contradictory yet ge-
nealogically related images of "Red Riding Hood." Thus, though
not representing a "flight" from the bloody chamber, the plural
closure of Carter's narratives allows "departure," breaking with
"the specular relations" which rule the coherence of a subject or
text (Cixous, "Castration or Decapitation"), and imag(in)ing a different kind of self-reflexivity, one pouring out of touch, voice, and
blood. Like the older literary versions of "Red Riding Hood," then
Carter's three stories leave the protagonists within the bloody
chamber, where they work to transform and multiply our fixed
image of both fairy-tale heroines and chambers.

And, as I hope I have shown, just as listening for the multiplicity
of folktale voices revitalizes the fairy tale, by acknowledging the
folkblood of storytelling, so too is the economic and symbolic
revaluing of women's menstrual and birth blood essential to the
transformation of the heroine's subjectivity. Formerly identified
with life itself, blood's "natural" value has been "covered over by
other forms of wealth: gold, penis, child." In patriarchal econ-
omies, women—who represent these "blood reserves"—are exploited because both profit and pleasure require the spilling of
their blood (Irigaray 125).[38] Carter's stories expose such an economy as a voracious preying on human life, and especially on lower-
class or otherwise marginalized women's lives. These stories
defiantly represent lifeblood as empowering, as in the last scene of
"Wolf-Alice," when "with infinite slowness," that "master of the visible," the fairy tale's magic mirror, gives way "to the reflexive
strength of its own material construction," and records the Duke's
and Wolf-Alice's bloody humanity (126).

I have argued that Carter revives the lost voices of "Red Riding
Hood" by negotiating story with story, (were)wolf with (girl)wolf.
But this transformation works only if we are willing to read these
stories intertextually, within the volume *The Bloody Chamber*, and in
the broader wonder tale tradition. Otherwise, "Wolf-Alice" would
display at best a female protagonist who remains an inarticulate,
though crooning, new Eve, identified primarily by her sexuality
and nurturance. By retelling all three "women-in-the-company-of-
wolves" stories, along with the shorter narratives that they inscribe,
as stories within a dream, the later cinematic version of "The Company of Wolves," written by Carter and Neil Jordan, corroborates

the need for intertextual reading. The film's story-within-and-against-other-stories technique not only successfully represents the process of working through an image to undo the distortions of dreamwork, but also performs the lively multiplicity of the storytelling process in a variety of ways. Finally, like the tales, the movie re-values female blood, but does so by reinterpreting blood-line as narrative tradition, and by foregrounding the girl's active role as storyteller within a primarily female genealogy.

Meta-narrative is most definitely the name of the game in this parodic, deliberately overly-symbolic movie. The conventions of horror and psychological movies mingle with animatronics,[39] as "Red Riding Hood" is invoked on at least three significant levels. First, as narrators and characters succeed each other in the framing and embedded narratives, *The Company of Wolves* represents the social history of the fairy tale as genre.[40] Class interests compete over time, as the medieval folktale is appropriated by the upper classes in the eighteenth and nineteenth centuries, and then by the family-centered interpretations of twentieth-century psychoanalysis. For example, the peasant related stories within the protagonist's dream can function as wish fulfillment against upper-class privilege, as when the wronged girl turns the greedy aristocratic wedding party into the wolves that they are. On the other hand the bourgeois-family frame seeks to restrict, though unsuccessfully, the storytelling process to a fixed set of scenarios and symbols.

Second, by telling and retelling stories within stories, and in different situations to differing effects, the movie reproduces the process of storytelling itself. In the first evocation of "Red Riding Hood," for instance, when the protagonist dreams that her older sister has been devoured by wolves, a smile of satisfaction passes over the dreamer's face. Within the dream, though, the older girl's death functions as a warning to the younger one, which granny, who wishes to protect her from all sorts of wolves, underscores by telling the story of a woman whose handsome but mysterious groom was "hairy on the inside." The girl's mother, however, who is more concerned with reassuring her daughter about sex, tells her that "if there is a beast in man, it meets its match in women too." And when the girl herself tells a wolfman story, the point is again different: the wolf may not be worse than those rich people whose wolfish nature her story exposes. And a final turn of the screw. The girl tells this story while her father is out hunting a huge wolf that turns back into a human when killed.

Third, and most importantly, in this Chinese-box narrative the girl actively and critically participates not only in the process of (primarily women's) storytelling, but in the related determination of choices. The older girl's death is presented as a "Don't stray from the path" story, but the protagonist asks "Why couldn't she save herself?" Resisting the warning exemplified in the gruesome story of the werewolf bridegroom, the girl unequivocally states "I'd never let a man strike me," and asks instead how "real wolves" treat their females. As she pursues her curiosity, she begins to tell stories herself—to her mother, and then to the wolf she has met and befriended. By telling her mother a story she claims to have heard from her granny, the girl places herself squarely within the female line of storytelling, but the story itself challenges both older women's dichotomous interpretations of heterosexual relationships, since it explores the intertwined issues of violence and transformation within a social, rather than a demonic or animal, context. And finally, through a story, the girl consoles the crying wolf, a transformation of the man she wounded when he seemed intent on devouring her. Her story is itself about a wounded wolf, but a she-wolf "from the world below" who was a girl "after all." After straying from the path, this wolf encountered both violence and healing; remembering what she had found, she then descends once more. Symbolically representing her own wounded self in this way most obviously establishes communication with the wounded he-wolf. But the wise girl storyteller faces the limited nature of human knowledge and avoids the traps of simple morals.[41] "That's all I'll tell you, for that's all I know" she concludes while stroking the wolf: straying from the path is necessary to acquire knowledge but what that leads to cannot already be known.

The next day, the girl's mother recognizes her as one of the two wolves who leave the grandmother's cottage for the open forest. Is this a liberating and happy ending? Certainly, the girl's self-reflective transformation as a storyteller and a (girl)wolf is an unequivocally critical response to Perrault's victimizing text, which the cautionary story of her sister's death had called up in the beginning. As the dream spills back into life, however, not only does a pack of wolves pull apart the Victorian playhouse, but the terrified dreamer awakens when a "real" wolf breaks into her room through the window. In a violent move, this image undoes much of the woman-centered initiatory storytelling of the stories within the dream. After all, the young girl appears again as a victim of her own sexuality and of deadly appetites. Re-enter Perrault unfortunately, since that final image would seem to confine any transformation of sexual politics to the dream world and punish the girl. Viewers are confronted with another potentially tragic ending, which undercuts the wondrously utopian powers of storytelling as developed in the rest of the movie and which also contrasts dramatically with the last scene of Carter's story "The Company of Wolves."[42]

Visually, there is no happy ending. But perhaps this punitively regressive image need not be considered final as the ongoing process of storytelling reasserts itself in the movie's last words, when a female voice repeats Perrault's tongue-in-cheek moral, reminding the audience that "now, as then," a "simple truth" (such as "it was all a dream") can only be a seductive fiction.

* * *

With its appeals to several traditions at work within the "tale of wonder" genre (the literary, the children's literature one, and the oral), Carter's project cannot simply be summed up as "taking a patriarchal form like the fairy tale and rewriting it"—a description of *The Bloody Chamber* "to"which, in a 1985 interview, Carter responded in this way: "Not really. I was taking the latent image—the latent content of those traditional stories and using that; and the latent content is violently sexual. And because I am a woman, I read it that way" (Goldsworthy 10). For Carter, the highly concentrated meaning of a fairy tale image is valuable to her precisely because of its "latent" and varied possibilities, as her Foreword to her own English translation of Perrault's tales emphasizes:

Perrault's versions...became the standard ones, and through translation and continuous reprintings and retellings entered back into the oral tradition of most European countries. My own grandmother used to tell me the story of "Red Riding Hood" in almost Perrault's very words, although she never spoke a single word of French in all her life. She liked especially to pounce on me, roaring, in personation of the wolf's pounce in Red Riding Hood [sic] at the end of the story, although she could not have known that Perrault himself suggests this acting-out of the story to the narrator in a note in the margin of the manuscript. (*Fairy Tales* 13)

In Charles Perrault's fixed text of "Little Red Riding Hood," the image of the wolf pouncing to eat the little girl already spills into that of the "most dangerous beasts of all," human males sexually attacking their pretty preys, as Perrault's not-for-children-only moral makes clear.[43] But in the margins of the text and in performance, this image spills out again as another disguised attack, though one which brings pleasure to the storyteller and her audience. The grandmother, whom the wolf in the tale both impersonates and personifies, turns the tables by playfully mimicking the act of devourment. And the image spills over once again into what Perrault omits, but the grandmother's reversal invokes: the girl's actual feasting on her grandmother's flesh in oral tradition. Then, in the movie, this image transforms itself into the huntsman's seductive imitation of the wolf, which repeats itself with a difference when later the "real" wolf—but could it be the girlwolf now?—bursts through the window.

Clearly, one text, no matter how authoritative, cannot contain this tale-telling image. In whatever form of performance, its "violently sexual" latent content escapes identification with heterosexual seduction or rape, and reaches for a woman-centered reciprocal dynamics of storytelling. It explodes into voices. Although itself a forcefully gendered perspective, Carter's self-conscious exploration of this multi-valency complicates any either/or, inside/outside construction of gendered identity, or of gendered narrative forms.

4

IN THE EYE
OF THE
BEHOLDER

"WHERE IS BEAST?"

ONE OF THE MOST POPULAR TALES OF MAGIC, "Beauty and the Beast" is known as sub-type C of "The Search for the Lost Husband" (AT425) to folklorists, who have counted approximately fifteen hundred versions. This tale's history and diffusion exemplify the vital interaction of folk and literary texts.[1] The most widely known "Beauty and the Beast," by Madame Jeanne-Marie Le Prince de Beaumont, appeared in *Le Magasin des Enfants* in 1756. In it, Belle remains with Bête to save her father, who angered the powerful beast by stealing a rose, the gift his favorite daughter Belle had requested. Bête treats her like a queen, she grows fond of him, but she refuses his nightly marriage proposal. Bête allows Belle to visit her sick father only after she promises to stay no longer than a week. Her envious sisters conspire to keep her longer, however, and she returns to find Bête on the verge of death. Begging him not to die, she promises to marry him. Bête turns into a prince, and the fairy who advised Belle in a dream rewards her virtue, reunites her with her father, and punishes her sisters.[2]

While this specific plot of "Beauty and the Beast" developed fairly recently in France, by grouping it together with the much older "Cupid and Psyche" (AT425A) and "East of the Sun, West of the Moon" (AT425B) sub-types, Aarne and Thompson's classification helps modern Western readers to understand far better the tale's symbolism and affect. In "Cupid and Psyche"—the most famous version is Apuleius's second-century A.D. literary rendition in *The Golden Ass*—the heroine is sent to an invisible bridegroom, and her sisters convince her he must be a monstrous serpent. Breaking her promise to her husband, Psyche holds an oil lamp over his sleeping form: though she falls in love with the divinely handsome youth she sees, a drop of oil awakens him, and he leaves in anger. After taking revenge on her devious sisters, Psyche submits to the four impossible tasks her jealous mother-in-law sets for her. Magic helpers and Cupid himself assist Psyche, but only when Jupiter intervenes is Venus appeased. Cupid and Psyche's marriage is, thus, celebrated by the gods and the couple conceive their child, Pleasure. In "East of the Sun, West of the Moon," the heroine marries an animal or an invisible bridegroom—in the Italian folk version "King Crin" and in Straparola's sixteenth-century literary tale "Re Porco," a pig.[3] Once again, she cannot resist looking at his true features; once again the handsome youth leaves, falling into an enchanted forgetfulness. She sets out on a long and difficult journey to find him, picking up along the way three magic objects—oftentimes nuts—which she eventually uses to buy three nights with her husband from his new wife or betrothed (see Sautman). The first two nights, he lies in a drugged stupor. On the third night he recognizes her, and they are reunited.

The most significant links between "Cupid and Psyche" and "Beauty and the Beast" are the mysterious nature of the husband, whose invisibility or bestial appearance is the supernatural effect of divinity or enchantment; the broken tabus, which in all cases concern knowledge of the other or of one's self; a virgin's sexual initiation in both a psycho-familial context, involving sisters, fathers, and mothers-in-law, and a more broadly social one, involving mortals and immortals in the case of "Cupid and Psyche," and merchants and gentry in "Beauty and the Beast"; and the valorization of beauty over pride and vanity. Most obviously, the two tales dramatize the reconciling of physical and spiritual beauty in each member of a heterosexual couple, which leads to a physical and psychological transformation—Psyche turns into an immortal, the Beast into a Prince; Cupid grows out of being an enfant terrible, and Beauty is no longer daddy's girl—and an overall balanced union of eros and soul. "Beauty and the Beast" also shares both the heroine's self-sacrificing yet active nature and the dramatic urgency of the bridegroom's disenchantment with the "King Crin" sub-type: Beauty finds a close-to-dead Beast; the forgotten wife arouses her husband's memory on the third and last of the nights she has bargained for.[4]

Thinking of "Beauty and the Beast" in this broader textual network helps make sense of Beast's complex, appealing nature. Though not described, allowing readers and illustrators to join Psyche's sisters in forming the picture of a serpent out of Cupid's invisibility, his "*deformitas* conceals *monstrum*" (a wonder, a manifestation), making him admirable rather than repugnant, divine rather than sub-human (Henein 46).[5] While today the Beast is usually read as a warning not to judge by appearance, history and anthropology give us further insight by connecting animals with gods even more explicitly than Apuleius does. As Jack Zipes notes, "the transformation of an ugly beast into a savior as a motif in folklore can be traced to primitive fertility rites" and sacrifices to dragon-like "monsters" (*Breaking* 8).[6] Cupid's multiple images as "saevum atque ferum vipereum malum" ("dire mischief, viperous and fierce" Apuleius 100), as boy with no manners or respect, as erotic god of love, as invisible presence in the dark, and as faithful husband in the end also map out a number of well-known directions for exploring the "noble Beast" metaphor.[7]

Placing "Beauty and the Beast" in its larger folkloric and literary context highlights as well the family's centrality in this narrative. In general, the heroine's emotional and social ties to her family determine her future with her own new family.[8] Though Ruth B. Bottigheimer rightly contrasts Psyche's isolation within the human world to Beauty's bond with her father, in both cases it is the father's doing which delivers the heroine into her new and mysterious situation.[9] In Apuleius, the king asks Apollo's oracle how to find a husband for the daughter everyone admires but no one wants to marry; in de Beaumont's narrative, by breaking off a rose from the Beast's garden, the merchant unwittingly initiates the process that will separate him from his beloved Beauty. He could be seen, in other words, as a concealed helper, but certainly both fathers have the role of sender or power in Proppian terms. Either explicitly or through the highly symbolic rose, the narrative announces the heroine's move into a different psycho-sexual and social role through marriage, in many cases arranged marriage. Her adjustment to this role is the rest of the tale's subject. She must get to know—but not too quickly—her husband; rethink old ties with her malevolent sisters and her doting father;[10] and, in Psyche's case, negotiate with a mother-in-law and produce a child, the sign of her successful marriage.[11]

But what are the social and ideological dimensions of this rite of passage? Comparisons are again fruitful. Marriage is clearly staged as a social contract: in "King Crin," the baker's daughters agree to marry because the pig's royalty seems an adequate reward; in Apuleius, the gods request Psyche's "dreadful wedding" because it will ultimately bring harmony to mortals and immortals (100). "Beauty and the Beast" is more complex, for it enacts several possible solutions to the conflict between the nobility and the middle class in eighteenth-century France. For Zipes, the story puts the bourgeoisie in its place. Beauty's marriage to Beast chastises the overly ambitious sisters and rewards Beauty's "innate" virtue, which in de Villeneuve's 1740s version is clearly associated with a rediscovered noble lineage (*Breaking* 8). As for Gary Alan Fine and Julie Ford, de Beaumont "proposes a distinctly bourgeois solution of a marriage market" by connecting virtue to wealth rather than birth ("The Reflection of Middle-Class Life" 94). In my opinion, resolving this conflict depends on both the writer's and the readers' class allegiance. De Beaumont's text, for instance, offers an aristocratic and a bourgeois perspective on marriage, if only because she was herself an impoverished lady who became a governess, and who assumed she was writing for upper- and middle-class French and English young girls. A fine line separated gentry and upper bourgeoisie at the time.[12]

Regardless of class value, Beauty is initiated into married life within a patriarchal frame: whether she is a willing object, victim, heroine, or all three, both father and husband benefit from the exchange. Though often reluctant to give Beauty to the Beast, in Andrew Lang's version the father actually suggests her as a replacement for himself.[13] Whatever his level of willingness, the father gains riches and, in the end, happiness. For Beast, the all-important "side" benefit of Beauty's love is the disenchantment that restores him to his rightful place in society. Acquiring Beauty as a wife also grants him beauty as a token within a socio-economic exchange. Her willingness to resign herself to Beast is the necessary condition for the transaction's success. Giving herself up to keep her father's word gives her future husband reason to trust her; in fact, the heroine's momentary betrayal in "Cupid and Psyche" and "East of the Sun, West of the Moon" can only be expiated by sacrificing all and undertaking impossible tasks to gain him back. In all texts, the heroine's self-sacrifice and devotion to the male, whether father or husband, contrasts sharply with competitive, untrustworthy traits found in other females. The fairy in de Beaumont's "Beauty and the Beast," for instance, supports Beauty only because she would sacrifice her life to save her father's. Self-effacement and concern for her family are Beauty's virtues; wealth and social position with a prize-male are her reward, but as the object of exchange she has no real control over whether she can retain this reward.

Like "Cupid and Psyche" and "King Crin," then, "Beauty and the Beast" represents marriage as a social and ideological institution.[14] While stories like "Bluebeard" expose the failures of marriage to an extreme, "The Search for the Lost Husband" cycle repeatedly reenacts the patriarchal exchange of women, and affirms women's collusion with the system. Reading "Beauty and the Beast" along with its folk and literary analogues reveals not only its specific psycho-sexual, familial, and political implications as a tale of female initiation, but also the construction of its appeal.

The representation of Beauty's character helps explain why her role can be so appealing to women readers. The frozen object of male desire, Snow White's only possible development is self-destructive reproduction; Beauty, in contrast, participates in constructing her seemingly well-balanced and joyful future. Like Psyche and the forgotten wife in "King Crin," she is an active heroine whose physical and psychological journeys provide most of the narrative "suspense" and whose decisions—right and wrong—advance the plot. In all three sub-types, the heroine, however sadly, chooses to go to her invisible or animal husband. Psyche walks "resolutely" to the top of the hill where she is to meet the "marvelous" husband she obviously equates with death (Apuleius 101). Though the baker's youngest daughter well knows that the royal pig killed her two sisters on their wedding nights, she persuades her father to agree to her own marriage to Crin. And Beauty, though she believes the monster will eat her, sheds no tears when she explains that she "will deliver" herself "up to all his fury" (de

Beaumont in Opie and Opie 187). This dignified, resolute, and courageous character may be the object of an exchange, but she turns her victimization into heroism. Whether swayed by evil counselors, or by her own curiosity to break her promise of "not looking" or by staying away for longer than a week, she takes responsibility and pays dearly for it, especially in the case of Psyche and the forgotten wife. The heroine's determination to find her lost husband or to reanimate Beast is admirable—a clear sign of her affection and integrity.[15]

But Psyche's journey would not have succeeded if Cupid had not saved her from her unredeemed curiosity: her psychological growth remains somewhat questionable. Beauty's is not. Regret at breaking her promise, concern for the dying Beast, and a desire to show her "gratitude, esteem, and friendship" indicate where her values lie (Opie and Opie 193). Her physical and psychological journey also has a different intensity to it. Beauty does not have to confront the underworld as Psyche does, or the powers of the (super)natural world—the man-eating winds—as the forgotten bride does. Though Beast might be threatening, everything in his mysterious palace obeys Beauty. And Beauty's developmental task in this narcissistic and elegant fantasy world is, thus, the opposite of Psyche's or the forgotten bride's. They enjoy their husbands' mysterious nocturnal visits, displaying a sexual attachment not matched by the trust, sensitivity, responsibility, common sense, and intellectual affinities which by today's standards would presumably make for a solid marriage. Beauty's relationship with Beast is solidly built in this way, but her oedipal attachment makes her sexually "immature." These heroines' journeys, therefore, explore different realms of experience, though for the didactically-inclined minds of eighteenth-century well-educated readers, who were quite likely personally familiar with arranged marriages, Beauty has perhaps the more advantageous starting point.[16]

For all these heroines, however, the courage, determination, and dignity they exhibit on their journeys help them to become sexually and psychologically "mature" women, ready to assume, depending on the tale, the elevated social position of minor goddess or queen. While they certainly "deserve" this position, they seem unaware of what their initiation has required of them. Like the strength of other active fairy tale protagonists, Beauty's heroism bears the marks of collusion with the patriarchal system, developing along the lines of submission and self-sacrifice. Betsy Hearne argues that Psyche's task is obedience and Beauty's is insight (15–16); in my opinion both learn that *compliance* is the female virtue their worlds honor and reward.[17] Marriage is their path to success—and an arduous one, with fear and violence along the way, which demands the channeling of desires.[18]

But Beauty gains far more than most fairy tale heroines, active or not, because her submission and sacrifice transform another being, and more specifically, a sexually and/or socially threatening male. A virtuous, insightful, determined woman can change a beast into a person—such is Beauty's power.[19] Ancient and clearly related to our ability to produce new life, this belief in women's transformative powers has been reduced within patriarchal ideology to the popular "kiss a frog" motif, complete with its more realistic posing of the question "How many frogs will I have to kiss before I find a prince?"[20] Undeniably, giving "new life" to another being is glory hard to resist; more disturbingly, the hope of a metamorphosis brought about by her endurance and sacrifice has left many a woman the victim of physical or psychological abuse inflicted by a "beastly" man whose nobility only she can see.[21]

Doing justice to the complexity of this narrative will, therefore, require a merging of its positive significance as the story of a developing heterosexual relationship and its implicitly critical assessment of social norms shaping such relationships. As Betsy Hearne suggests, "Beauty and the Beast" is a multidimensional "metaphor for strong emotions," shaped profoundly by historical and ideological forces, such as a new literary tradition in the eighteenth century, "innovations in book-making and printing" in the nineteenth, and "the influence of psychological interpretations, new media techniques, and mass media distribution" in the twentieth (3–4). Zipes, Bottigheimer, and others have written about which culturally and historically specific views of love and marriage its most famous versions embody. I wish to claim that the tale's insidiously patriarchal appeal depends most on the active but self-effacing heroine—a protagonist with agency whose subjectivity is construed as absence and whose symbolic reward is in giving rebirth to another.[22]

However, if we redirect our attention to de Beaumont's classic

"Beauty and the Beast," its gender politics are not so straightforwardly conservative. This tale stages an ambiguity which problematizes its own ending and magic. When Beauty declares her
love for Beast, fireworks, lights, and music grandiosely punctuate
his transformation. Yet something is amiss:

> [E]very thing seemed to give notice of some great event: but nothing
> could fix her attention; she turned to her dear Beast, for whom she trem-
> bled with fear; but how great was her surprize! Beast was disappeared, and
> she saw, at her feet, one of the loveliest princes that eye ever beheld; who
> returned her thanks for having put an end to the charm, under which he
> had so long resembled a Beast. Though this prince was worthy of all her
> attention, she could not forbear asking where Beast was. (Opie and Opie
> 194–95)

Beauty's question marks a moment of hesitation which the text's
happy ending proceeds to ignore, but cannot fully recuperate.
After the prince explains how a wicked fairy made him monstrous
and senseless, Beauty is "agreeably surprized" that he and Beast
are one and the same. Her civilized and moderate joy, however,
hardly matches her earlier emotional outburst: "No, dear Beast,
said Beauty, you must not die; live to be my husband; . . . Alas! I
thought I had only friendship for you, but the grief I now feel con-
vinces me, that I cannot live without you" (Opie and Opie 194).
The transformation is magical, and the prince incarnates an ideal
combination of virtue, wit, and looks—but, for the moment at
least, Beauty's own wonder when she realizes it is Beast she loves
seems to have the stronger fascination.[23]
    Where, indeed, is Beast? Is transformation "real" or does it re-
sult from Beauty's new perception of him? Does the change answer or betray Beauty's desire? And what kind of transformation
has she undergone herself? Who has tamed whom, and how have
social dynamics shaped this apparently magic moment? The many
versions and variants of "The Search for the Lost Husband" suggest a variety of answers. In "Cupid and Psyche" the groom does
not change—he has always been a god—but Psyche becomes immortal once Jupiter "authorizes" her marriage to Cupid. In de Villeneuve's text, Beauty's transformative powers are limited.
Though Beast turns into the prince of her dreams, he does not
awaken until his mother arrives to ensure that a union of the two

is socially desirable. In the anonymous *L'Amour Magot,* a nymph courted by a monkey turns into an animal herself: both are punished for their "passion déréglée" (unruly passion).[24]

Modern and postmodern authors continue to exploit and explore the metaphorical power of "Beauty and the Beast" by amplifying and interpreting the problematic nature of Beast's transformation and Beauty's ambiguous response to the prince. Where is Beast—the beast in our loved one and the beast in ourselves—after the transformation?[25] Fear may raise this question—a particularly appropriate reading if we think of de Beaumont's text as a colonial narrative of othering[26]—yet desire also plays a part. The Beast's disappearance poses problems of perception, but also of an emotional excess which at first the prince's handsome gentility apparently cannot contain. In Jean Cocteau's 1946 movie, for instance, Beauty has a mixed response to Prince Ardent's looks, and when asked if she is happy, she answers: "I'll have to get used to this" (Hearne 82).

Is Beast's metamorphosis desirable, then? And whose desire is at work? The finale of the eighteenth-century text calls for fireworks, but Beauty's momentary hesitation hints at a different story, which other folk and literary versions have explored, and modern and postmodern versions delight in investigating. Cartoons in the animal groom tale tradition often show the beast's reluctance to become human, turning the magic of transformation into a joke (Mieder). Not taking Beast's transformation for granted generates many possible narratives, in several forms and mediums, with various purposes and effects. Here I will focus on four such contemporary revisions of "Beauty and the Beast." Ron Koslow's TV series stresses the impossibility of Beast's physical transformation, but its updated, heavily mimetic interpretation center-stages his inner transformation. In Tanith Lee's science fiction story, no transformation is required: Beauty simply discovers her affinity with the alien. One of Angela Carter's two rewritings ends with Beauty's new perception of Beast as a man faintly resembling a lion, suggesting that his physical transformation may not be what the tale is about, while in a startling reversion her second rewriting concludes with Beauty willingly turning beast.

Within this questioning framework, the crucial problem for female listeners/readers and writers becomes their interpellation as women. If beauty is in the eye of the beholder, Beauty is also in the hold of a narrative eye which claims to represent her in specific phases of her psycho-sexual and social initiation. One need not be a Freudian to realize that "Beauty and the Beast" depicts a woman's struggle to reconcile sexuality with "love." More prosaically, moving from her father's to her husband's house also maps Beauty's transformation through "courtship" from daughter to wife—the source of the narrative's dynamic structure and energy which build toward Beast's outer transformation. How then does Beast's disenchantment affect Beauty's development within the tale? Certainly she can take her rightful place as the wife of a rich and powerful man, but this metamorphosis betrays her desire and decision-making. Having acknowledged her love for Beast, the heroine suddenly faces an emotional and social situation she has not bargained for, but into which she has been "magically" traded. Jacques Barchilon has good cause to note that the Beast's transformation occurs when Beauty abandons her childhood fantasies and accepts reality. When she comes to terms with Beast, and can conceive a happy future with him, he disappears. When the fear goes away so does the beast: a "charming irony," writes Barchilon (*Le conte merveilleux* 10). Yes, but also a magic trick which leaves *almost* no trace of Beauty's desires and losses.

* * *

In its unrevised updating of tale's classic themes and gender dynamics, the 1980s CBS "Beauty and the Beast" series is a case in point. Catherine, a New York assistant district attorney plays "Beauty"; Vincent, a strangely leonine and noble being who lives in the city's underground tunnels with a community of marginals, is the mysterious "Beast." Worlds apart socially but brought together by their common ideal of justice, these two creatures fall in love. Most of the episodes present the two as a team working against crime in the alienating upper world of New York City, which is contrasted to the under world of "Father" Jacob's uncorrupted community of outcasts. Like Beauty's relationship with Beast while she is his prisoner-guest, Catherine's involvement with

Vincent, though intense to the point of telepathy, remains platonic for a long time. In the two-hour episode that inaugurates the second year of the series, the two protagonists begin by describing their bond as extraordinary: having conquered Vincent from the start, Catherine's "beauty, warmth, and courage" will undoubtedly continue to change his life, while she declares that his spiritual presence is stronger than love or friendship in her new life. I will focus on the development of their relationship to highlight its reliance on an apparently active heroine whose life-giving energy demands her own self-denial and death as well as its subordination to patriarchal, and specifically male homo-social, dynamics.[27]

In this same episode, the dramatic struggle between Vincent and his own dark side, literally a Vincent dressed-in-black and with a penchant for mischief and violence, becomes central.[28] The previous season's cliff-hanger scenes are repeated. Catherine walks toward a mysterious cave "below the catacombs." Though a terrifying roar is heard within, she says she must go: "He is my life. Without him, there is nothing." Even more horrible roaring is followed by Catherine's screaming of "Vincent!" In the new season's episode, we now *see* what is happening. Yes, he is attacking her, but her voice has quite literally stopped him "dead." Desperate, she kisses him and brings about his resurrection-transformation, symbolically marked by a dream-like sequence with blooming roses, fireworks, and water imagery.

Father goes in and finds the two in a classical Pietà-like composition that visually emphasizes the complexity of the transformation. Like Mary, Catherine holds a human being to whom she has given rebirth, but unlike Christ, Vincent is now alive, more "human," feeling "blessed" by Catherine's love. Three observations can help to place this scene. First, the transformation occurs in a typically unmarked, isolated space, outside his and her social worlds. Vincent says he "must" leave the community to struggle with the beast within him; Catherine says she "must" confront Vincent alone when he is "lost" to himself. Second, as Father tells Catherine, this struggle and rebirth process is not new to Vincent. As an adolescent he fought a less potent but similar dark figure; after being restrained, his vital signs seemingly stopped, but he then simply came back to life. That time, Father saved him from the "dark nights." Third, although Vincent remembers nothing of his previous life for a while, his loyalties to Jacob and Catherine remain intact; and in fact his relationship with her becomes more intense.

Clearly enough, this TV episode builds around the conventional social, psychological, and sexual *topoi* of initiation in narrative. The neophyte's liminal position forces him to rely on cultural knowledge and support given by special figures, to confront his fears alone, and to grapple with the troubling, yet transforming nature of sexuality. Vincent meets all the requirements. His beastly side vanquished, he can now assume his place in the community, becoming even more of the "scholar" his first crisis had made him, and even less dependent on Father, whose principles he has internalized. Psychologically, a "new peace," a "contentment" accompanies Vincent's resolution of his inner struggle and his knowledge of Catherine's love. The actual sexual union remains an ellipsis: though Catherine's kiss intimates it and her pregnancy is telling, the event itself is not narrated. Only sexuality's transformative powers—positive and negative—are displayed. Vincent is reborn, but also less "extraordinary," for his telepathy with Catherine is seemingly lost. This preoccupation with himself also closes Vincent off from another gift, the "extraordinary" child she bears him. Their "connection" has truly taken a life of its own, but self-absorbed Vincent does not recognize it. Though transformed, then, his initiation into love is not over.

As he competes with the sinister Gabriel in the last few episodes, Vincent's next struggle is for fatherhood. Which of the two males offers more to Catherine's child? Vincent can telepathically hear the pounding heart of the baby as the birth nears, and his struggle to enter the building where Catherine is held prisoner parallels the struggle of birth. His screams are presented in counterpoint to Catherine's. Is this "natural" bond stronger than the imprint Gabriel establishes by making sure that *his* face is the first one the baby sees? Gabriel has great power, seven Rembrandts, and an understanding of how death feeds on life. All this he wishes to give to the extraordinary child he names Julian. Vincent has different gifts: his conquered bestiality; his love for Catherine; and his alternative, caring community. In a foreboding hallucinatory dream, Vincent finds himself dreaming of a snow-covered landscape where a single red rose grows—a strange invoking of Beauty's fa-

ther in the Beast's garden. Vincent searches for his son, and predictably, "natural" fatherhood eventually wins. With the help of
Diana, who is investigating Catherine's murder, Vincent saves his
child from physical and spiritual death and returns with him to
the nurturing underworld. The last scene focuses on the child's
christening, as Vincent renames him Jacob—Father's name.

Here the normalization or domestication of "Beast," accomplished by the transforming love of "Beauty," does not culminate
in his marriage. What matters is that Catherine's sexual encounter
with Vincent changes him enough to allow him to father beauty
through her. After giving birth to Vincent's son, and informing
him of the child's existence and beauty, Catherine dies. Her function is over: though she appears on screen for a moment, looking
upon the christening, the real "trinity" is the father, man, and son.
Diana, Catherine's possible replacement in Vincent's life, receives
no special attention among the celebrants.

Furthermore, in the last two episodes, caring for his son represents Vincent's lasting tie with Catherine. The Beast now incarnates Beauty: Vincent is a father whose bond with his son is
entirely natural and healing. When the child is sick, Vincent "Can
feel him dying." "Can't you feel it?" he asks Gabriel, the false and
devil-like father: "Bring him to me: let him live. . . . He needs more
than my blood; he needs me." With the child in his arms, the
chained Vincent is the tame, feminized image of a loving parent.
He calls the beautiful baby "son of Catherine," and his flowing
hair contributes to revealing his lasting inner transformation, that
internalization of beauty/Beauty/Catherine which allows him to
call the baby "my son," but also makes the actual Catherine unnecessary, obsolete.

If Beast has become Beauty by replacing her, where is Beast?
Functionally, the strong, skillful, smart yet marginal Diana replaces Beast by doing his dirty work for him. Diana's method of in-
vestigation is to "penetrate" the mind she is after—in this case,
Vincent's. While there was no imagining him at first, once they've
met she cannot forget him, and actually she gives up her lover, security, and job to help him. In the process she becomes more and
more like a pursued fugitive, an alienated "Beast" in the city jun-
gle. She is his helper, and eventually his avenger. Once in
Gabriel's secret headquarters, she finds that Vincent is about to

kill him. She stops Vincent by telling him to take care of the crying child: life and beauty thus prove to be more important than death, confirming Vincent's successful transformation. Diana herself kills Gabriel, the angel of death. Enacting Beast's vengeance with Catherine's gun, Diana has symbolically become Beast, and while on one level the gun may seem to bring Catherine back into the scene, on another it further sentences her to that kingdom of death from which she cannot return.

Despite the romantic packaging, the primary focus of this narrative is therefore not Catherine's but Vincent's psychological, social, and sexual development as son, lover, and father. Updated but not transformed, the gender politics of "Beauty and the Beast" remain unchanged, becoming if anything more dangerous thanks to the initial pseudo-feminist presentation of Catherine's character. A determined, strong-minded New York professional, she chooses Vincent over two other "suitors" who operate in her social world, and who consider power of one kind as their game. In their love for Catherine, however, they resemble Vincent closely; eventually, by contributing to bring her killer to "justice," they turn from opponents into Vincent's helpers. Why does Catherine choose Vincent, then? Because Catherine's bond with him has the appeal of the "extraordinary": she can transform *him* like no other being. What the narrative glosses over, however, is the shattering of Catherine's "beauty, warmth, and courage" in the process. Though Catherine's quest ends happily on a symbolic level—Vincent and Jacob have life and love—it also requires her death. Her presence would inevitably disrupt the father/son unity. To which world, for instance, would Jacob belong if his mother were alive?[29] At the beginning of the series, Vincent's outcast status as Catherine's social other fulfilled the requirement of one of TV's most rigorous formulas—a heterosexual and heterogeneous couple who unite to fight crime and corruption.[30] In an interesting reversal, the second part of the series ends happily because Catherine is present only symbolically—heterogeneity recuperated through Vincent's feminization. Catherine's sacrifice is thus her reward, and once again "Beauty" is not the subject, but the object of the Beast's quest—the metaphorical power informing the narrative, the agent of transformation, but not its focus. The magic of this TV "Beauty and the Beast" simply re-produces Beauty's collusion with the patriarchal world of father and Beast, and glamorizes her self-denial.

In *From the Beast to the Blonde*, Marina Warner briefly discusses the CBS series as an example of "current interpretations" that "attempt . . . to face up to the complicated character of the female erotic impulse," but are also threatening to women consumers because they "focus on the Beast as a sign of authentic, fully realized sexuality, which women must learn to accept if they are to become normal adult heterosexuals" (312). Tanith Lee's "Beauty," in the 1983 *Red as Blood: Tales of the Grimmer Sisters*, participates in this insidious project: even though Lee's collection of short stories ambitiously transforms the fairy tale to foreground women and their desires, "Beauty"'s feminist utopianism is weighed down by an essentialist representation of both Beast and Beauty.[31]

In her novella "Beauty," Lee wishes to remain true to her heroine's self-fulfillment. The setting is Earth and the future. No wars, no poor people, the weather is artificially controlled, this world's family structures, life styles, and entertainment seem familiar, though its sexual relations seem freer and the arts thrive. Estar, a young girl with "green-brown hair" and an "unrested, turbulent spirit" has an extraordinary destiny (168). The aliens who control the Earth without ruling over it bestow on Mercator Levin, her father, a pale green rose as a sign of their demand for one of his children. His other daughters have commitments and interests, so he chooses Estar, who is surprised by the alien summoning even though her earlier wish for a rose and her pale green clothing unconsciously seem to have foretold this fate. Estar leaves a home that was never "home" to her, and a family that made her feel like a guest. She nevertheless is angry with the aliens for depriving her of "her only chance at becoming human" (178). Once in the alien host's house she exercises her "autonomy," yet complains about being held against her "will" (179). As seasons pass, however, she becomes increasingly comfortable with the alien's heavily camouflaged presence, until it is obvious to her family that she has fallen in love. The problem, as one of Estar's sisters puts it, is "the way they *look*" (193): the word among humans is that the aliens disguise themselves so thoroughly because "they" are ugly. When the alien agrees to show himself naked to Estar, she returns to her family and spends a week of "temporary oblivion, aping the release of death" (198). Her relatives—and the reader—believe the alien's ugliness has shocked her¹ out of love, but when dreams of him make further oblivion impossible, she returns to the alien. A double revelation follows. First, he "*was* beautiful. Utterly and dreadfully beautiful. Coming to the Earth in the eras of its savagery, he would have been worshipped in terror as a god" (202). Shamed by her own inadequacy, she left "humiliated and made nothing." But second, the alien finds her "strangely, alienly lovely" (208). Not only wanting to be her lover, he also informs her that while she looks human she actually belongs to his species. To defy their sterility, the aliens have devised a technologically astute plan: for each green rose, a spirit is waiting to come "home" from Earth. Having found her "raison d'Estar" (178), the heroine gladly agrees to love "spontaneously, but without any choice" (208). Uncomprehending yet certain, her family and other humans remain in the dark.

The connections with "Cupid and Psyche" are quite explicit. Estar is named after a planet "meaning the same as the Greek word *psyche*" (168); a child-sacrifice to the gods is suggested (175); before seeing the alien, Estar dreams "of coupling in the dark, blind, unseeing" (195); her sister persuades her she must look at him and "know" him; the end suggests that the two "aliens" will have a child together. The rose, the family, the sisters' suitors, the invisible servants, the telepathy, and the water near which the alien's beauty is revealed obviously make "Beauty and the Beast" an intertext as well. Less explicit analogies, however, point to issues of gender and narrative construction: as in "Cupid and Psyche," the alien does not change form and Estar's fulfillment comes from recognizing her innate affinity with the alien—which is Psyche's and Beauty's task as well.

That neither Estar not the alien physically changes significantly affects how "Beauty" answers the question "Where is Beast?" At first, considering the alien to be "a superior, wondrous monster," Estar dared him: "'This is the house of a beast, . . . Perhaps I could kill it . . .'" (184). Later, Beauty senses a lie in her own words and is ashamed. Quite simply there is no Beast in "Beauty," a narrative move that exposes xenophobia as a defensive mechanism grounded in misunderstandings and blind superiority. The tabu against looking naturally complements such willful blindness. Fed by occasional sightings of "some inches of pelted hairy skin, the gauntleted over-fingered hands, the brilliant eyes empty of white" (176), the human-centered, humanistic gaze assumes that the aliens are concealing ugliness. An implicit gossip tabu—"and this was almost never spoken of" (176)—then closes off any possible refutation of this faith. Such circles of certainty are powerful. When Estar does look and sees beauty, thereby challenging the human-centered tabu, does she think the alien is beautiful only because she is one too? Would Lyra or Joya, her human sisters, have the same reaction? Ultimately, even the phantom of the "Beast" vanishes for Estar. It continues to endure only in the earthlings, whose willful ignorance leaves them "brutes" or *bêtes*—children, who will not or cannot learn about what stands before them.

If the alien is no beast, then Estar has no need to change him, but neither must she change herself, needing instead simply to acknowledge her nature—her reason to be, and to be with the alien. The two "changes" her father notes in Estar after her first stay with the alien are only in the eye of the beholder. If she no longer dyes her hair green, that is because the aura of the green roses now surrounds her, and if she looks sad and distant at times, the fact is that she always has, though with less intensity and self-consciousness. The alien is therefore the catalyst for an event, not a transformation. Treating her like a child, he reassures her of her autonomy even while knowing where her path will take her. Recognizing herself as a child in his company, Estar "inhumanly" comes to see that love is a matter of being, not choice. "If I were human," she thinks, "it might offend me" (208). But what humanly may seem a sacrifice now seems a privilege. Taming or being tamed is not the issue: "she loved him with a sort of welcome, the way diurnal creatures welcome the coming of day" (187). Their love is founded on sameness, rather than the attraction for what is "unlike, incompatible" (191). Estar has little to change in a world she finds herself so essentially a part of.

In "Cupid and Psyche" mortals also recognized Psyche's godliness before she did. Nevertheless, when Jove makes Psyche immortal to appease her mother-in-law, Venus, Psyche still undergoes a token transformation. In Lee's text, Estar's innate superiority is ensured genetically: the god-like beings are her kin. Such predestination—some see the light because they are made of light—has its own relation to basic fairy tale themes. Cinderella does not become a princess, but comes to be revealed as one, and unpromising heroes eventually find their way in the right circumstances because they are "heroes." As Nicolaisen has argued, such narratives return to an existing order, rather than create one ("Why Tell" 61–71), and, while those who consider fairy tales to be literature for children tend not to emphasize this possibility, this inherently conservative vision has interpretive power. The gender implications of such looking and telling are similarly constraining. A fully compliant heroine, with a neatly packaged, unproblematic self-centeredness, Estar is a Beauty who can say good-bye to "Beast" without hesitation or regret because transformation gets raised only to be made unnecessary. Though Estar's look is shaped by her alienness, her true culture, these forces are also her essence—her soul's nature in its "freedom and beauty" merges with the alien, and, like his order, her look proves to be not "in-human" but "un-human," and explicitly superior. The alien order is thus naturalized, and so is the magic of the fairy tale's limited and constraining representation of change.

In her two revisions of "Beauty and the Beast," Angela Carter engages the fairy tale by exposing its traditional tabus against looking and telling to a spotlight which projects varicolored "shadows" of Beauty's performance as problematic subject of transformation.[32] In the Latin tale, Cupid warns Psyche that during their visit her sisters will ask her about his physical appearance. If, however, she talks with them, she will then want to look at his face, which will bring about their separation and unhappiness. Simpleminded and lonely, Psyche cannot resist making up stories about the husband she has never seen. Breaking the gossip tabu thus paves the way for violating the tabu against seeing. Inextricably bound together, seeing follows telling as Psyche's ordinary but contradictory stories lead the sisters to guess the extraordinary nature of this husband, whose "divine beauty" becomes visible, and therefore immediately lost, to Psyche. She sees a *monstrum*, but not of the kind she was made to fear.

Published in 1697 as "Riquet à la Houppe," or "Ricky of the Tuft," Charles Perrault's literary version of "Beauty and the Beast" forges a very different link between telling and seeing. In exchange for marriage, an ugly little prince endows the beautiful but stupid woman he loves with intelligence. When the princess, no longer a *bête*, refuses to keep her promise because he is ugly, or visibly a *bête*, he explains that she has the power to bestow beauty upon the one she loves. "'If that's so,' the princess said, 'I wish with all my heart that you may become the most charming and handsome prince in the world.' No sooner had the princess uttered these words than Ricky of the Tuft appeared before her eyes as the handsomest, most graceful and attractive man that she had ever set eyes on" (Zipes, *Beauties* 56). While the woman's new-found intelligence is widely recognized at court, implying that Ricky's gift is truly transforming, Ricky's own transformation is not necessarily so apparent:

> Some . . . say that the princess, having reflected on her lover's perseverance, prudence, and all the good qualities of his heart and mind, no longer saw the deformity of his body nor the ugliness of his features. . . . They also say that his eyes, which squinted, seemed to her only more brilliant for the proof they gave of the intensity of his love. Finally, his great red nose had something martial and heroic about it. (Zipes, *Beauties* 56-57)

In contrast to "Cupid and Psyche" here the princess's words and looks are encouraged, not proscribed, and work to her advantage, not her loss; furthermore, she, like Psyche, undergoes a transformation, while appearance or visibility is at issue for both Ricky and Cupid. Has Ricky's physical transformation occurred or not? Perrault's two morals tie beauty and intelligence to the "charm" of love: "We find what we love is wondrously fair, / In what we love we find intelligence, too" (57). As Barchilon remarks, "whether Riquet is handsome or ugly depends solely upon the princess's way of looking at him" ("Beauty and the Beast" 6). Stories and looks, telling and seeing, have the power to transform, but the ontological status and the effect of such change are ambiguous. The transformed being may very well be what our word or eye has wished into existence; and "real" or not, the transformation may either embody what we agree to speak of and see within social norms—"realistic" indeed—or incarnate the transgressive voice and peek.

By articulating story and look, writing and gaze, voice and glance differently in "The Courtship of Mr. Lyon" and "The Tiger's Bride," Angela Carter loosens without losing the magic of

Beast's transformation to shed light on the question "Where is Beast?" Though she updates and anglicizes the props and setting—cars, taxis, trains, and telephones, a Queen Anne dining room, a spaniel, a Palladian house hiding behind cypresses, London's hotels and theaters, thick-cut roast beef and whisky—the *fabula* or story line in "The Courtship of Mr. Lyon" is so similar to de Beaumont's "Beauty and the Beast" as to be more a version or imitation than a transformation. Carter's language and focalization, however, complicate matters, shifting her tale toward Perrault's ironically ambiguous "Ricky of the Tuft." Her text exposes the machinations of its magic without explicitly renouncing it, leaving the reader to reflect on the power of words and looks.

The narrative begins with a vignette:

> Outside her kitchen window, the hedgerow glistened as if the snow possessed a light of its own; when the sky darkened towards evening, an unearthly, reflected pallor remained behind upon the winter's landscape, while still the soft flakes floated down. This lovely girl, whose skin possesses the same inner light so you would have thought she, too, was made all of snow, pauses in her chores in the mean kitchen to look out at the country road. Nothing has passed that way all day; the road is white and unmarked as a spilled bolt of bridal satin.
> Father said he would be home before nightfall.
> The snow brought down the telephone wires; he couldn't have called, even with the best of news.
> The roads are bad. I hope he'll be safe. (*The Bloody Chamber* 41)

"We" look here upon a rather familiar fairy-tale situation and landscape—young woman at the window at dusk, a place and time of transition, the unmarked winter snow. As tradition requires, the narrator is external. Extraordinary and ordinary also merge, for while the snow has "a light of its own" and the girl appears to be made of it, she stands in a "mean kitchen," doing her chores and worrying about her father. The girl's loveliness and the "spilled bolt of bridal satin" unmistakably make her into a bride-to-be, with attendant expectations of spilled blood.

Elegantly done and nothing new. And yet the shifting focalization puts us in familiar Carter territory by undermining the external narrator's reliability even while serving it. Who is looking? Clearly, the girl searches the winter landscape from inside the window for signs of her father's arrival, but she in turn is not only observed by us (designated by the indexical "you") but also by an external focalizer who thinks it knows how we see. Who is looking at the snow? The external focalizer, or the girl? Though we are not told, the "as if" in "the hedgerow glistened as if the snow possessed a light of its own" marks a gap between the words/the look and the focalized object. The uncertain simile may be confirmed by the landscape's later "unearthly . . . pallor," which builds towards the animation of nature, but the "reflected" nature of that pallor, which could result from the onlooker's light as well as the moon's, leaves the simile even more unstable. If "we" look at the girl this way, we still must ask whether "that same inner light" that makes her "all of snow" is "reflected" as well. Whatever the case, the narrator clearly expects "us" to see her as inanimate and animate at the same time, for this perception lets the snow-covered road point to her future as bride.

We are invited to share in the naturalizing gaze that sees Beauty as unmarked, ambiguously animate snow, but we are also exposed to Beauty's own look, and therefore to the question of how *we* are to look. At the end of the scene, for instance, Beauty wishes to see her father walking up that road—which perhaps points symbolically to Beauty's unresolved oedipal attachment, but also unbalances the totalizing equation of that road with marriage. And "we"/"I"? While we could buy into the gaze that supports the external narrator, always working to appear omniscient and objective, and thus consent to the naturalization of Beauty's initiation process, we could also follow the cues of disturbance, and observe how focalization affects the narrative's coherence and credibility.[33]

Though the narrator remains external throughout, the focalization, or visual perspective, is often character-bound. When for instance Beauty's father comes to the Beast's house, even if the description may initially seem "objective," the knocker is seen through his eyes: "This door was equipped with a knocker in the shape of a lion's head, with a ring through the nose; as he raised his hand towards it, it came to him this lion's head was not, as he had thought at first, made of brass, but instead, of solid gold" (42). Sometime later when Beauty first sees the Beast, he is different from the vast and angry "leonine apparition" (44) her father had seen:

she could not control an instinctual shudder of fear when she saw him, for a lion is a lion and a man is a man, and though lions are more beautiful by far than we are, yet they belong to a different order of beauty and, besides, they have no respect for us: why should they? Yet wild things have a far more rational fear of us than is ours of them, and some kind of sadness in his agate eyes, that looked almost blind, as if sick of sight, moved her heart. (45)

While "in his confusion" her father had seen a being larger than life, with features like those of the inanimate knocker—"eyes green as agate," "golden hairs"—and "claws" which "pierced the sheepskin" of his coat, she sees a lion of extraordinary beauty, with rational fear of humans, and agate eyes which are "sick of sight." Though she recognizes the Beast as "the death of any tender herbivore," and herself as "Miss Lamb, spotless, sacrificial," his "bewildering difference" attracts her. And, after all, she is the one eating "a cold bird," just as her father had earlier dined on "roast beef" in the company of the abstaining Beast (45, 43).

Later, one evening, Beauty and the Beast exchange a crucial look. Flung at her feet and licking her hands, Beast "gazed at her with his green, inscrutable eyes, in which she saw her face repeated twice, as small as if it were in bud" (47). Still "inscrutable," his eyes are no longer "sick of sight," for in their green meadow Beauty's reflection is beginning to blossom. The naturalizing gaze works "on some magically reciprocal scale": as she turns into the promise of life, he offers her a new vision of herself. But, then shocking her, Beast goes off "on all fours." The process of transformation is only beginning, and before it is completed, Beauty must break her own promise and betray Beast's vision of her. Back in London later in the spring, she and her father enjoy the wealth that "monstrous" yet "benign" Beast has given them, but the image smiling back at Beauty in the mirror is that of a "pampered, exquisite, expensive cat"—a pretty face, but "not quite the one she had seen contained in the Beast's agate eyes" (48, 49). When the Beast's faithful spaniel arrives, "her trance before the mirror" easily breaks and she rushes to save the lion.[34]

The garden still wintery, his house in disarray, the Beast lies in his "modest bedroom" that is filled with the roses she had sent him, all dead: "How was it she had never noticed before that his agate eyes were equipped with lids, like those of a man?" Beauty wonders, "Was it because she had only looked at her own face, reflected there?" (50). She then touches and kisses him, and she sees his fingers begin "painfully" to stretch and his "meat-hook claws" to withdraw.

> Her tears fell on his face like snow and, under the soft transformation, the bones showed through the pelt, the flesh through the wide, tawny brow. And then it was no longer a lion in her arms but a man with an unkempt mane of hair and, how strange, a broken nose, such as the noses of retired boxers, that gave him a distant, heroic resemblance to the handsomest of beasts. (51)

A magic transformation surely, but one that leaves its work visible. Through Beauty's eyes the Beast becomes Mr. Lyon, and from these same eyes come tears "like snow." Embracing that naturalizing vision first found in the external focalizer and then in the lion's green eyes, she not only transforms and reincarnates the beast, but through an act of "magical reciprocity" she comes to see herself as he and the external focalizer/narrator wish to see her. The ex-Beast and ex-Beauty then eat "a little breakfast": is it a vegetarian one? I doubt it, for the Lamb has become Mrs. Lyon.

In its updated "and they-lived-happily-ever-after" charm, the story's last scene is ordinary, yet extraordinary: "Mr. and Mrs. Lyon walk in the garden; the old spaniel drowses on the grass, in a drift of petals" (51). The focalization is external, camera-like and at a distance. What we see is "magic," but also the product of a "freezing" process—the metamorphosis of flowing tears into snow, of life into picture. And, true to the tradition of "Beauty and the Beast" and "Ricky of the Tuft," Beauty's transformed vision of herself also transforms Beast. The scene is frozen, and confined to the garden; "they walk," it seems, in slow-motion. Though the two are "happy-ever-after," the petals have fallen and the spaniel is old. It may be spring, but Beauty is no longer in bud—like the "bolt of bridal satin," her blood has been spilled. This final cameo naturalizes *and* de-naturalizes the traditional female initiation pattern leading to marriage. By placing it within a specific social order, the cameo illustrates the fairy tale's collusion with bourgeois and leisurely carnivorousness. It is a "common or garden enchanted"

ending (Carter, *Sleeping Beauty & Other Favourite Fairy Tales* 128).
The external narrator quietly triumphs—yet the scene's "objective" naturalization is produced by the work of focalization.

If telling a certain story implies a way of looking, breaking away
from that telling does not necessarily transform the internalized
gaze. If "The Courtship of Mr. Lyon" problematizes the external
narrator through multiple character-bound focalization, "The
Tiger's Bride" insists on how external focalization insidiously informs character-bound perception as well, since any transformation must comply with or contest that gaze. How we see ourselves,
in short, is predicated upon how we are seen. "The Courtship of
Mr. Lyon" resolves this subject/object relation by setting it within
comfortable conformity. The framed naturalizing image of "life"
reflected in Beast's eyes, Beauty remains objectified as she gives rebirth to Mr. Lyon—her subjectivity is thus founded on self-effacement. In "The Tiger's Bride," however, the painful, joyful splitting
of the subject/object of focalization is a necessary step in the
difficult process of turning the younger "eye" into the exuberant
"I"-narrator who acts upon her desire.

All the characters in this story remain nameless, and the "de-
cembral" setting, desolate northern Italy, hardly meets the Russian
father's and daughter's expectations of exotic sunshine (51–52).
Expectations of parental love are equally disappointed. "My father
said he loved me, yet he staked his daughter on a hand of cards,"
the heroine relates, noting precisely that "You must not think my
father valued me at less than a king's ransom; but at *no more* than a
king's ransom" (54). She is lost to the Beast, and "La Bestia" here
is a rich Milord with "the Devil's knack at cards" and "a mask with
a man's face painted most beautifully on it" which conceals his features "but for the yellow eyes." He gives her a "white rose, unnatural, out of season," which, as the card game proceeds, she
nervously rips apart (52–53). Carried off as winnings to the Beast's
dismantled palazzo, "an uninhabited" place (57) filled with horses
and wind, the young woman's only company is a mechanical doll
that not only looks like her but also holds up a magic mirror reflecting the father's self-pity and the girl's own pale face. The
small simian valet informs her that the Beast wishes to see her
naked once, "after which she will be returned to her father un-

damaged" with money and gifts (58). Full of human pride, she refuses, and interprets the Beast's two tears (which turn into diamonds) to be signs of his shame. When he takes her riding in the "wilderness of desolation," however, he inverts the situation by revealing his own "great, feline, tawny shape," appearing before her as a tiger with "annihilating" eyes like "twin suns" (63–64). Awestruck, she herself disrobes, exposing her flesh to the Beast's and the horses' look. He then keeps his promise, but rather than return to her father, the woman enters the tiger's room. While his "purring rocked the foundations of the house," she lets him lick her skin, lick it off:

And each stroke of his tongue ripped off skin after successive skin, all the skins of a life in the world, and left behind a nascent patina of shining hairs. My earrings turned back to water and trickled down my shoulders; I shrugged the drops off my beautiful fur. (67)

This story has a double relationship to the fairy tale. To begin with, some of the most jarring departures are in fact part of the "Beauty and the Beast" narrative tradition. The father losing the daughter at cards, the metamorphosis into animal, the rose, the life-giving river, the hunting, and the jewels are other common motifs that Carter aptly reinterprets.[35] "The Tiger's Bride" also revitalizes both the tale's transformative force through knowing "the self disguised as other" (Canham 14),[36] and the significant rewards of honor and humility—not to be confused with pride and humiliation.[37] In this case, the familiar tabu against looking affects both "Beauty" and "Beast"—she refuses to be seen, he wears a mask—and their eventual disrobing is therefore a "reciprocal pact": a willing exposure, but one that reveals the tabu against unmasking of any kind and, more specifically, animal sexuality to be socially constructed. The tabu against gossip is also implicitly violated, since even after growing her fur she uses language to tell us about her experience—a transformed self that nevertheless still reminds us of our humanity. Like "Beauty and the Beast," "The Tiger's Bride" tests social mores by focusing on the family, but in Carter's story the father's hypocrisy and weakness underscore for the daughter and ourselves the rottenness of a social order that trades (female) bodies to sustain some privileged souls. Finally, while the heroine willingly honors her father's promise, yet bravely rejects the Beast's offer, she has no allegiance to the father. Her attachments are to the horses and to the excitement of hearing old wives' tales about tiger men.

And yet, while the strong ties with the fairy tale make the final transformation a powerfully magic happy ending, in Carter's version that magic is awry. Both narratively and visually, this story poses the question "Where is Beast?" quite differently. "My father lost me to The Beast at cards" (51), the cool autobiographical voice tells; the girl watched it happen. From the very beginning, the "we"—at times represented by the indexical "you"—knows what happened through her words and eyes. But what the I-character saw in herself and others at the time is not what the altered I-narrator sees. The younger "eye"'s vision has been transformed into what "we" are exposed to: a protagonist who now knows how women being seen as objects had shaped her own seeing of humans—male and female—, gods, and, of course, beasts. As her father desperately gambles, for instance, the younger version "watched with the furious cynicism peculiar to women whom circumstances force mutely to witness folly" (52). And yet, though she sees his folly and his hope, his selfishness and sentimentality, this "I" does not speak. "I saw . . . I saw . . . I saw," she says, fulfilling our expectations of a careful "I-witness" with a detailed perception of places, people, and feelings. But much of this in-sight soon proves to be mediated, indirect, already materially and culturally framed. To this younger "eye," the scene reflected in a mirror is like a collection of masks—her father's "wild hope," the Beast's "still mask," her own "impassivity," even the faces on the cards. This cluster of images ironically revises her extraordinary expectations of Italy as "the blessed plot where the lion lies down with the lamb" (54, 52, 51).

What kind of knowledge is this? Clearly a knowledge of what conceals *La Bestia*, rather than what he is. The "fuddling perfume," the all too symmetrical mask, the "growling impediment" in his speech—all camouflage she knows not what (53–54). Significantly, though primarily sight but also smell and hearing grant her knowledge of the masks, there is no reference to taste — a telling absence, since her last meeting with the tiger takes place "between the gnawed and bloody bones," making "the fear of devourment" a legitimate response (66, 67). At the card game site, touch or feeling seems reserved for the weather. The extraordinary cold that envelops her is, of course, an external correlative of her father's actions—a typical Carter strategy for showing how "myths" turn human relations of power into something as natural "as the weather"—but "we" have no direct access to him. Gazing into mirrors at masks leads the tiger's "bride" to feel that "all the world was locked in ice" (55). She carries this vision to the Beast's remote palazzo; only the "sprightly appearance of life" she notes in a "dashing black gelding" gives her hope (55). Loving horses, she thinks them more noble than humans, though the fact that *La Bestia* has "given his horses the use of the dining room" (57) does not change her image of him, locked as it is in the beast mold. She sustains her proud attitude—after all, she is human!—for though she despises her father, she sides with him in matters of honor. Nor does she submit to the "disdain" and "queer superciliousness" of the simian valet's look (57).

What is important here is the heroine's confused perception.[38] An external, but not impartial or "natural" focalization, the humanistic, patriarchal gaze, conditions her responses, even though she realizes that this order victimizes her. Nowhere is this more evident than when she rebels against the Beast's apparently insulting demand. Rape is the beastly act everything she knows has prepared her for, but to be looked at naked is "the abominable" (66). Continuing to see herself as her father does—a precious pearl, or meat to trade; in any case an object—she cannot conceive of the Beast's looking at her flesh as anything but a one-way pornographic gaze that fantasizes, objectifies, and others her. By refusing to serve as a visual object of desire, she assumes she is forcing *La Bestia* to behave as beasts are expected to.

However, to her surprise, he shows himself not as beast but as *monstrum*. Moved by his self-restrained ferocity and his solar eyes, when she shows herself to him, she finds her own perception of the "fleshly nature of women" transformed (64). Looked upon by horses and tiger, in the midst of nature, she is neither "natural" nor, as she fears, a "frail little article of human upholstery" (64). Rather than othering its object, the tiger's gaze requires instead another subject's engagement, acknowledges "no pact that is not reciprocal" (64). By showing the tiger she "would do him no harm," she thus admits and takes responsibility for the *monstrum* within herself: "I felt I was at liberty for the first time in my life" (64).

What the tiger's sight liberates her from is her own otherness, constructed by that gaze which made her a "wild wee thing" as a child, and a treasure to be traded later (56). She now recognizes how her own compliant eye, externalized in the clockwork maid's "blue, rolling eyes," had viewed herself as the "cold, white meat of contract," lying under the "indifferent gaze" of those similar "eyes that watch you" at the marketplace but "take no account of your existence" (66). The pornographic gaze had informed her everyday vision. What she labeled "abominable" when proposed by the Beast was actually "ordinary" without her knowing it. The mechanical doll, no longer her double, can go back to her father; she can separate from him with no regrets because his appearance in the magic mirror no longer touches her. The subject of her own transformation, her own rebirth, she instead—"white, shaking, raw,"— approaches the tiger "as if offering, in myself, the key to a peaceable kingdom in which his appetite need not be my extinction" (67).

As my own rhetoric must have signaled, this metamorphosis of the furiously silent daughter into the tiger's bride appeals to me. It subverts the humanistic and patriarchal order. It values the flow of tears and water over the "for-ever" of diamonds, thus unlocking a frozen world.[39] It lets a female protagonist reject a self-effacing subjectivity, and embrace—literally—an exuberant and undomesticated one. It turns the war of the sexes into a fleshly encounter based on a reciprocal, male and female pact of life. Most of all, it neither betrays Beauty's desire nor belittles the Beast. Wishing to luxuriate in the image of two beautiful tigers, the triumph of the pleasure principle, the narrator's language carries my desire. But throughout the telling, the eye-work makes it uncomfortable to view this magic as "natural." No return to nature, no simple reversal of the human/beast dichotomy. This transformation does more than reinforce the ancient mythic link between animals and gods, or debunk the more recent Western association of bodily pleasures with devil and beast, or reject the objectification of humans as mechanized means of production. Carter's magic can only be the product of a differently framed look, a new *order* that privileges the "naked," neither as pornographic objectification nor as "natural" state, but simply because it is unmasked.

In its search of essences, such unmasking cannot of course fully do away with masks. "I was unaccustomed to nakedness," the protagonist notes as she takes her clothes off near the bank of the river:

I thought the Beast had wanted a little thing compared with what I was prepared to give him; but it is not natural for humankind to go naked, not since first we hid our loins with fig leaves. . . . I felt the most atrocious pain as if I was stripping off my own underpelt, . . . (66)

The tiger's abrasive tongue continues this stripping, exposing "shining hairs" (67), as if she was as hairy on the inside as the were-wolves in other Carter stories.[40] If we choose to go with the narrative "flow," this somewhat Marcusean liberation of the pleasure principle does homage to the higher nature of the beast within us, the beast that will save us from the age of mechanical reproduction—and Carter's own participation in the Sixties' sexual and political revolution lends this reading some support. But, such "nakedness" does not come naturally, for the transformation takes place not in a garden of Eden, but on the tiger's "carnivorous bed of bone" (67). Furthermore, when the protagonist admires her pelt, her "beautiful fur," more than her raw skin, this fur could be yet another "mask," liberating rather than oppressive perhaps, but still not her inner being. And, finally shedding "all the skins of a life in the world" (67) has not led her to renounce language—a fact that distinguishes her from the tiger. Though the "fur" might grow naturally, "beautiful fur" (67) can only be the product of labor—her pain, his tongue; and it can only be beautiful to the educated eye, caught in the elaborately staged look the narrator provides us. Carter's magic may mark one order more desirable than another, may even privilege "wild beasts" over "human careless-ness," but she also signals, through its *visual-education* component and its verbal artifice, the magic's own hard work.

When read with one another, "The Courtship of Mr. Lyon" and "The Tiger's Bride" further interrogate the Beast's transformation and its relation to Beauty within the tale's tradition.[41] "The

Courtship of Mr. Lyon" visualizes his transformation by making
Beauty its informing power, but leaves Beauty's own desire unex-
plored, though socially conditioned. Both figures seem tame in
the end—carnivorous, but in a civilized way. "The Tiger's Bride"
reverses all this. And yet the two texts do not simply contradict
each another, but represent two different visions of magic that the
ordinary, whether oppressive or liberatory, can hold, two consciously ambiguous appreciations of this magic.

Both stories employ telling and looking in ways I have already
discussed, and explore their ties to the dynamics of power—of devouring the other or not, of transforming flesh into meat or meat
into flesh. One rewards the sacrificial lamb with a Mr. Lyon willing
to lie down with the lamb, but on his own terms; the other shows
how "the lamb must learn to run with the tigers" (64), with the reward the extinction of neither. In this way "The Courtship of Mr.
Lyon" moves toward the prescribed, toward a comfortable patriarchal order, while "The Tiger's Bride" visualizes and verbalizes the
forbidden. But read closely, the former tale parodies its normaliz-
ing magic by pointing to its carnivorous frame, while the latter tale
makes its own enchantment suspect by constructing it so conspic-
uously. In either case, the lamb cannot remain passively vegetarian
when the carnivore is at work. The more crucial issue is therefore
what to view as food (meat or bud) and what as flesh. Traditionally, the beast is what we devour or what devours. Kill or be killed.
But, however differently their *fabulas* may develop, both Carter's
stories resist consuming the Other, whether beast or beauty, and
thereby raise open questions of desire and power to the reader's
attention. By dwelling on emotional, physical, and material excess,
Carter thus does not recuperate but amplifies Beauty's moment of
hesitation in de Beaumont's text.

But always with a keen awareness of the costs. Both Mrs. Lyon's
and the tiger's bride's successful initiations may be a matter of
"eye" rather than "I." In neither tale is the heroine a free agent,
nor is the visual and linguistic symbolic order simply subverted.
Similarly, whether the father's, Beast's, or Beauty's, desire never
operates freely; and so the betrayal or fulfillment of Beauty's desire must be considered within a larger narrative/visual framework. Gaining access to the construction of their own subjectivity,
as the tiger's bride does, liberates women only partially within a

genre which, as Mrs. Lyon's contentment suggests, is often used to constrain gender. In both stories, Carter intertwines gender and narrative concerns to comment on how the classic fairy tale plots women's "developmental" tasks and desires within patriarchy in more ways than thematically and psychologically. The questions at work here do not simply concern Beauty's self-fulfillment or desire as she gains control over the path of her initiation process, but also investigate how narrow that narrative path is, and how it shapes the heroine's conforming or contesting journey.

Furthermore, in Carter's parodic imitations of "Beauty and the Beast," multiple focalizers, voices, places, and cultures expose the complex narrative mechanisms of the fairy tale as an ideologically variable "desire machine." Even as we joyfully succumb to Carter's magic, we still must confront its construction, power, and dangers. The wonder of fairy tales comes to reproduce its own workings and make them visible; in this way, Carter sustains and renders suspect her own re-visions, showing that the magic of the fairy tale is its own beast.

5

"BE BOLD,
BE BOLD, BUT NOT
TOO BOLD"

DOUBLE AGENTS
AND BLUEBEARD'S
PLOT

NOWADAYS BLUEBEARD'S NAME evokes the image of a man with a dark secret, a number of murdered wives, and a blood-stained key. Everybody knows that. But perhaps because "Blue-beard"'s gruesome theme is not deemed appropriate for children, now considered the primary audience for classic fairy tales, people are not as generally familiar with the details of the homonymous tale. Published in the 1697 *Histoires ou contes du temps passé*, Charles Perrault's "La Barbe-Bleue" tells the story of a rich man with a blue beard, "which made him look so ugly and terrifying that there was not a woman or girl who did not run away from him."[1] The first part of the tale describes the "beauties and riches" that convince the younger daughter of a "lady of quality" to marry him. (An older sister, Anne, becomes her companion.) A month later, Blue-beard announces he must go on a journey. Leaving his young bride with keys to all his apartments and jewels, he warns her not to enter "the little room at the end of the long corridor on the ground floor." While her neighbors explore the mansion, the girl breaks her promise and rushes to unlock the door to the forbid-den room. Inside, "the floor was covered with clotted blood of the dead bodies of several women suspended from the walls. They were all the former wives of Bluebeard, who had cut their throats one after the other. She thought she would die from fright, and the key to the room fell from her hand." No matter how hard she tries to clean it, the tell-tale key remains stained with blood. Re-turning earlier than she expected, Bluebeard condemns his wife to death. During the quarter of an hour she is given to pray, the young wife and her sister Anne hope for the arrival of their brothers who are to visit that very day. Just as Bluebeard is about to cut off the young woman's head, the two brothers burst through the gate and kill him. The widow shares her wealth with her siblings and marries "a worthy man" who makes her "forget the miserable time she had spent with Blue Beard" (Zipes, *Beauties* 31–35).[2]

Charles Perrault appended two morals to "La Barbe-Bleue," which one translation gives as:

> "Ladies, you should never pry,—
> You'll repent it by and by!"

and

> "Then the husband ruled as king.
> Now it's quite a different thing;
> Be his beard what hue it may—
> Madam has a word to say!"

The first message warns women to resist curiosity which equals trouble; the second chides men for losing their authority thanks to the feminine "vice" of talk. In Johnson's translation, both morals nostalgically look back to a time of innocence and absolute male power and both blame women for the change. Though just as playfully ironic, Perrault's French text is not as explicit in its woman-blaming. As Zipes's more literal translation shows, Perrault's first *moralité* seems to be a universal, non-gendered warning: "Curiosity, in spite of its charm, / Too often causes a great deal of harm," though it eventually turns to the second sex or *sexe*, euphemistically rendered as "ladies" in translation. The second moral does not refer to women's talking, and it does admit that Bluebeard's behavior is unacceptable: "No longer are husbands so terrible, / Or insist on having the impossible." The French text does however betray a certain insecurity about household power: "And whatever color his beard may be, / It's difficult to know who the master be." Whether in a more crudely sexist translation or in the original, Perrault's two morals still uphold absolute patriarchy as a "paradise," lost when women's curiosity opened the door to the bloody chamber.[3]

As the most authoritative version of "Bluebeard," it should not
be surprising that Perrault's narrative has led literary retellers and
commentators, especially in the nineteenth century, to identify
the tale's central theme and crime as women's curiosity. The key is
the central motif; women are targeted as the primary audience for
the tale's apparent cautionary message. In *The Hard Facts of the
Grimms' Fairy Tales* and in *Off with Their Heads!* Maria Tatar has recently shown how this interpretation depends on reading "Bluebeard" as an echo of "the Genesis account of the Fall," which not
only identifies Eve, and thus every woman, "as the principal agent
of transgression" but also infuses "her act of disobedience with
strong sexual overtones" (*Off with Their Heads!* 96). The result in
some literary versions of "Bluebeard," and in Perrault's and Bechstein's especially, is an explicit condemnation of the heroine's curiosity, but total silence on the ethics of the husband's serial
murders.[4] Such editorial comments have encouraged psychoanalytical interpretations that view the bloody key as a sign of the
heroine's sexual knowledge and betrayal.[5] Bruno Bettelheim's
reading is typical:

"Bluebeard" is a tale about sexual temptation. . . . However one interprets
"Bluebeard," it is a cautionary tale which warns: Women, don't give in to
your sexual curiosity; men, don't permit yourself [sic] to be carried away
by your anger at being sexually betrayed. There is nothing subtle about it;
most of all, no development toward higher humanity is being projected.
(301–2)

When considered within a folkloristic framework, however, such
cautionary readings appear narrow and unconvincing—yet another reminder that relying on one or two texts for interpretation
is dangerous, and that the narrator's/editor's comments are ideological variables which cannot determine the tale's semantics.
Tatar, for example, draws on the related tale "Mr. Fox" and examples from *The Thousand and One Nights* to show how curiosity can,
when "paired with intelligence," prove to be "life-saving" rather
than "self-defeating" (*Hard Facts* 178). Tatar claims that following
Perrault's cue writers and critics have turned a tale of adventure
based on a prohibition/violation sequence into a cautionary tale
"rehearsing the perils of curiosity or celebrating the power of
craft" (*Hard Facts* 178). Evoking earlier folkloristic research, espe-

cially E. Sidney Hartland's, in re-reading the structural and thematic role of curiosity, Tatar comes to provocatively fresh conclusions with both narrative and gender implications. Thus, as Catherine Velay-Vallantin's careful work has also shown, exploring the rich and varied folkloric tradition of "Bluebeard" is an important step toward a feminist reading of the tale and its contemporary re-visions (*L'Histoire des contes* 43–93).

Take, for example, what E. Sidney Hartland identified in 1885 as the tale's "Forbidden Chamber" (C611) motif. Clearly, this prohibition need not have a cautionary value, nor does it have to affect women alone. In fact, the knowledge gained by exploring the bloody chamber in such tales is often instrumental to the hero's or heroine's deliverance.[6] If the "Forbidden Chamber" rather than the "Bloody Key" is treated as the tale's central motif, then "Bluebeard" is no longer primarily about the consequences of failing a test—will the heroine be able to control her curiosity?—but about a process of initiation which *requires* entering the forbidden chamber. Sexual curiosity, with its implication of betrayal because it occurs behind her husband's back, is not the issue. The heroine's knowledge of her husband, of herself, and of sexual politics is what matters. The test is whether she can acquire this knowledge and then use it cleverly enough to triumph over death.[7]

Focusing on initiation and survival helps us recognize that "Bluebeard" (AT312), "Rescue by the Sister" (AT311), and "The Robber Bridegroom" (AT955) are sister tales.[8] All three tale types appear in the Grimms' collection. Published as *KHM* 62 in the 1812 edition, and then omitted as too close to Perrault's French version, "Bluebeard" (AT312) begins with a king stepping out of a "golden coach" and asking a man in the forest "if he could have his daughter for his wife." The man happily agrees, but the girl is scared of the king's blue beard, which "made one shudder whenever one looked at it." Before leaving with her husband, she makes her brothers promise to come to her rescue if they hear her screaming. Bluebeard as usual soon leaves his wife, giving her the keys and threatening her with death if she uses the "little gold key." Dead women hang from the walls of the forbidden chamber and blood streams toward the horrified girl. When the blood-stained key betrays his wife, Bluebeard allows her to pray before she dies. She cries out from the window to her brothers; just as he is about to "plunge his knife into her heart," the three brothers charge in and kill him. After hanging Bluebeard "in the bloody chamber next to the women he had killed," the girl and her brothers leave with his treasures (Zipes, *Brothers Grimm* 660–63).

Survival and initiation are even more explicitly central to the Grimms' "Fichter's Bird" (AT311; *KHM* 46). Through magic, a sorcerer abducts a beautiful girl, the oldest of three sisters. He offers her everything she desires with one exception: "You may go wherever you want and look at everything except one room, which this small key here opens. If you disobey me, you shall be punished by death." He also makes her promise that she will carry an egg wherever she goes while he is gone. Upon entering the forbidden room, the girl finds "a large bloody basin . . . filled with dead people who had been chopped to pieces." Horrified, she drops the egg into the basin. The blood stains it, and though she "wiped and scraped," she "could not get rid of the spot." The sorcerer returns, sees the blood-stained egg, cuts off the girl's head, chops her up, and throws the pieces into the basin. The second sister's fate is the same, but the youngest sister is "smart and cunning." She leaves the egg in a safe place before entering the forbidden chamber: "But, oh, what did she see? Her two sisters lay there in the basin cruelly murdered and chopped to pieces." Setting "to work right away," this girl "gathered the pieces together, and arranged them in their proper order. . . ." The older sisters come back to life and rejoice in seeing her. When the sorcerer returns, examines the egg, and sees that the girl has "passed the test," he promises to marry her. His magic power over her, however, is gone. The clever girl tricks him into carrying her sisters back home in a basket filled with gold. She in the meantime makes a "false bride" out of a skull, jewels, and flowers, and places "her" at the window. Rolling herself in honey and feathers the girl leaves the house unrecognized. The returning sorcerer encounters this "strange bird," who tells him that his young bride is ready and "looking out the attic window." When he and his friends are gathered inside the house, the girl's brother and relatives set the house on fire, burning them up (Zipes, *Brothers Grimm* 167–70).

Though represented differently, the agency and initiatory experience of the heroine are equally significant in the Grimms' version of "The Robber Bridegroom" (AT955; *KHM* 40), a tale well known in the British tradition as "Mr. Fox." A miller's beautiful daughter is promised to a rich man she neither loves nor trusts: "Whenever she looked at him or thought about him, her heart shuddered with dread." She goes to visit him one day "in the dark forest"; he is not home, and a parrot's song warns her to leave because the place belongs to murderers. Ignoring the song, she explores the house until she finds an old woman with a bobbing head. When the girl asks about her bridegroom's whereabouts, the old woman replies that "You think you're a bride soon to be celebrating your wedding, but the only marriage you'll celebrate will be with death." Taking pity on her, the old woman hides the girl when the murderers, who are also cannibals, return, dragging another girl in. They kill her by giving her three different wines to drink, chop her up, and salt her. Having "noticed a ring on the murdered maiden's little finger," one of them chops it off; though it falls on the hidden girl's lap, the robbers fortunately do not find her. The old woman and the girl escape after the men have eaten and drunk a drugged wine. The girl tells her father what happened, then repeats the story at the wedding, as her increasingly nervous bridegroom remarks, "My dear, it was only a dream." When however she produces the finger with the ring to prove that her story is true, the bridegroom and his crew are executed for "their shameful crimes" (Zipes, *Brothers Grimm* 153–57).[9]

The initiatory pattern and other commonalities of these three tale types become even more evident if we consider folk versions that are closer to the oral tradition than the Perrault or Grimms' texts are. How the girl comes under Bluebeard's power varies. She marries him of her own free will; she is offered by her father; she is traded; she is tricked or captured. Reasons for choosing to marry him include money or, in some cases, her attraction to a special feature—sometimes even his beard.[10] While not perhaps significant in themselves, the many reasons given for the marriage multiply interpretive possibilities: Perrault to the contrary, then, the girl is not always the guilty party. As for the Bluebeard figure, he is inevitably presented as Other, belonging to a different class, land, or world altogether. He may be an ogre, a vampire-like creature, a cannibal, or even the Devil himself. Certainly a stranger, he is also a mysterious being who usually presents himself as a rich man with a beard, be it blue or green, or a silver nose in an Italian version, as the visible clue to his otherness.[11] The heroine's test in itself requires a knowledge of death/otherness and forces her to use her cleverness in the name of life/the familiar. The forbidden chamber can therefore be the husband's bloody chamber, a room where the heroine is asked to consume human flesh, or Hell itself. She tricks the Bluebeard figure: by sending an animal messenger to her family; by not carrying the key, flower, egg, or other object entrusted to her into the forbidden room; by making him believe she has eaten the human hand or foot he gave her; by exposing him in public through her "dream."[12] In the process of saving herself, she often saves earlier victims—her sisters, a young prince. The girl reassembles their bodies, applies a magic ointment, or pulls them out of Hell.[13] Even when she does not literally rescue others, she contributes to the general welfare, by sharing her dead husband's riches or by pointing her finger at the criminal and thus putting a stop to the murders.[14] And, in most cases, the girl does not passively rely on chance for rescue. She initiates her own rescue by sending an animal helper back to her family, or she plans and executes her own deliverance.[15]

"Bluebeard" and related "Forbidden Chamber" tales (AT312, AT311 and AT955) are therefore tales of initiation in which the protagonist successfully confronts death because she is bold and clever or because she has strong community ties. Bravery, not simply curiosity, lead her to unlock the forbidden chamber, especially when her husband tells her that her sisters are dead, and that she will be too if she disobeys. She must be clever to see him not as the Law but as the enemy. Sometimes she does not trust him in her heart; other times, though proven to be false, he holds her in his power.[16] Surviving requires clever deception and siding with her human allies, which again reinforces the social dimension of this initiation. In the face of death, she relies on her family, her sisters or brothers, and more broadly humankind, the community (to which the Bluebeard figure does not belong), to re-establish a link with life. In AT312 tales, brothers or parents save her when called upon.[17] In some AT311 versions, the murdered women themselves advise her, or she relies on her mother's support at home.[18] The Grimms' "Fichter's Bird" has her brother and relatives destroying the sorcerer, his cronies, and his castle, once the girl and her sisters are safe at home.[19] And in AT955 versions, the girl's parents believe her story and plan the fake wedding ceremony to trick her bridegroom. Once he is exposed, whether turned over to the authorities, or even lynched as in the North Carolina "Old Foster" tale, the whole community takes part in punishing him.[20] In many versions, the girl marries again, and happily; in some cases, the future husband has provided her with helpful information during her trial.[21] In other versions, she simply returns to the bosom of her family.[22] Regardless of the details, the tale's resolution reaffirms the protagonist's membership in a variety of social groups—humanity, women, family, the town—and establishes her right to make a home for herself with her own kind. She is transformed by the experience.[23]

Female disobedience is therefore hardly the point. Focusing on the initiatory pattern redeems the heroine, restoring her to her place as the tale's rightful protagonist. But this is not the whole story. Emphasizing the bride does not necessarily place her husband or husband-to-be in a subordinate role, since he remains the other subject of this double-plotted narrative.[24] Pursuing independent though related goals, each functions as means and obstacle in the other's plot. By crossing the threshold of the bloody chamber, both have trespassed, and blood marks them both. Both also want knowledge of, and power over, the other. Not only is the plot double—she wants his riches or love, he wants her life—but Bluebeard and his wife are themselves duplicitous, yet another aspect of their doubling one another. Or as one Kentucky narrator puts it, "Whenever he married the last time, he got his match" ("The Fellow That Married a Dozen Times," Campbell 246).[25]

Duplicity and doubling structure the plot or *fabula* of "Bluebeard" tales. To give an extreme example, in the Ozark AT311 "How Toodie Fixed Old Grunt," Toodie still marries the well-to-do Old Grunt, even after two older sisters successively "showed up missing," because her "folks talked her into it." Her boyfriend Jack discovers the sisters' bodies and warns Toodie; she blinds Old Grunt with pepper when he tries to kill her. Jack and Toodie then cut Old Grunt's head off and throw the body into the cistern where his victims lie. "About three weeks after that Toodie told everybody that her husband had run off and left her," and soon she has her parents and Jack move in to help her with the farm. Inevitably, "she and her Jack got married, and raised a big family, and they all lived happily ever after" (Randolph 63–65). Clearly, Toodie is Old Grunt's double, right down to using the same explanation for her spouse's disappearance. I have already noted that in AT312 versions the bride's deceptions mirror her husband's, though not as pronounced as Toodie's. To disregard her bridegroom's strange features or even to be attracted to them, the bride must have some affinity with Bluebeard. If the fox's "popular lore attributes" are "cunning, greed and cowardice" (Carter, *Virago* 231), then the "Bluebeard" heroine is not just foxy, but foxlike—tricky, often greedy, reluctant to confront her enemy in the open or alone.[26]

An initiatory plot that exploits duplicity and doubleness not surprisingly will often sustain itself through duality. While its plot builds on doubling, "Bluebeard"'s clear-cut resolution, magic-tale style, can only come from privileging duality as binary opposition. One force or the other must be destroyed—no room for ambiguities at the end of fairy tales. Even when, in some versions, the girl simply escapes the robbers' cave and marries her loved one, the Bluebeard figure pursues her to her new home; for her to be safe, he must be killed.[27] But even before the ending, representing the two characters as extreme opposites sustains the story thematically (death/life), even as their doubling complicates this dichotomy: in a British tale, the "diabolical" Captain Murderer meets his match in "the dark twin," not the fair one. In the Ozark tale, for instance, despite the doubling subtext, Old Grunt and Toodie are explicitly and primarily set up as opposites, one doing the work of death, the other of life; Toodie actually planting flowers on the ground covering the cistern. The evil giant in the Breton "Comorre" rules over "the country of black corn," while Triphyna's country is that of "white corn" (Soupault 165), and in other Breton versions the Bluebeard figure becomes murderous when his wife becomes pregnant, further underscoring their death/life dichotomous symbolism (Velay-Vallantin 48).[28] We know that characters and conflict in fairy tales are extreme; thus, even though initiation demands a death-like experience, the heroine's contiguity with life sets her starkly in opposition to Bluebeard's death drive.

Because the struggle between life and death in "Bluebeard" is played out over the bodies of women, what this initiation story's value is for women today, and what its simultaneous doubling and duality signify in terms of sexual politics, are questions which must be addressed. Margaret Atwood's, Angela Carter's, and Jane Campion's re-visions of "Bluebeard" tales supply answers by investigating the female protagonist's agency and by foregrounding doubling within the frame of the double-plot. Each writer self-consciously engages specific versions of "Bluebeard" and highlights the heroine's collusive agency, but resolves the doubling/duality tension differently. The cumulative performative effect of their re-visions is itself double: empowering female protagonists as well as readers/viewers, while interrogating the fairy tale's naturalizing of gender dynamics. Doing so involves focusing on agency, but also on the protagonist's voice, on her ties to other women, on her implication with Bluebeard's plot, and more generally, on socio-economic dynamics.

In the partial retelling of "Bluebeard" embedded in her story "Bluebeard's Egg," Margaret Atwood foregrounds doubling by exploring the female protagonist's perception of herself as trickster.[29] Sally, the third wife of a heart specialist, is taking a night course called *Forms of Narrative Fiction*. Her assignment is to rewrite "a variant of the Bluebeard motif" from a specific point of view (176). What Sally remembers of the story she has listened to in class is a wizard abducting three sisters successively; a test/gift egg, and a forbidden chamber with the blood-filled basin; the third sister reassembling her older sisters' chopped-up bodies; and the wizard promising to marry her. Even though it ends *in medias res*, the version is obviously the Grimms' "Fichter's Bird," and "There was more, about how the wizard met his come-uppance and was burned to death, but Sally already knew which features stood out for her" (177). Wanting to do something "clever," more clever than the other students, Sally decides to write the story "from the point of view of the egg." This strategy, she believes, will allow her to answer the question: "How does it feel, to be the innocent and passive cause of so much misfortune?" (178). This idea comes to her when she begins to think of her husband Ed as the egg and of herself as the clever one who helps him/it remain intact, unblemished. Not simply "the princess" whom her husband, like the unpromising fairy-tale hero, is lucky enough to marry, Sally feels that her cleverness protects and saves Ed: "if it weren't for her, his blundering too-many thumbs kindness would get him into all sorts of quagmires, all sorts of sink-holes he'd never be able to get himself out of, and then he'd be done for" (162). But these "sink-holes," as she uncomfortably admits, are other women, whose hearts and blood might soil Ed's "monumental and almost energetic stupidity" (161), his "lamb-like" innocence. Like the egg with which the sisters in "Fichter's Bird" are tested, he has no idea of the danger she is rescuing him from: "these troops of women, which follow him around everywhere, which are invisible to Ed but which she can see as plain as day" (170).

Doubling occurs on several levels. To begin with, though "Bluebeard's Egg" is not five pages long, it does fulfill the requirements for Sally's assignment: a "transposition" of "Bluebeard"—in this case the "Fichter's Bird" version—which is "set in the present and cast in the realistic mode," and told from a specific point of view (176).[30] While identifying with "the cunning heroine" (177) by posing as trickster, Sally also self-consciously doubles as the Bluebeard figure, the wizard. After all, she hunted Ed down (161); she is the one objectifying her husband (*My darling Edward,* she thinks. *Edward Bear, of little brain. How I love you*" 160); and she is the one who feels no qualms in erasing other women (*"Trouble with your heart? Get it removed,* she thinks. *Then you'll have no more problems*" 165). Therefore, Sally's conscious identification with the heroine who defeats the wizard in "Fichter's Bird" depends on Sally's own tendency to join the wizard in objectifying and victimizing human beings. "A free woman in an unfree society will be a monster," Angela Carter notes (*Sadeian Woman* 27), and yet, because Sally accepts the restricting plot in which a woman's survival depends on her being recognized as the "true bride," she ends up doing Bluebeard's dirty work herself—the reason, perhaps, why the third girl's escape in "Fichter's Bird" does not seem to stick with her, or why there is no Bluebeard in Sally's recasting of the story.[31] Furthermore, her seemingly clever orchestration of married life does not save Sally from being victimized herself. Eventually she recognizes herself as the "false bride" that a re-evaluated, perhaps even "enormously clever" Ed might soon discard (181). When Sally enters the forbidden chamber—Ed's studio, with its self-exposing and objectifying heart machine, and the alcove in which she sees him patting Marylynn's behind—she must finally

admit that Ed fooled her. While correct in interpreting "his ob-
tuseness" as "a wall" (171), and in suspecting that if he were the
wizard his forbidden room "wouldn't even be locked" (178), Sally
must now confront what she clearly feared and closed her eyes to:
the room where she imagined him healing and restoring life can
also be a place for betraying and "killing" women—herself included.

Sharon Rose Wilson has shown how "Bluebeard's Egg" echoes
and parodies the mirroring or doubling at work in the gender dynamics of "Fichter's Bird,"[32] while rejecting any move to duality in
the end.[33] Though Ed becomes more sinister and Sally more obviously vulnerable, in "Bluebeard's Egg" neither character "defeats"
the other. Instead, Atwood extends the doubling by foregrounding the "alive" egg: "one day it will hatch. But what will come out of
it?" (182). Earlier, Sally realized "she's fed up with her inner
world; she doesn't need to explore it. In her inner world is Ed, like
a doll within a Russian wooden doll, and in Ed is Ed's inner world,
which she can't get at" (173). Unblemished and "innocent" (178),
the egg is thus an appropriate and safe image of her inner world
and Ed's as well, since he is in her "inner being." By the story's
end, however, Sally fears the egg, which glows "softly as though
there's something red and hot inside it" (182). Both in Ed and in
Sally, that being is "almost pulsing," coming alive. Will it mean
new life for Ed or Sally? Atwood's text does not choose. Since Ed is
de-objectified, dangerous but alive, the egg might contain his life,
and, to survive, Sally, like the girl in the Italian "The Three
Chicory Gatherers," might have to break it. Or Ed's coming to life
in Sally's worldview might instead mark the frightening but potentially promising renewal of their relationship.[34] Or perhaps, when
Sally steps from her room with a view down into the cellar, she
could be witnessing the beginnings of her own rebirth, as a
woman no longer under the spell of Bluebeard. By underscoring
doubling, the condition for the liminal phase of rites of passage,
even when Sally is becoming aware of her difference, no "rebirth"
is ruled out.[35] Initiation is not accomplished, but is in process.

The narrative itself reinforces this doubling and ambivalence.
"Bluebeard's Egg" is focalized through Sally, but told by an external narrator: unlike the protagonist of "The Robber Bridegroom"
tales, Sally does not tell her own story. We do hear her dialogues

with Ed and her friend/rival Marylynn, and Sally is an active talker, but she predominantly uses words to hide or to trick—which Ed and Marylynn also seem to do. As a brief exchange between Sally and Ed demonstrates (179), the unspoken rule is to pretend that telling and thinking are the same when you are talking, but are not necessarily identical when another talks. Atwood builds her narrative strategy on this ambivalence. Although Sally basically lacks her own point of view until the end—she sees herself through Ed—her role as focalizer is paradoxically more productive and believable than the role of narrator would have been. Within the external narrator's seemingly objective framework, Sally's perspective emerges as "voice" in Cixous's terms, full of contradictions and mixed allegiances. This "voice" is potentially more transforming than her active but blind agency in the text. We can therefore hope to hear her as a narrator when the egg hatches.

Why does Atwood insist on this doubling, this refusal to give in to duality? On the one hand, it clearly rules out facile happy endings: "femininists" (180) should not be smug about seeming power gains because our actions and perspectives may very well be instrumental to a patriarchal plot. On the other hand, this strategy shifts us away from the seemingly natural "battle of the sexes" embodied in "Bluebeard" stories, and toward a nuanced understanding of patriarchal sexual politics as a social construction that oppresses both women and men. Here and elsewhere, Atwood sides with women, but she also exposes and ridicules various types of "femininity," and, by revealing the constraints and fears motivating men, she undercuts "masculine" plots to subjugate women as well. In "Bluebeard's Egg," reflection and calls for action, irony, and sympathy can coexist because doubling sustains a process rather than forcing a statement. The story's inclusion of men's fears and its push for knowledge may seem luxuries in the general context of gender politics, and perhaps they are, but they are productive, and not trivial luxuries.

This vision shapes Atwood's more recent "Bluebeard" retelling in *Good Bones*. "Bluebeard ran off with the third sister, intelligent though beautiful, and shut her up in his palace," the story begins. Everything there is hers except whatever lies behind the forbidden "small door" ("Alien Territory" 82, 83). We are told that she is in love with him, "even though she knew he was a serial killer," and because "she loved him, she wanted to understand him. She also wanted to cure him. She thought she had the healing touch" (83). In this version, Atwood nonchalantly picks and chooses from Perrault's text, where the female protagonist willingly overlooks Bluebeard's alienating features, and he offers her riches and comfort; from the Grimms' tales, where the girl thinks herself clever; and even from Béla Bartók's opera *Duke Bluebeard's Castle*, where the girl believes she will transform his world through love. But in Atwood's version Bluebeard's other women are easily found in the "linen closet, neatly cut up and ironed flat and folded," and the protagonist slips the one who "looked like his mother . . . into the incinerator" (83, 84). Inside the forbidden room, lies instead "a small dead child, with its eyes wide open." "I gave birth to it," the Bluebeard figure claims, "It is me" (84, 85). The woman then falls out of love, but he takes her "deeper" for "suddenly" there is "no floor" (85). Like Bartók's Judith, she moves into darkness.

This ending may seem gloomy and hopeless, a triumph for duality and a slap at female curiosity.[36] When read in context, however, this "Bluebeard" changes. It is section six of "Alien Territory," a seven-part text which with "The Female Body," its similarly structured companion text, not only suggests how destructive "Bluebeard"'s sexual politics are for both women and men, but also offers embodied compassion as a way out. In "Alien Territory" [AT] and "The Female Body" [FB] Atwood exposes Bluebeard's plot as a ritual of masculine self-conception which feeds on a denial of the human body, by simultaneously under- and over-valuing the female body. When "he conceives himself in alien territory" (AT 75), that "alien territory" is a metaphor for the body, even though "he" might view it metonymically as female. Represented as a "topic," with such accessories as "garter-belt," "head," and "Reproductive System," this female body has "been used as a door-knocker, a bottle-opener, as a clock with a ticking belly." A commodity and "a natural resource," even in its Barbie simulacra it is mutilated and rejected (FB 39–46). "One and one equals another one" (FB 44): within a patriarchal framework, biology turns into a formula for women's commodification and interchangeability. And yet, with his existential Aloneness, "he" may realize "he's lost the Female Body!" and thus he may try to recapture it: "Put it in a pumpkin, in a high tower, in a compound, in a chamber, in a house, in a room. Quick, stick a leash on it, a lock, a chain, some pain" (FB 46). Just as in the "Bluebeard" stories, women here are sacrificial victims or phoenixes in flight. Mirror-like, "Alien Territory" investigates the demands and strategies of this plot from within, from "his" perspective.

Simone de Beauvoir has best explained how the West has dichotomized gender dynamics through the body. Because man fears mortality, the condition of humanity, he believes himself to be in alien territory and chooses instead to conceive of himself metaphysically—like a god. Atwood's fiction fleshes out de Beauvoir's scholarly words. "Having a body is not altogether serious," we hear; "men's bodies are detachable" and not "dependable" (AT 81); they are reason for "intimidating" comparisons (AT 78). Above all, though:

What men are most afraid of is not lions, not snakes, not the dark, not women. Not any more. What men are most afraid of is the body of another man.

Men's bodies are the most dangerous things on earth. (AT 79–81)

What epitomizes the mirroring effect of sections six and seven of "Alien Territory" is that in Bluebeard's forbidden chamber the body, female and male, is killed over and over again. As in "Bluebeard's Egg," doubling is a narrative strategy that leads us to disturbing but transformative knowledge. Both men and women are alienated from themselves and their "significant others"; both assume a mythic or metaphysical life within the no-body plot; both continue to mutilate themselves and to move into the other as if entering "alien territory."[37]

The end of section five in "Alien Territory" suggests a new beginning: "In the gap between desire and enactment, noun and verb, intention and infliction, *want* and *have*, compassion begins" (82).[38] Sections six and seven can be read as enactments of the two sides of "compassion." As noted above, section six's retelling of "Bluebeard" exposes compassion's destructive aspect: attracted to Bluebeard's suffering, the woman ultimately suffers for him. There is no happy ending. The seventh section of "Alien Territory" looks for reasons why women are attracted to "those ones" who "offer nothing" but "have bodies" which "are verbalized" (85,

86). "Because if they can say their own bodies," the narrator hope-
fully suggests, "they could say yours too. Because they could say
skin as if it meant something, not only to them but to you" (88).
This section explores the alternative to Bluebeard-driven plots by
employing "compassion" as a "sharing" of emotions and a re-evaluation of the body—a possibility for reciprocal and embodied
recognition which parallels the red and hot promise of Bluebeard's egg.

Does Atwood supply a "happy ending"? This clever writer puts
us in process, with no simple resolution, no closure—only the
double-edged signs of compassion. Section six's dark ending not
only opposes but mirrors the promise-filled close of section seven.
Both involve suffering—largely psychological in the first scenario,
primarily economic in the second. And why, in the very beginning
of section seven, do "those ones" have no explicit referent or an-
tecedent? Are "those ones" like "beggars, whose gift is to ask" (AT
86), meant to parallel the wizard's initial disguise as beggar in
"Fichter's Bird," which section six has just recalled? And when
"those ones" tell a woman that her body "is made of light" (AT
88), are they performing just one more disembodying trick? While
this image mirrors the light that women were to bring to Bluebeard's dark castle, there is a difference. The "beggar's hands" are
on the woman's body, blessing it—at least for now. In "Bluebeard's Egg" and "Alien Territory," Atwood therefore privileges
doubling not simply as a strategy to retell Bluebeard tales, but as a
method for problematizing the female protagonist's trickster-role.
Furthermore, by insisting on the self-reflective, liminal aspect of
initiation, Atwood resists any dichotomized view of genders as
"naturally" alien territories.

Angela Carter goes about things differently. In "The Bloody
Chamber," her "Bluebeard" revision, she contextualizes and complicates the female protagonist's victim-role, reflects ambiguously
back on the process of initiation, and highlights the seductive
socio-economic dynamics of sex-gender oppression. Reproducing
the tension between doubling and duality already active in "Bluebeard," Carter increases it until the tale's dualistic resolution can
only be seen as a temporary disentanglement from doubling. In
Carter's short story, the forbidden room holds the mutilated remains of a Breton Marquis's three wives: the embalmed naked

body of the first; within an Iron Maiden, the pierced and bleeding body of the second; and crowned by a bridal veil and white roses, the grotesquely beautiful skull of the third. When wife number four—a pale adolescent pianist, "innocent but not naive," discovers this horror, she drops the key and the indelible bloody stains on it betray her to the murderous husband. The young bride's minutely detailed, hauntingly visual, and soul-searching account reveals that she self-consciously viewed her innocence as an asset—she exchanged her virginal body for her husband's riches. However, having opened the forbidden door, she soon realizes that death, more than sex, is the ritual he wishes to enact and she is apparently fated to pass through. Her martyrdom will place her for eternity in his crypt. But inspired by her mother's courage, and comforted by a blind piano-tuner, the young woman decides to escape this fate, and does. After her mother kills the Marquis, the heroine turns the castle into a school for the blind. The contents of the bloody chamber are "buried or burned, the door sealed" ("The Bloody Chamber" 17, 40).

In "The Bloody Chamber," as in other "Bluebeard" stories, doubling and duality, ambivalence and opposition strongly shape the characters. Both the unnamed fourth wife and the Marquis have "white" faces and are associated with lilies; furthermore, her pretense mirrors his: "With the most treacherous, lascivious tenderness, he kissed my eyes, and, mimicking the new bride newly awakened, I flung my arms around him, for on my seeming acquiescence depended my salvation" (34). In age, class, economics, knowledge, power, and motivation, however, the two are sharply distinguished. Analogously, the bride learns she has inherited her mother's spirit and courage, her "nerves and a will" (28), and yet the two women are set up in opposition to one another through the mother's youthful heroism—she not only "defiantly beggared herself for love" but at one point also "shot a man-eating tiger" (8, 7). Nor does the doubling/duality strategy stop here. While the "eagle-featured" mother (7) is clearly the nemesis of the father-like, "leonine" husband (8)—she eventually descends on him like an "avenging angel" to save her child from hell (39)—her Medusa-like wildness is a mythic match for Bluebeard's mastery. When confronting each other, they look like two lions, one white-maned and the other black-bearded. An eerie resemblance also haunts the seemingly antithetical husband and lover. An older man of massive bulk and riches, the Marquis's violently eroticizing gaze seeks to control. The young, "slight" piano-tuner is poor, sweet, and blind. Yet both men have walking sticks, and the husband's all-seeing eyes nevertheless display an "absolute absence of light" (9), while the lover sleeps "in a room at the foot of the west tower," where the bloody chamber is also located.[39] The doubling/duality comes full circle when the young woman, having finally seen the bloody chamber for what it is, is struck into self-recognition when she faces the piano-tuner's "lovely, blind humanity, . . . his tender look" (32).

Carter's performance of "Bluebeard" narratives also plays out a generic tension between repetition and opposition. As in Perrault's "Blue Beard," Carter's young woman marries, for money, an unappealing man she does not love. Before leaving on an unexpected trip, the husband in Carter's story also grants his wife everything but access to an underground room. The bloody key predictably betrays the girl's transgression, and a family member rescues her from death. Finally, the irony, luxurious descriptions, and artfully constructed mirrors in both stories are clearly the work of accomplished stylists. But Carter's departures are even more striking. The socio-economic disparity between bride and groom is much greater; the mother, not the brothers, serves as the family avenger; and the tale itself is told by the young woman in the first person and after the fact. "The Bloody Chamber" also unsettles Perrault by drawing on other "Bluebeard" versions and a variety of other intertexts. The references to Breton versions, the openly initiatory details from other French "Bluebeard" tales, and the playful allusion to Charles Dickens's retelling, "Captain Murderer," all revise our understanding of Perrault's version even as Carter reproduces its plot.[40]

Carter's narrative doubling pushes for knowledge. "The Bloody Chamber"'s first-person retrospective style of narration embodies what Danielle Roemer has called Carter's "doubled voice" strategy.[41] The narrator's sensual style both uses and exposes seduction as a trap. The survivor looks back on her victimizing experience from varying distances: an oscillating focalization that tricks readers—and women readers specifically—in and out of identification with the heroine's disturbing *mélange* of displayed cleverness

and passivity.[42] Perrault's "Blue Beard" heroine is the appropriate
model for shaping the protagonist's contradictory victim-role.
Comparing Perrault's heroine to other folkloric "Bluebeard"
brides makes it easy to blame her for her own troubles, since she
agrees to marry the man, she rushes to satisfy her curiosity, and
she remains uncharacteristically passive, a victim whose rescue depends on chance and prayer (see note 15). "The Bloody Chamber"'s unnamed first-person narrator, focalizer, and main agent is
also a "virtuous" yet "willing victim," but her own awareness of this
ambivalence opens the door to furthering our knowledge of the
bloody room of collusion.[43] Her memory of herself as a seventeen-
year-old attending the opera on the eve of her wedding crystallizes
both collusion and doubling within an explicitly economic frame:

> That night at the opera comes back to me even now . . . the white dress;
> the frail child within it; and the flashing crimson jewels round her throat,
> bright as arterial blood.
>   I saw him watching me in the gilded mirrors with the assessing eye of a
> connoisseur inspecting horseflesh, or even of a housewife in the market
> inspecting cuts on the slab. I had never seen, or else had never acknowl-
> edged, that regard of his before, the sheer carnal avarice of it. . . . When I
> saw him look at me with lust, I dropped my eyes but, in glancing away
> from him, I caught sight of myself in the mirror. And I saw myself, sud-
> denly, as he saw me. . . . I saw how much that cruel necklace became me.
> And, for the first time in my innocent and confined life, I sensed in myself
> a potentiality for corruption that took my breath away. (11)

The archetypically liminal figure of the bride-to-be appears here
in different lights. Though the frail, innocent "child" finds herself
reduced to "meat" (poor thing), when she turns away from Bluebeard, her view of herself mirrors his. That "extraordinarily precious slit throat" (11), the choker of rubies, is another ambivalent
sign foreshadowing both the Marquis's plan to decapitate her and
her own deliverance, since his aristocratic grandmother had the
necklace made after the French Revolution as a remembrance of
how she had escaped the guillotine. And yet this choker also
marks her "potential for corruption": she might be "dead meat"—
after all, her breath gets taken away—but she also seems to enjoy
the cruelty that goes with the "luxurious defiance" of privilege
(11).[44] Carter reminds us how victimhood for women often carries

with it the dangerously seductive companions of "willingness" and "virtue."

On the one hand, the narrator's attention to material conditions undeniably promotes an unflinching and self-implicating understanding of heterosexual sado-masochism within a socially exploitative society.[45] Like the *Tristan*'s *Liebestod*, the "willing victim," the image of the girl wrapped in white muslin and red ribbon is presented as exciting, or "voluptuous," precisely because it carries "such a charge of deathly passion" (10). When later in the master bedroom the package is unwrapped, the process not only replicates the (dis)robing rituals in non-literary French versions of "Bluebeard," but also "the etching by Rops" in which a man "in his London tailoring" examines a girl "bare as a lamb chop" (15).[46] Glancing in the mirror, the young bride recognizes that she and the Marquis are "the living image" of the etching, which represents the "[m]ost pornographic of all confrontations" (15). After the Marquis, still wearing his smoking jacket, "impales" the quasi-naked virgin, she is left wondering whether in his orgasm she has seen the face behind the inscrutably impassive mask or not (17–18). As for the Marquis, he does not kiss the girl but the rubies of her choker, a fetishizing essential to this sado-masochistic ritual in which the encounter of two bodies, two individuals, is in fact merely a gendered, socio-economic interaction.

The psychological fall-out is predictably confusing for the young bride. "I was aghast to feel myself stirring," she notes, and later, "I longed for him and he disgusted me" (15, 22). This is not an example of "manipulation by the narrative to sympathise with masochism," Avis Lewallen to the contrary (Lewallen 151), but rather a painful recognition from within of masochism's presence in sexual and economic exploitation. Having marketed her child-like innocence, the girl must now look to her buyer for self-worth. Her collusion leaves its mark on her body in the "heart-shaped stain" he impresses on his bride's forehead (36); symbolically, this collusion causes her narration to oscillate between naive expectations of sex and knowing descriptions of economics.[47] Carter's mirroring of pornography ultimately does not endorse heterosexual sado-masochism, however, because destructive relations are not presented as natural, but as symptoms of specific repressive socio-cultural dynamics. Though the bride pities "the atrocious loneliness" of the Marquis inevitable in someone fated to take pleasure only from his own *enfer*, this pity makes the Marquis no less a "monster" (35). What it does suggest is that the very structures that support his privilege repress his own capacity for compassion. Preserving his blue blood, his riches, his power apparently depends on his isolation, his criminal reproduction of beautiful symbols of death.

On the other hand, Carter's story in its appeal to religious imagery simultaneously sets the protagonist's aspiration to be a "virtuous victim" within the history of "Bluebeard" narratives while parodically stripping the self-serving qualities away from this representation of victimhood. The bride's words make the Marquis not simply a being favored by God—"On his arm, all eyes were upon me. The whispering crowd in the foyer parted like the Red Sea to let us through" (10)—but a deity himself: "The light caught the fire opal on my hand so that it flashed, once, with a baleful light, as if to tell me the eye of God—his eye—was upon me" (29). Seeing all, including her entry into the bloody chamber, he will punish or reward her, in both cases with death. His "little nun" (17), she compares herself to "a penitent" (27), and lets him "martyrize" her hair (19). But of course, her husband is also the Devil— a figure whose kingdom, or *enfer*, is hell (21)—who wishes to corrupt the girl's innocence, who has bound Huysmans's *Là-bas* "like a missal" (16), who blasphemes during orgasm (18), and who possesses "chthonic gravity" (35). In the girl's narrative, the husband, whether he is seen as God or Devil, seems to hold absolute power, leaving the girl not simply a victim, but a martyr—a lopsided St. Cecilia, in fact, as the girl's imagery and specific observations bear out.[48]

The religious significance of the girl's sacrifice works on different levels to disparate effects. First, by pursuing her metafolkloric or archeological project, Carter reactivates the Christian and pre-Christian religious dimension of "Bluebeard." Representing Bluebeard as the Devil strongly invokes Italian and French folk versions, and in Brittany, the scene of Carter's story, "Bluebeard" has traditionally blended the profane with the hagiographic. Carter's stylistic experimentation and her protagonist's religiously based self-righteousness both find their precedent in the already mentioned Breton version "Comorre," in which Triphyna, who has committed no sin, is married to a most evil giant who murders her. She is finally resurrected by Saint Veltas. Carter and the Breton tradition both root this good/evil struggle in a fertility/sterility dichotomy. Though Carter's heroine believes Bluebeard is taking her to his "legendary habitation" to "bear an heir" (8), she soon realizes she is fated to die. Similarly, Comorre's four dead wives tell the pregnant Triphyna he will kill her because he believes his first-born will kill him (Soupault 165–174; see also note 28). A second level of religious significance appears when Carter, by stressing the bride's role as sacrificial victim, reactivates those initiatory features of "Bluebeard" which Perrault tersely erased. In several French versions, the bride victim's ceremonial robing and disrobing become her method for gaining time. While ritually dressing up as a bride for her death, she responds to Bluebeard's requests to come down for the "ceremony" by singing back the items of clothing she has put on. Or conversely, in some versions, the bride must go naked to her death. Carter exploits both possibilities. "Go, now," "The Bloody Chamber" husband commands, "Bathe yourself; dress yourself. The lustratory ritual and ceremonial robing; after that, the sacrifice" (37). The woman returns wearing only the "white muslin shift, costume of a victim of an auto-da-fé" (37), and the red choker, but "once again, of my apparel I must retain only my gems; the sharp blade ripped my dress in two and it fell from me" (39).

On yet another level within this retrospective first-person narrative, the religious framework, which seeks to provide a foolproof representation of the heroine's innocence and virtue, shows itself as a victimizing, self-serving ideology—iconoclastically working in tandem with the more common sexual commodification of women through marriage. Though certainly the heroine presents herself as a martyr while displaying little saintliness, the most telling point here is that the religiously sanctioned subject position of "virtuous victim" not only fosters her passivity when she is fated for "immolation," but also lets the narrator justify that passivity. Though bold and courageous in the bloody chamber, she does very little indeed to defeat death. Slipping right into the martyrdom form of initiation, she accepts her fate, hoping all the while to be saved. "I've done nothing," she admits to the comfort-

ing piano-tuner, "but that may be sufficient reason for condemn-
ing me" (37). Is this "doing nothing" a mark of virtuous innocence
or the complacency of a fated passive figure waiting to be rescued?
And who is actually being taken in? Especially when describing her
preparation for their "last rites" (36), the narrator's language foregrounds the initiation's religious aspects as a method for re-constructing her lost innocence, for cleansing herself of collusion
with the devil, and for justifying in hindsight her acceptance of
fate. Victim-blaming is not my purpose here. Rather I am pointing
out contradictions in the heroine's narrative as hints to religion's
status as a readily available ideological refuge or mask which still
seduces women into victimhood. "The Bloody Chamber"'s protagonist believes she has lost, like Eve, the "charade of innocence and
vice" her husband has engaged her in, that "game in which every
move was governed by a destiny as oppressive and omnipotent as
himself" (34). Condemnation or salvation thus depends on some
higher power, or to put it more bluntly, without her mother, this
self-reflective bride would be dead.[49]

Carter's re-presentation of Perrault's heroine, then, explores
her socio-economic motivations for entering the bloody chamber
of collusion while parodying her masochism in order to build resistance to it. The narrator's double-voiced confessional mode bal-
ances self-exposure and self-protection in a presentation that
cautions against sexual, economic, and symbolic seduction even as
it lulls the teller into self-righteousness. This sustained narrative
doubling apparently finds a clear-cut resolution in "The Bloody
Chamber," which in a way it has to if the bride is there to tell her
story in the past tense. The narrator's "avenging angel" mother descends and saves her child (39) by putting "a single, irreproach-
able bullet" through the Marquis's head "without a moment's
hesitation" (40). Acting in accordance with her "*maternal telepathy*"—which Carter playfully updates by having the heroine crying
to her mother on the telephone about gold taps, rather than sending the traditional black dove or similar coded signs of a cry for
help—the mother intervenes and restores her daughter to life. Inspired by her mother's presence, the passive victim-to-be even
rushes to help her struggling "lover" unbolt the gate and let the
avenger in (39). As the story ends, she settles down into a quiet,
middle-of-the way life with her mother and her piano-tuner.

Is duality reasserted? On the level of *fabula*, yes, life triumphs over death. But, complicating the traditional masculine/feminine opposition, this duality is not naturalized. Life is to death not as woman is to man. Rather, "Woman" as metaphor for fertility gives way to a mother-daughter bond which is socially, economically, and emotionally specific. This bond is affirmed in the face of another mother-daughter relationship which colludes with Bluebeard's plot. The girl's "old nurse" teases the bride-to-be about the Marquis's previous wives, and while admiring her engagement ring, warns her that "opals are bad luck" (9). But this mother figure, who keeps "back copies of society magazines" in a trunk under her bed (10) and treasures her "little store of holy books" featuring "woodcuts of the martyrdom of the saints" (28), also rejoices in the "marital coup" which not only will transform the girl into "her little Marquise" (9), but wed the "richest man in France" to her own "saint Cecilia" (12, 38). Having unwittingly nursed the protagonist into victimhood, this woman is "scandalized" when the mother rushes to the rescue following the girl's phone call: "—what? interrupt milord in his honeymoon?—" (40). Terribly disillusioned by the marriage's outcome, this "false" mother dies.[50]

As for the "true" mother, neither the Marquis's gravity nor his riches seduce her, and she gives her daughter up "reluctantly" (7, 10). The "daughter of a rich tea planter" in Indo-China (7), this woman has lived unconventionally, even eccentrically. Always prepared for the violence lurking in the ordinary, she carries her dead husband's revolver in her shopping bag. She also listens to her daughter's music, silences, and cries, acting resolutely to revive her "heart." Hers is another economy, a marginalized one that the oedipal norms and the "blood banks" of women's commodification and martyrdom have exiled to the margins. The mother's actions place her with the many clever and bold heroines of "Bluebeard" stories, and with the heroines' often older female helpers as well (see note 18). Only readers who believe that fairy-tale heroines are hopelessly entangled in patriarchal values will be surprised that the mother's eccentricity is the key to her success.[51] As Danielle Roemer notes, though "an agent of the past" like the Marquis, the mother has a "history of strong-mindedness." And while not consistently, fairy tales have center-staged this alternative. As Carter remarks in the Introduction to *The Virago Book of*

Fairy Tales, "That I and many other women should go looking through the books for fairy-tale heroines" enacts "a wish to validate my claim to a fair share of the future by staking my claim to my share in the past" (xvi). Carter therefore gives her easily-taken-in heroine a future by revising the "good" mother into the powerful and active keeper of an alternative economy of desire.[52]

Only because the resolute and wiser woman saves the hesitant younger one can she then look back on her experience and tell her story. The agency that brings a "happy ending" to a potentially tragic plot also stimulates the narrator's self-reflection. The *fabula*'s liberating outcome may rise out of extreme opposition and action, but the protagonist's initiation remains to be reviewed, retold, and thus resolved. And is she initiated? Certainly the heart-shaped blood stain her husband inscribes onto her forehead with the magic key stands as experience and narrative. Most obviously this sanguine tattoo proclaims a number of initiations—sexual (she has lost her virginity), epistemological (having entered his hell, she recognizes herself as one of his victims), ritual (she is reborn after an encounter with death), and spiritual (no longer blinded by gems, her heart now guides her). But Carter takes matters further. Since in Bluebeard's plot the stain signifies the woman's guilt, our heroine first sees it as "the mark of Cain" or "the caste mark of a brahmin woman" (36). But having survived his plot, in her re-vision of it the stain reflects her "shame" (41)—not at having disobeyed her husband, but at having been "bought with a handful of coloured stones and the pelts of dead beasts" (18), at having belonged to "the fated sisterhood of his wives" (29). And still the heart-shaped stain's significance spreads for it is the sign of an alternative economy of blood relations, the mark of women's alliance and a third-eye vision. And invoking Charles Dickens's version of "Bluebeard," in the style of an in-joke not uncommon in Carter's writings, it can even be an ironic reflection on the self-righteousness of its bearer. In "Captain Murderer," as retold by Dickens, the villain's "milk-white horses" have "one red spot on the back, which he caused to be hidden by the harness" when they pull his wedding carriage. "For the spot *would* come there, though every horse was milk-white when Captain Murderer bought him. And the spot was young bride's blood" (Philip). Could Carter be referring to her clever but passive and unwise protagonist as a "horse's arse"?[53]

Though she advocates action and courage to move out of victimizing plots, Carter thus continues to show how precarious any resolution built on binary oppositions will remain—even when one pole is a quite understandable self-righteousness. If the doubling strategy makes "The Bloody Chamber" disturbing and leaves its "happy ending" dubious, it nevertheless relentlessly counts "the ways in which women can be complicit with what captivates and victimizes them, even or especially in their adventurousness." Only after recognizing these ways can we "change what we desire" (Jordan, "Dangers" 130). "The Bloody Chamber," thus, mimics the tense doubling/duality of "Bluebeard" stories, but makes it resonate for women today by reflecting on their/our sexual and religious seduction, the contradictory open-endedness of initiation and its knowledge, and the economics of sexual politics. Agency, voice, and mother/daughter ties are represented as vehicles for change, but still we are warned of the shifting, even contradicting values they assume in different contexts.

Margaret Atwood and Angela Carter both offer an initiatory reading of "Bluebeard" which also acknowledges its warnings, its cautionary function. For these writers, however, it is not "sexual curiosity" per se that is at stake. Jane Campion's *The Piano* radically asserts the initiatory value of "Bluebeard" tales precisely by subverting commonplace interpretations of sexuality and disobedience in the "forbidden chamber." As it thematizes agency and voice, inscribes duality within a historical and cultural script, and provocatively exploits a specific form of doubling, mimicry, to contradictory effects, the film emphatically affirms the strong, though dangerous, power of carnal knowledge. Ada McGrath, *The Piano*'s protagonist, is a small, solemn-looking Scottish woman who willfully stopped speaking at the age of six. Sparse written notes and a sign language she shares with her daughter Flora keep her in touch with the world. Flora is Ada's communicative voice, but her rosewood piano is the outlet for her inner, symbolic language. Her "mind's voice" (9) frames the movie, announcing her "elective mutism" at the beginning, but informing us that she is "learning to speak" at the end (122), even though silence continues to affect her.[54] Not much else is explained about Ada. Like the movie's other characters, the audience must listen for her feelings by attending to her body and dress language, her reluctant though direct gaze, and her music.

The historical and cultural context for her eventual transformation is represented in a clear, unnuanced way. In the middle of the nineteenth century, Ada is married off to a man she has not met. Dressed in dark Victorian clothes, she sails with her illegitimate nine-year-old daughter to "the bush" of New Zealand. She is met by Alisdair Stewart, her new husband, a utilitarian settler who accumulates land that he then hopelessly tries to clear. Having no use for Ada's piano, he abandons it on the beach. Handed from father to husband, silent and unprepared for the muddy darkness of her new surroundings, Ada appears to be the classic victim of Victorian repression and oppression. And yet, stubbornly rejecting this subject position, she cleverly and imaginatively transforms the circumstances themselves, and her obtuse husband as well, "for silence affects everyone in the end" (9). To do so, however, she must enter the "forbidden chamber."

Having glimpsed Ada's strong emotions and her piano playing, George Baines, a neighbor, proposes an exchange to her husband: a parcel of Baines's land, in return for the piano and piano lessons from Ada. Feeling violated to the core, Ada protests violently in a desperate note, "NO, NO, THE PIANO IS MINE! IT'S MINE!" (42). Her angry husband replies by demanding her submission to his authority: "we are a family now, all of us make sacrifices and so will you.... You will teach him. I shall see to that!" (42). Baines's hut, where the lessons take place, is a "forbidden chamber" in more ways than one. It is certainly the symbolic site of women's victimization. When she goes there, Ada is reified or commodified by the two men's trade, and like Bluebeard's dead wives, she is soon being "dismembered" by Baines's sexual preying on her "parts": the nape, a leg, her arms, her clothes. Not simply the "hell" that Flora calls it (81), though, the hut is also the site of a profoundly transforming initiation process.

Unlike Stewart's house, surrounded by mud and burnt tree stumps, Baines's shack blends into the mossy bush, signaling his close relationship to the land and to the Maoris.[55] In this liminal place, where social rules as the Victorian characters know them are suspended or put to the test, the possibility for a new form of exchange arises. "Do you know how to bargain?" (52), this illiterate white man or *pakeha*, his clothes loose and colorful, his face partially tattooed, asks Ada. His direct question changes her status from trade to trader, to "willing" victim perhaps, but also potentially to clever trickster. Though "free will" is out of the question for Ada, by negotiating with Baines to buy back one black piano key with each visit, and thus exploiting his sexualization of their lessons while holding it in contempt, she is exercising will of a kind. Once having crossed the threshold into the forbidden, already prostituted by her unwitting husband to obtain more land in the name of the normative values of family and sacrifice, Ada risks prostituting her body to regain her piano, which is more vital and necessary to her than her uncomprehending husband and social conventions, or a body which is hardly her own.

Her boldness leads her to unexpected knowledge: discovering that self-expression and communication need not be antithetical, she gradually repossesses her body. In the face of an openly repressive patriarchy, Ada had "very powerfully removed herself from life" (Campion, *Cinema Papers* 7) by abandoning ordinary language and projecting herself onto the piano, where she artfully expresses feelings and desires which go unheard in the society surrounding her.[56] The piano embodies Ada, standing as a displaced version of her own flesh which repressive social norms have already taken from her. In the liminal space of the lessons, the distance between her surrogate, externalized self and her bodily self shrinks. By expressing her emotions through her music, Ada exercises some control over the piano/body exchange with Baines; in this marginal space at least, her music acquires social meaning and power. During the "lessons," Ada concentrates her efforts on a difficult, obsessive, highly charged piece of her own composition that articulates her capacity for improvisation as well as her confusion before newly-experienced sensations, for Baines's purchased touching of her body affects the music. When, for instance, "unnerved" by Baines's erotic stroking of her arms, "she changes the music to something brisk, almost comical. Baines feels suddenly ridiculous, his mood broken. He takes his hand away" (60). And yet, having acknowledged Baines's touch in her music, Ada becomes curious about both him and her own body. When a frustrated and confused Baines denies himself as an active listener of her music, she is the one who moves further into the "forbidden chamber," away from her piano and behind the red curtain that hides his bed. Though dispossessed of both her piano and her body, Ada defiantly continues to claim them as her own, and even acknowledges their affinity by impetuously extending her musical, self-expressive exploration to the realm of carnal discovery and interaction. When Baines suddenly calls the deal off—"The arrangement is making you a whore and me wretched" (76)—Ada has won back her piano; however, she finds herself missing Baines when she plays. With her music transformed from enforced solipsism to engaged experimentation,[57] she returns to Baines on her own terms, reappropriating her body as a site for self-expression and communication, though neither site is free or safe.

However, unlike "Bluebeard" heroines, Ada does not enter the "forbidden chamber" as part of her husband's deliberately criminal plot. By substituting a culturally established script for an aberrant, individual pathology as the force setting the narrative in motion, Campion makes Baines and Stewart not only partake of Ada's initiation but also find themselves transformed as they follow her into an unfamiliar place. Both men's curiosity and their troubled relation to the conventional gender role models of the time affect how *The Piano* develops. Just as their other features clash, the two men react differently to their new knowledge. Intrigued by her powerful attachment to the piano and the emotional release that accompanies her music, Baines wants to touch Ada, and is driven to propose the terms which lead to their meetings in the forbidden room. Baines, however, is not prepared for his own transformation. Because Baines "listens," Ada's piano voice can open the door to revising the conventional "master/ slave" plot which they would seem to be enacting. He first finds himself hearing her music when he is alone; soon, naked, he is polishing the piano with sensuous devotion. He even becomes jealous of the piano as the object of Ada's affection. Instead of purely instrumentalizing Ada's love for the piano to gain access to her body, Baines comes to recognize the intimate, constrained affinity between Ada's body and her music. Active listening transforms him, and arouses his desire for a reciprocal exchange of pleasure. He takes his shirt off when he uncovers her arms; he stands naked before her when he asks her to undress for more keys; if she is "stiff" when he "kisses and touches her with feeling and affection," touched by "her stillness, he too becomes still" (62). A genuine open-minded curiosity and his abandonment of the predatory script that objectifies women's sexuality are, within the film's romantic terms, his salvation. Baines calls off the bargain and returns the piano to her because he has no hope of touching Ada the way her music has touched him.

Likened to Beast by at least one reviewer,[58] Baines's transformation sharply contrasts with Stewart's. Though Stewart does not recognize the piano as the key to Ada, her willful aloofness nevertheless attracts and threatens him. Since he refuses to listen when she does articulate her desires, he can do no more to win her affection than to mimic the "alternately paternalistic and authoritarian husband" model. His first sudden experience of the forbidden has a frightening effect on him. When he witnesses Ada's and Baines's reciprocal passion, his own curiosity leaves him in a child-like, helpless, unexpectedly voyeuristic role. Seeking to recover his authority, he locks her up in his "civilized" home,[59] but Ada tricks him further into the "forbidden chamber" by cleverly appealing to his new-found curiosity. Celebrated as one of the most modern and feminist moments in the movie, since it portrays "a woman exploring her libido without any kind of romantic attachment or sentimental quality" (Campion, *Cinema Papers* 9), the scene in which Ada sexually manipulates Stewart while refusing to be touched by him further exposes his vulnerability and his fear of improvisation and passion. As a result, when he is given the telltale piano key he quickly falls into a well-known script that mimics "Bluebeard." He violently punishes his disobedient wife by chopping off her finger. To no avail. Excited and ashamed, he is about to rape Ada, when her unflinching eyes meet his. Caught at his most exposed, he "hears" Ada's voice. Whether Ada actually sends a telepathic message to Stewart, or whether he realizes he must protect himself from his own desires by mimicking her unspoken words, Stewart does not actually "listen" to Ada, but merely repeats "her" words as they fulfill his wish: "She said, 'I have to go, let me go, let Baines take me away, let him try and save me. I am frightened of my will, of what it might do, it is so strange and strong'" (115). Even if they are Ada's words, what they might mean to her does not matter to Stewart. Having entered his own Hell, he has discovered himself, like Bluebeard, to be a violent coward. "I wish her gone," he announces to Baines, "I wish you gone. I want to wake and find it was a dream, that is what I want. I want to believe I am not this man. I want myself back; the one I knew" (115).

Thus, while one man yearns for salvation, the other desires a retreat into safety through forgetfulness. Almost flaunting the opposition between them, *The Piano* nevertheless presents this duality as different reactions to a common experience of forbidden pleasures on a culturally and historically framed testing-ground. Though they would have more social power than Ada in their social world, be it Scotland or New Zealand, Baines and Stewart are as unprepared as she is for the self-discovery initiated by their liminal experiences. Baines takes the risk of improvising, of acting out new knowledge; afraid of his own actions in uncharted territory, Stewart resorts to the authority of the well known. Whether to the Maoris, to the under-water strangeness of the land, to Ada's music, to the pull of unexpectedly strong emotions, or to their bodies and minds, both men respond to encounters with "the other" by mediating them through a cultural Victorian script.[60] Explicitly displayed as part of that script is a retelling of "Bluebeard" that activates in *The Piano* the particular form of doubling known as mimicry, which here functions as imitation, mockery, and miming.

Organized by the local Reverend, and staged in the school hall, the humorous yet chilling shadow play version of "Bluebeard" lies at the very heart of the movie.[61] Together with the forty-odd members of the audience, including Ada, her husband, Flora, and several Maoris "in their best European dress" (63), we watch "the young maid" come "upon each and all of Bluebeard's missing wives, their severed heads still bleeding, their eyes still crying" (65). The amateurish theatrics—animal blood, piano music, candle light—increase the scene's drama and its absurdity. When, however, the large shadow of Bluebeard that is cast upon sheets appears to attack his young wife with an axe, two of the Maoris in the audience run to her rescue, shouting war cries as they corner the "whimpering" actor, "an umbrella held spear-like above him" (66). Following this interruption, which terrifies much of the audience and makes "the corpses come very much to life" (66), the

Maori warriors are introduced to the theatrical devices and to the women playing Bluebeard's victims.

Certainly a moment of comic relief, this scene also has important functions.[62] Most notably it quotes, to the point of parody, from a cultural script very familiar to the Victorian *pakehas*. Mirroring the whole movie's relationship to "Bluebeard," this staged *mise en abyme* produces multiple effects through mimicry. Though the performance sets out to convey the tale's conventional message, the audience's reactions to the play cloud that message, foregrounding instead the retelling's performative aspect. The young woman enters the forbidden closet, the blood-stained key tells on her, the angry husband raises his axe. His warning—"Women, resist your curiosity! It only leads to danger"—is typical of nineteenth-century European popularized retellings, whether serious or farcical.[63] Though not condoning Bluebeard's murders, for justice requires his death, such versions above all warn women to keep their place and to distrust their own desires. In the New Zealand settlers' performance, the cut-out banister behind Bluebeard's shadow as he comes upon his wife caricatures an erect penis, which, when linked to the dripping blood in the closet, would seem to refer, however humorously and indirectly, to the presumed sexual nature of his wife's betrayal—though to twentieth-century eyes the banister could just as easily seem to be an inflated icon of patriarchal authority.

When the two Maoris run to the heroine's rescue, however, a different, disruptive, and transformative form of mimicry also occurs. This intrusion brings the performance to an abrupt end. The Maori do not recognize the Western fictional conventions at work—"E Nihe, E Nihe he Kohuru, he kohuru?" (subtitled: "Nihe, Nihe, is this murder?"), one asks, and is answered "E te whanau keite pai-he takaro tenei" (66, subtitled: "Everything is fine, this is just a game"). More importantly though, the Maoris' disapproval of the *pakehas'* "fearsome though familiar" script paradoxically brings the plot to its conventional close.[64] The young bride is rescued by "brothers," who do not fear the treacherous and powerful tyrant. That the "wives" return to life because they fear their rescuers, rather than recognizing them as kin, only adds to the irony of this cultural misunderstanding. "That is very, very nice" mumbles the uncomprehending Aunt Morag after introducing the "actresses" to the Maoris, and we can perhaps agree, since through the encounter the message of "Bluebeard" now embraces new possibilities.

The movie's larger re-interpretation of "Bluebeard" echoes this shadow play in several ways. Most obviously, when Ada disobeys her husband—betrays his trust, as he tells her—he takes an axe to her and chops off her left index finger, thus re-presenting the dramatic core of the staged performance. Mockery also pervades these performances. Both Bluebeard and Stewart are cowards, deflated authority figures hiding behind conventional screens. As he watches Baines giving Ada pleasure, Stewart's voyeuristic, wet-dream-like experience of passion is even mimicked by the dog's licking his hand. However, this mimicry extends beyond simple repetition or parody of "Bluebeard." Just as the staged performance unexpectedly turns into the unstated revelation of the affinity between (*pakeha* or white) women and the colonized, by playing up to and against audience expectations, *The Piano* renews and proclaims the social value of carnal knowledge and initiation in "Bluebeard."

To begin with, the language of the body is no longer marginalized, displaced, or contained in the forbidden chamber, but uttered defiantly within the larger world. As Baines and Ada learn to communicate through musical and bodily signs, words and writing also lose their social primacy. Stewart desperately tries to prevent this shift. What drives him to violence, after all, is not Ada's and Baines's carnal encounter, which Stewart even experiences voyeuristically, but Ada's written profession of love. The key, then, is not the button she drops while getting dressed at Baines's hut, but the piano key, indelibly "marked" with the words "Dear George, you have my heart, Ada McGrath" (94). Though signifying differently for each character, this key binds the power of body and language together for all. What horrifies Stewart, who is accustomed to repressing the body, is the key's written articulation of the flesh's unspoken desire. Having intercepted this mute message from Ada to Baines—an illiterate but bold interpreter—, Stewart finds the key a confession of guilt which he replaces with Ada's bloodied finger in his own message to Baines: "if he ever tries to see her again I'll take off another and another and another!" (104). However, just as the dead woman's index finger speaks when the heroine in "Mr. Fox" holds it up to prove the criminal's guilt, Stewart's violence does not silence Ada. As in the staged performance, language and communication are at issue, but by foregrounding the language of the body and its dialogue with the language of words, *The Piano* opens channels of translation between the body's signs and other languages.[65] Like Cixous's *écriture féminine, The Piano* signs the body "back into semiosis, from which it has been exiled by dualist, metaphysical philosophies and theories of representation" (Banting 228). What is unspeakable in the play stubbornly refuses to be repressed in the movie. Speaking a language of its own, it transforms the characters who have the courage to "listen" and be touched, even to the point of translating Ada's relationship into conventional language. She chooses to re-learn how to speak.

The Piano also underscores the social value of carnal knowledge and initiation by celebrating a fruitful, though undeniably dangerous curiosity. Punished for her disobedience, Ada does not internalize guilt. When Stewart locks her up, she instead continues to experiment with the body's language. When he attempts rape, she fights back; when maimed, she resists death's call as a self-inflicted condemnation. In the highly dramatic scene when Ada has her mutilated piano thrown overboard with her destiny literally tied to it, in the silence of the ocean her will chooses otherwise and she fights her way back to the surface. Losing her finger and her piano marks her, but she herself is not lost. Continuing to choose risk-taking over submission, improvisation over passivity, Ada embraces the imperfections of human language and life and simultaneously refuses to accept patriarchal punishment. With her will to live comes a transformation into a new, social being. In the movie's final scenes Ada, dressed in light clothes, her face radiant, is learning to pronounce words, while a better-groomed Baines shows his affection and Flora does cartwheels in the garden. Clearly an alternative family to the Stewart household, by living in Nelson they also provide *pakehas* like Campion with a more positive reconstructed past.

Finally, *The Piano*'s strongly performative aspect displays to Campion's spectators the varying value of even relentlessly social narratives in the face of human desire. Ada's triumph is not absolute. What late twentieth-century viewers know, but Baines, Ada, and the others do not, is that the lovers' improvisation mimics the script of romantic passion, that radical impulse which *The Piano* sets against the predictable, bland uses of passion in today's Hollywood film. The silenced, guilty woman who drowns is a familiar *topos*—the tragic outcome of a woman's romanticized boldness. Exploited dramatically and aesthetically at the movie's end, this image is nevertheless shattered by Ada's choice to live. In a precisely analogous way, *The Piano* plays up to and against a victimizing, commonplace understanding of "Bluebeard." Here the life-affirming trickster, by leaving the victim within her behind, emerges to defeat the monster husband. And yet, Campion's fresh look at the romantic impulse and at "Bluebeard" is fractured by spectators' awareness that for all Ada's courage, historical circumstances inscribe her relationships with men, and her very choices, in ways which make her survival in body and will exceptional. Though we can exult in Ada's rejection of a mythic, easeful death ("What a death! What a chance!" 121), history allows her to "be bold, but not too bold." We are grateful that she can tell her story, but some of us want more for her.

Regardless of qualification, "be bold" is the motto that inspires the three different feminist lenses focused on "Bluebeard" that I have been describing. Since they pursue knowledge as self-criticism of collusion, Margaret Atwood's and Angela Carter's re-visions are more deconstructive. Atwood's ironic and philosophical self-reflection finds the Bluebeard within women and names the fear that leads to the masculine construction of the bloody chamber. Carter's seductive and confessional self-portrait of the "victim" exposes the socio-economic interests supporting heterosexual sado-masochistic relationships. Jane Campion's transformation of "Bluebeard" is more affirmative, for self-discovery leads more straightforwardly to empowerment. Her romantic and eerie *fugue* dismembers and remembers the female body, proclaiming its knowledge and celebrating the courage it takes for women to survive the forbidden chamber. Put to different feminist uses, then, a gruesome fairy tale often deployed against women becomes recuperated as the story of successful, socially meaningful female initiation. "Bluebeard"'s plot-sustaining dynamics of simultaneous doubling and duality are reformed to articulate and further our knowledge of gendered relationships in varying scenes.

EPILOGUE
PEOPLING THE BLOODY CHAMBERS
"ONCE UPON MANY TIMES" AND "ONCE UPON ONE TIME"

THE REVISED MAGIC OF POSTMODERN FAIRY TALES
overtly problematizes mimetic narratives, gender identities, and
humanistic conceptualizations of the subject, calling into question
the naturalized yet normative artifice of the tale of magic. These
antimythic narratives, however, are not all performatively the
same. While exploring how variables such as narrative frames,
voice, focalization, and agency intersect and reflect on one another, my aim has been to make visible—in the fairy tales and in
their postmodern performances—gendered patterns of complicity and resistance, differing socio-economic and historical dynamics of gender representations, the making or unmaking of a
heterosexual project, and the varying impulse to enact fleshed
knowledge in narrative.

And yet my effort to distinguish among these postmodern wonders is not directed at classifying per se. When I first began this
project, the identification and definition of "postmodern" fairy
tales seemed a significant goal in itself; then, I worked towards a typology of contemporary and, more specifically, postmodern revisions of fairy tales. But as I pursued my research in the magic
forest of classic fairy tales, I became less fearful of losing myself
there and more interested in the intricacies and intersections of
its many ways. At that point, I re-conceived of my project as the exploration of a small area of that intertextual forest, with an eye to
the proliferation of its creative paths and branches; to the tricks
played by its mirrors strategically placed in it to reflect, refract,
and frame me and other women; and to the signs that other
women had left in their own journeys through this wonder-ful and
pseudo-natural funhouse.

This is not to say that I gave up entirely on my initial quest to
map postmodern fairy tales. I distinguish "postmodern" retellings
from other contemporary fairy tales on the grounds of narrative

strategies (doubling as both deconstructive and reconstructive mimicry) and subject representations (self-contradictory versions of the self in performance). And I discuss the effects of this postmodern self-reflexivity on the images of "story" and "woman" as projected by classic fairy tales: destructive in Coover's and Carter's re-visions of "Snow White"; re-constructive in Carter's short stories "The Tiger's Bride" and "The Company of Wolves"; subversive in Atwood's "Alien Territory" and Carter's "The Bloody Chamber." But these distinctions are hardly the point.

Throughout this book, for instance, Angela Carter's demythologizing narratives have exemplified the transformative powers of postmodern magic and its interpellation of women. I have focused on selected stories, but her entire 1979 collection can be seen as a sustained re-vision of the fairy tale. *The Bloody Chamber* performs the multiple meanings of its title: Bluebeard's forbidden *room*, a high-class bedroom, a windowless cell, the grandmother's house, a castle's vault; but also the *legislative assembly* which—as village, family, "man"kind, or Lacanian mirror—sets developmental and social norms for Carter's heroines to follow; the *body's cavities*, most metaphorically the womb, then the orbit of the eye, the chambers of the heart, the interstices of the brain; and the *space for holding charge* in an explosive book, for holding narrative fire in the destructive war of the sexes. In and out of these lords' and ladies' chambers, women's blood is spilled; at times, Carter arrests its theft, at others, she re-values its flow. The encounter of beast and beauty, human and other, woman and man is enacted in every room: as the masks peeled off in one scenario are refracted differently in another, suspicion lingers but dynamics shift. In the mirror of such contained intertextuality, the stories I have discussed reflect on each other through the work of repetition against itself. If we read the collection teleologically, almost in linear progression towards some sexual and narrative liberation, the transformation of the mirror in the bloody chamber is positively magic: from inorganic speculum serving the masculine gaze in "The Bloody Chamber," to dream-like but porous matter in which to envision our futures, in "Wolf-Alice." But these images still hinge on the "Snow Child," disembodied at the center of the book. If we read the stories in juxtaposition to one another, talking back at each other, Bluebeard's mirror has transformed but not shattered: the ending of "Wolf-Alice" could be another "seeing is believing" trick. The construction of each reading is shaken by the emerging of another tunnel, another underground chamber, another story, another audience.

Carter's more recent "Ashputtle *or* The Mother's Ghost: Three Versions of One Story" plays in an analogously serious way with images, themes, and the audience's construction of "Cinderella" tales (AT510A). Here, the protagonist's association with ashes projects varying self-reflections of the classic Cinderella: in part one, "The Mutilated Girls," the child is the ashen "imitation" of her mother's will, a grayish puppet of maternal ambition; in part two, "The Burned Child," she is the survivor who does not turn away from mourning, yet thrives on cannibalism; in part three, "Travelling Clothes," she is the disfigured girl who welcomes death, but unexpectedly travels her own way. In all three versions, "mother love...winds about these daughters like a shroud": like ashes in the hearth, mother love holds the promise of self-renewing fire, a small domestic "wonder," which evokes "both awe and fear" in Ashputtle (Carter, *Old World Wonders* 115). The three versions also thematize marriage in different ways. The economic and social significance of marriage frames the psychological conflicts in the first two tales, either by exposing the violence perpetrated on young girls through arranged marriages or by illustrating the gain and pain of women's rivalry. The third story, perhaps recalling both the lower-class association of a wedding with one's first pair of shoes and the AT510B tradition (see Perco's analysis of Northern-Italian "Cinderellas"), turns the coffin-like image of the tiny slipper in "The Mutilated Girls" into the opportunity for adventure and not exclusively economic fortune.

In these three tales which cluster to form another un(w)holy narrative of death and resurrection in the name of the mother's ghost, Carter also thematizes storytelling as a multiple, curious and always staged dialogue. In "The Mutilated Girls" the reader is represented as a narratee, but like the girl submissive to the wishes of a clever but nevertheless bullying narrator and orchestrator: "you"/we are interrupted right away, asked to take note of what "we are not told" in well-known domesticated versions; then "you"/we are not allowed to pursue other plots, but are instead imperatively required to imagine gory details and are left with the feeling that like the girl "you"/we have not been "well" looked after, no matter what the intentions of the "I" (*Old World Wonders* 110, 112, 115, 116). The narrator of "The Burned Child" mimics the external, matter-of-fact style of classic fairy tales and Carter's "The Snow Child." But when order is re-established in the end, the slippage between the narrator's "She [the girl] did all right" and the mother's "'Now everything is all right'" destabilizes narrative objectivity and implicitly constructs a space for readers to evaluate that order: is it "right" or just "alright" for some (118)? "Travelling Clothes" enacts the magic trick of journeying into a dead fiction (death itself, motherhood, women's subjectivity, generosity in small things, and most of all the fairy tale) to know it anew, reread-ing its worn maps and tracing one's own path. This appropriation is not the privilege of writers or scholars alone (Haase, "Response" 244); it's what fairy tale listeners and readers have done and will continue to do since the meanings that fairy tales "generate are themselves magical shape-shifters, dancing to the needs of their audience" (Warner, *From the Beast* xxiv). Whether we are analyzing folklore or "folklorism"—the "performance of functionally and traditionally determined elements outside their local or class com-munity" (Moser in Haring 187)—we must pay attention to its re-ceivers, "the relations of transformation that occur when cultures converge," the production of new interpretive frameworks (Har-ing 194).

And yet Warner laments the naturalization of the fairy tale pro-duced by Disney and Ladybird Books: "This is one of the prima facie problems of corporate reach in the global village" (*From the Beast* 416), she writes, and "there are grounds for profound pes-simism about the narrative possibilities that remain" (417). I agree that Disney-like uniformity reproduces and sells itself internation-ally by turning the fairy tale into a standard values-and-dreams package. Children are especially vulnerable: "they can be moulded, and the stories they hear will become the ones they ex-pect" (410). The warning is an important one, but I'd wish to tem-per it with the reminder that the reproduction of culture, even in a trans-national economy, is not simply mechanical.

My readings throughout have focused on postmodern wonders for adults which feature women characters, reflect on their ho-mosocial and heterosexual tasks in a patriarchal world, and resist and transform their naturalized images. To suggest the vitality of this struggle over the production and reception of magic in a broader context (after all children are the primary intended market for fairy tales today and many classic tales feature children as protagonists), I will now outline the ways in which two recent musicals participate in the domestication of the fairy tale as *children's literature* but to very different effects. *Into the Woods*, a Broadway musical which opened on November 5, 1987 and then successfully toured the United States, was written and directed by James Lapine with music and lyrics by Stephen Sondheim. *Once Upon One Time* was first produced at Kennedy Theatre in Honolulu on September 20, 1991, and then again in the summer of 1996, following staging of the completed trilogy, which included "Once Upon One Oddah Time" and "Happily Eva Afta." Written by Lisa Matsumoto, directed by Tamara Hunt, with music by Paul Palmore, it was Matsumoto's M.A. thesis in Children's Theatre at the University of Hawai'i, and it uses Pidgin English along with some Standard English.

Both shows retell familiar tales which take us into the woods or "da forest." "Cinderella" (AT510), "Little Red Riding Hood" (AT333), "Snow White" (AT709), "Sleeping Beauty" (AT410) are part of both musicals. In addition to this common repertoire, *Into the Woods* features "Jack and the Beanstalk" (AT328), "Rapunzel" (AT310), and a "new" tale, "The Baker and His Wife," which exploits the common folk motif of the childless couple. And Honey Girl is the protagonist of "Shepherd Who Cried Wolf" (AT1333) in *Once Upon One Time*, which also includes a "Hansel and Gretel" (AT327A) story. The main narrative strategy in both musicals consists of intertwining the well-known plots of these tales and updating them through comedy so as to create a fairy-tale world directly related to today's. To this purpose, modern-day narrators cleverly mediate between fairy-tale characters and young audiences, just as music (along with dance in *Once Upon One Time*) appeals to contemporary tastes.

While both performances "domesticate" the fairy tale or bring it "home," their revisions are based on different interpretations of what "home" is. Briefly, *Into the Woods* centers on the value of family in an uncertain world and, in spite of its hysterical fractures, reinforces the dominant Disney-like psychologizing representations of the fairy tale as a predominantly parent/child narrative. And because women seem more volatile, the future of responsible parenting falls primarily on fatherly shoulders. *Once Upon One Time* rejects a parent/child model of socio-cultural interaction and engages in agonistic dialogue with the standardized fairy tale tradition and its psychological uses. It also center-stages the courage and smarts of girls in the face of sexist assumptions, a theme which the second play of the trilogy develops more fully.

But gender issues clearly intersect with "local" ones. In Matsumoto's "Once Upon One Time," the central concern is growing up, as in dealing with obstacles and conflicts within a larger community of peers and within storytelling traditions in Hawai'i. In other words, the issue here is negotiating self-image within one's community and the often imported narratives that script it. "Growing up" is represented as a series of never-ending confrontations (familial, broadly social, and narrative), where conforming and transforming coexist.

Most significantly, the final line "Deas always one happy ending waiting foa you!" addresses not just any child, but one who has had an ambivalent relationship with fairy tales themselves. In other words, the social contract established within the play and with the audience is not based on universalizing moral or psychological considerations. Rather, language and social experience are clearly shown to determine who is "in" and who is "out." For instance, this is what happens when Narrator 1 first introduces Da Prince:

(stage direction) The Prince enters dressed like a fairy tale prince with feathers in his hat and other ridiculous attire.
THE PRINCE: Mother! Mother! I am home! I just have to tell you about those dragons.
. . .

NARRATOR 1: Eh, you in da Peta Pan clodes? Who you tink you, intarupting da story, l'dat?
THE PRINCE: I am The Prince.
NARRATOR 1: Not in dis story, you not! Wus wit da clodes, brah? You look moa like one fairy den one prince to me.
THE PRINCE: And what is wrong with my attire?
NARRATOR 1: I don't know noting about one tiya [tire], but his clodes gotta go. I need one local prince. I wen say Da Prince, not The Prince.

When the character returns on stage, he wears sunglasses and jeans, and speaks Pidgin; another character, the Princess, remains an "extra" because she never undergoes an equivalent transformation. Standard English-speaking princesses and princes, like Disney characters, have set the norms, narrative and social, for fairy tale protagonists in the U.S. today. Have they spoken to and validated "local" experience in Hawai'i? It seems not. Quite consciously, in *Once Upon One Time*, Pidgin-speaking narrators and characters respond by telling and living out their fairy tales in conflictual dialogue with a pervasive tradition which is not however accepted as the model narrative. The Prince must become Da Prince; the Princess is "bad" (good-looking) but too "strange" to be accepted as part of the in-group; "da six menehunes" parody the stupidity and sexism of Disney's dwarves. In this revision the classic fairy tale is a story needing to be changed through the peer pressure of "dis Oddah story."

As I see it, then, *Once Upon One Time* puts the fairy tale to "domestic" uses, by representing "local" norms and humorously setting them in conflictual dialogue with "majority" ones. As such, Matsumoto's play participates in a broadly postmodern approach to entertainment, but also an established tradition of politically charged Hawai'i-based revisions of fairy tales (Bacchilega, "Adapting"). It imaginatively represents the efforts of children in Hawai'i to insert "themselves cunningly into daily struggles" and encourages them to "turn the course of events in their favor" (Zipes, *Spells* xxx) in a variety of social situations. It talks back at Disney's naturalized colonialism, intentionally (though not fully successfully) seeking to re-inhabit the world of the fairy tale.

"Peopling" the bloody chambers of the fairy tale, as I have shown, does not result a priori in a conservative or progressive transformation. My own appropriation of the fairy tale has worked to further the specific knowledge of mechanisms by which postmodern fairy tales multiply narrative and gender possibilities. These resist fool-proof categorization, not because fairy tales are essentially magical, but because their permutations have depended and will continue to depend on human desires, desires which are shaped by varying histories, ideologies, and material conditions. The wonder of fairy tales, indeed, relies on the magic mirror which artfully reflects and frames desire. Overtly re-producing the workings of desire, postmodern wonders perform multiple tricks with that mirror to re-envision its images of *story* and *woman.*

NOTES

CHAPTER ONE

1. For an important scholarly and ideological critique of Bly's books see the chapter "Spreading Myths About Iron John" in Jack Zipes's *Fairy Tale as Myth/Myth as Fairy Tale* along with the reviews he cites.

2. Throughout this book my focus is narrative; therefore, when I refer to "folklore and literature" I am actually considering the limited field of folk and literary *narrative* relations. My effort and purpose are to place the study of these narratives within their cultural context, with particular attention to gender ideology.

3. "Twice Upon One Time," the second chapter of Nancy A. Walker's study *The Disobedient Writer: Women and Narrative Tradition*, perceptively discusses women writers' revisions of fairy tales in the nineteenth and twentieth centuries. While "folklore and literature" is not her framework and my object of study is much narrower than hers, I perceive a strong affinity between our projects.

Walker perceptively analyzes feminist appropriations of biblical, fairy tale, specifically American, and autobiographical narratives; her effort to foreground each disobedient writer as an "astute reader of narratives—both literary and cultural—that tell persistent stories about her" (172) makes for a compelling example of intertextual and culturally relevant work.

4. Other book-length studies have been significant: see Stewart's *Nonsense: Aspects of Intertextuality in Folklore and Literature*, Stahl's *Literary Folkloristics and the Personal Narrative*, and Rosenberg's *Folklore and Literature. Rival Siblings*. Particularly relevant are essays such as Preston's "'Cinderella' as a Dirty Joke"; Roemer's "Graffiti as Story and Act"; and Mark Workman's insightful work from the 1987 "The Serious Consequences of Ethnic Humor in *Portnoy's Complaint*" to the most recent "Folklore and the Literature of Exile."

Works important to such intertextual approaches have been the 1957 *Journal of American Folklore* "Folklore and Literature: A Symposium"; Mary Ellen B. Lewis, "The Study of Folklore and Literature: An Expanded View"; Alan Dundes, "Texture, Text, and Context"; Richard Bauman, *Story, Performance, and Event*; Fredric Jameson, "Magical Narratives: On the Dialectical Use of Genre Criticism"; Italo Calvino, "Cybernetics and

Ghosts"; Joan N. Radner and Susan Lanser, "The Feminist Voice: Strategies of Coding in Folklore and Literature" in *Feminist Messages*; Katherine
Young and Barbara Babcock's special issue of the *Journal of American Folklore* on *Bodylore*.

5. For a concise and informative study of the fairy tale's thematics and a
significant bibliographical essay, see Steven Swann Jones, *The Fairy Tale*.

6. Among Zipes's many books on the fairy tale are also *Fairy Tales and
the Art of Subversion* (1983), *Don't Bet on the Prince* (1986), *The Brothers
Grimm* (1988), and the collection *Spells of Enchantment* (1991). Ruth B.
Bottigheimer's 1986 edited collection of essays, *Fairy Tales and Society*, and
her gender study *Grimms' Bad Girls & Bold Boys* (1987) have also con-
tributed to the social history of the fairy tale. Maria Tatar's books, especially *Off With Their Heads!*, develop a substantive critical analysis of fairy
tales as powerful narratives of punishment and reward.

7. The concept of "desire machine" appeals to me because it foregrounds the work that goes into producing a genre and its social effects: it
assumes Teresa de Lauretis's understanding of genres and genders as
"technologies," discourses (logos) producing (techne) representations of
story and (wo)man; it is also a playful allusion to Angela Carter, *The Infernal Desire Machines of Dr. Hoffman*.

8. Zipes acknowledges the dynamic interaction of mythic and antimythic fairy tales, and that is what interests me too; in addition, I would
argue with Walter Benjamin that the articulation or conflict of different
ideologies within individual tales is inevitable and that, thus, the anti-tale
is implicit in the well-made tale itself ("The Storyteller").

9. Zipes applies Roland Barthes's definition of "myth" to the fairy tale
and emphasizes its naturalizing, dehistoricizing, "freezing" effects. See
Zipes, *Fairy Tale as Myth/Myth as Fairy Tale* and Barthes, *Mythologies*.

10. I am referring to a masculine protagonist here because I am following Lüthi's lead.

11. In *The Fairy Tale as Art Form* Lüthi also quotes from Eliade's "Les savants et les contes de fées."

12. Lüthi cites from Eliade's *Rites and Symbols of Initiation*. I develop this
argument more in detail and in specific relation to the sub-genre of "The
Innocent Persecuted Heroine" fairy tale in *Western Folklore*.

13. Stone provides an excellent typology of feminist criticism of fairy
tales. Recently, folklorists like Satu Apo and Christine Goldberg have also
revised the Finnish School approach to folktale analysis from a more
woman-centered perspective.

14. Several feminist critics have reflected on this metaphor. As Nancy
A. Walker states, "in the work of modern feminist writers...the mirror of
the tale must be both examined and broken" (83).

15. See Elizabeth Grosz's entry on "The Subject" in *Feminism and Psychoanalysis*.

16. The *langue/parole* opposition cannot account for the dynamics of
folklore and literature, but its symbolic appeal is not altogether lost. In
Bogatyrëv's and Jakobson's essays, folklore functions mostly as langue and

literature as parole; for Propp, in strictly Saussurian fashion, the folktale's langue alone is a legitimate object of study, and its contrast with literature is built on evolutionary terms. With Bogatyrëv, the object shifts to the structure of parole, understood as an event of folklore; and with Bakhtin, this structure of parole is seen as part of a socio-cultural system. If we think of folklore in literature, it may function as langue or as parole. The limiting aspect of this however dynamic pair lies in its purely linguistic reference.

17. See Lindhal's "On the Borders of Oral and Written Art"; Stewart's *Nonsense*; and Preston's edited collection *Folklore, Literature, and Cultural Theory*.

18. This is Bal's term (*On Story-Telling* 27).

19. See Workman, "Narratable and Unnarratable Lives" and "Tropes, Hopes, and Dopes."

20. Here I am condensing and revising my earlier discussion of Derrida and Cixous which appeared in *Folklore, Literature, and Cultural Theory*.

21. "[I]f folklore is special, it is so chiefly insofar as it shows us especially clearly how expressive form and social function, individual creativity and collective tradition, personal action and communicative interaction, are interrelated in the kinds of communication we call art" (Bauman, "Conceptions" 16).

22 See my essay "Writing and Voice," for a more developed discussion, and also Bal's objection to Bakhtin as raised in *On Story-Telling* 1–2.

23. In *Structuralist Poetics* Culler distances himself from Derrida by stating that archi-writing "is a purely logical point, which someone concerned with the social can afford to neglect" since engulfing speech with writing erases a Western cultural distinction (133). In *On Deconstruction* (see "Writing and Logocentrism"), his treatment of writing is much more extensive and productive.

24. Françoise Defromont, "Metaphorical Thinking and Poetic Writing in Virginia Woolf and Hélène Cixous," in Wilcox, *The Body and the Text* 117.

25. And she does so avoiding two common pitfalls: relegating women to the oral and gendering genre.

26. I am paraphrasing Nicole Ward Jouve in "Hélène Cixous: From inner theatre to world theatre," in Wilcox, *The Body and the Text* 45; see also Banting's persuasive reading of Cixous. Gillian Bennett and Joan Radner have written extensively on systematic strategies of voice in women's folklore.

27. I am also not implementing "tradition and innovation"—Mieder, *Tradition and Innovation in Folk Literature*—or "tradition and creativity"—Bronner, *Creativity and Tradition in Folklore: New Directions*—because these paradigms, quite unintentionally, suggest a valorization of one or the other term of opposition; I like Nicolaisen's phrase "variation in repetition" for it foregrounds the dynamic and inextricable link of "tradition" and "performance" in folklore rather than their opposition to one another.

28. See Bal, especially 146–70.

29. This double movement of construction and deconstruction has proved to be particularly appropriate to those gender-oriented or more closely feminist approaches which seek to address the dynamics of subjectivity and agency. I have already identified this double movement in the work of Cixous; it has, against a specifically semiotic background, also shaped the work of feminists such as Teresa de Lauretis and Kaja Silverman; and Bal's own critical narratology has produced powerful readings of gender-ideology at work in the Old Testament and visual arts.

30. See Bal's definition of reading as a "practice of struggle" for power over signs (37–38).

31. See Culler, *Framing the Sign*.

32. I will not repeat here the authoritative narratives of postmodernism by Fredric Jameson, Jean-François Lyotard, Jürgen Habermas, and Jean Baudrillard: the debate over what postmodernism is, and how valuable it is to critical philosophy and social theory, has proliferated to a point that it has, for me, lost its poignancy.

For some discussions of folklore and postmodernism, see: John D. Dorst, "Postmodernism vs. Postmodernity"; Mark Workman, "Folklore in the Wilderness: Folklore and Postmodernism"; Bacchilega, "Folk and Literary Narrative in a Postmodern Context: The Case of the *Märchen*"; "Theorizing Folklore: Toward New Perspectives on the Politics of Culture" a special issue of *Western Folklore* edited by Charles Briggs and Amy Shuman; Pertti J. Anttonen, "Folklore, Modernity, and Postmodernity"; Peter Narvaez, "Chuck Berry as Postmodern Composer-Performer" and Dorst, "'Sidebar Excursions to Nowhere': The Vernacular Storytelling of Errol Morris and Spalding Gray" in Preston's collection.

Feminist interrogations of postmodernism, like post-colonial ones and even more pointedly feminist post-colonial ones, have had a sharp political edge. Even limiting our discussion to Western feminist practices, it is clear that postmodern theorists have much to learn from feminism; on the other hand, many feminists have come to acknowledge that postmodernism and political critique can go hand in hand, at least some of the way. In "Contingent Foundations: Feminism and the Question of 'Postmodernism,'" for instance, Judith Butler argues that a postmodern or poststructuralist understanding of the self-contradictory subject position of *even* the critic is "the very precondition of a politically engaged critique"; that "the critique of the subject is not the negation or repudiation of the subject, but, rather, a way of interrogating its construction as a pregiven or foundationalist premise"; that the construction of the subject is not equivalent to the determination of the subject: "on the contrary, the constituted character of the subject is the very precondition of its agency"; and that the deconstruction of "matter or that of bodies is not to negate or refuse either term" (*Feminists Theorize the Political* 6–7, 9, 12, 17). Among other interventions in this debate see *Feminism/Postmodernism*, edited by Nicholson; Benhabib, Butler, and Frazer, "An Exchange on Feminism and Postmodernism"; "Feminism and Postmodernism," *boundary 2*, co-edited by Ferguson and Wicke; and Babcock, specifically in relation to anthropology.

Significant to this debate from the folklorists' perspective especially are Margaret A. Mills, "Critical Theory and the Folklorists" and "Feminist Theory and the Study of Folklore." See also Nenola for an important European perspective on gender and the study of folklore.

33. Linda Hutcheon's own books on postmodernism have proliferated and I think of them as both useful and provocative (especially *A Poetics of Postmodernism: History, Theory, Fiction*); however, I still find her argument in this 1987 *Textual Practice* essay particularly lucid and rhetorically successful.

34. This is one of Butler's definitions of the performative:

Performative acts are forms of authoritative speech;: most performatives, for instance, are statements that, in the uttering, also perform a certain action and exercise a binding power. Implicated in a network of authorization and punishment, performatives tend to include legal sentences, baptisms, inaugurations, declarations of ownerships, statements which not only perform an action but confer a binding power on the action performed. If the power of discourse to produce that which it names is linked with the question of performativity, then the performative is one domain in which power acts *as* discourse. (*Bodies That Matter* 225)

Butler also explicitly addresses the dangers involved in reducing performativity to performance (see 234 especially).

35. Zipes provides a tentative typology of the "contemporary American fairy tale" in the last chapter of *Fairy Tale as Myth/Myth as Fairy Tale*. He also emphasizes the doubleness of these revisions and their varying ideological functions by playing out the various meanings of "duplication" as reproduction, repetition, and doubling.

CHAPTER TWO

1. The majority of tales have been collected in southern Europe (Italy and Spain especially) and in Ireland. Many of those collected in the Americas also come from the French and Spanish traditions.

2. Disney's popular movie version, which fixed this image even further, has attracted several critical studies so I will not dwell on it.

3. As noted in the introduction to "Snow White" (Opie), Basile's version explains that following her apparent death Lisa "continued to grow like any other girl," and the crystal caskets kept "pace as she grew," making this text "more satisfactory" to the Opies than the Grimms' version.

4. See Jones, "The Innocent Persecuted Heroine Genre: An Analysis of Its Structure and Themes." Jones identifies a number of fairy tales in which the female protagonist is subjected to repeated cycles of hostility, each involving rivalry, attack, and rescue.

5. Several studies provide information on oral versions of AT709: Nutt; Bolte and Polívka; Böklen; Edwards' carefully edited for classroom use "The Fairy Tale 'Snow White'"; most comprehensively, Jones's 1990 monograph *The New Comparative Method: Structural and Symbolic Analysis of the Allomotifs of "Snow White"*; and Ruf *Die Schöne aus dem Glassarg*.

6. In *The New Comparative Method*, Jones provides a useful overview of previous studies of AT709.

Psychoanalytical and psychological interpretations outnumber the sociologically-oriented ones, but initiation as psycho-sexual and social transformation can be seen as a common denominator. Here I refer to Bettelheim (194-215); Girardot; Gilbert and Gubar; and Barzilai.

7. For Bettelheim, daughters and mothers inevitably compete for the father's phallus; for Gilbert and Gubar, women within a patriarchal text are bound to. For Girardot and Barzilai, the mother's jealousy symbolically represents not growing up, a danger the protagonist must avoid. Barzilai, however, goes on to argue that the mother's behavior in "Snow White" when she rejects change is pathological, rather than normal. But, framing her feminist argument differently, one could also say that competitive and controlling behavior is the norm within what Nancy Chodorow represents as the reproduction of mothering.

8. As projection, reflection, prescriptive image, fragmented refraction, or anticipation, the mirror represents each critic's understanding of the relationship between the narrative "Snow White" and the world.

9. Some versions of "Snow White" introduce two beautiful women (the mother and the daughter) without detailing the younger one's origin. She is a wonder child simply because of her beauty and her name marks her beauty as pure or natural (e.g., Ermellina in "La scatola di cristallo," the Tuscan tale collected by Pitrè, as translated by Crane, 326–31).

10. In a Norwegian version, the woman finds the image of blood from her own nose-bleed falling on the snow so attractive that she wishes for a red and white child (Jones, *The New Comparative Method* 98); in Italian versions, it is the beauty of blood drops on milk or cheese that resonates in the woman's mind; in a Louisiana French version, "Snow Bella," the girl who pricks her finger while sewing, wishes for "a most beautiful daughter, whose cheeks and lips will be as red as this blood and whose skin will be as white as the snow falling outside" (Edwards 590); in a Catalonian tale, the queen sees a golden tangerine covered with snow and wishes for a child as white as snow and as gold as a tangerine (Jones 39). In other texts, Snow White's mother eats a rose petal (Basile), or a pomegranate seed.

11. In fact, in some cases the queen gives birth to a fruit or plant out of which the girl comes, fully developed though usually mute until the end of her initiation; see "La mela" in Pitrè, *Novelle popolari toscane*. For a fuller discussion of this "woman-as-nature metaphor," see Bacchilega, "The Fruit of the Womb."

I do not mean to suggest that there is something inherently "wrong" in the woman/nature association. My concern is with the way it has been essentialized through the popularization of selected "innocent persecuted

heroine" tales and ahistorically capitalized on to the purposes of gendered socialization of children in the nineteenth and twentieth centuries.

12. See Girardot's essay and Jones's study for a fuller analysis of the
color symbolism involved in the young girl's initiation. She is given white,
red, and black to mark her potential, which will come to fruition through
her relationship with men in the story (the huntsman, the dwarves or robbers, the prince). She will become whole when her heterosexuality stirs
the white (semen), red (menstrual blood), and black (ritual death) together; but white, as her name indicates, will remain her dominant at-
tribute, for purity and innocence are the core of her beauty. I do not
stress this reading in my text because the color symbolism does not per-
tain to the majority of "Snow White" versions.

13. In the case of a Louisiana French tale, "King Peacock," a fine man
with a gold carriage is rejected by a beautiful woman; in anger, he states
that she will soon have a daughter, "much, much prettier than herself"
(Jones 15). Here the mother figure is not cooperating and so both the
child and her beauty are presented as a punishment to her and as a realization of the man's desire.

Such versions, I believe, shake the ground under statements like this
one: "['Snow White'] with its disturbing notion of childhood innocence
preserved unsullied by a coma into sexual maturity—matching the Victorian ideal of a 'child-wife'—might be seen as a repressive male fantasy; it is
interesting to note that this text and the Grimms' were collected from
women, and that it is female jealousy, not male desire, that provides the
story's dynamic" (Philip 110).

14. In Pitrè's "La scatola di cristallo" an eagle plays the double role of
helping Ermellina and provoking the stepmother by giving her information on the girl's whereabouts. In the tale "Giricoccola" from Bologna
(Carolina Coronedi-Berti) the moon is called upon as judge of this
"beauty contest," and in the Gaelic "Gold-Tree and Silver-Tree" it is a
trout in a well (Edwards).

15. By shifting our attention to the mother's fears and wishes within the
dynamics of a mother/daughter relationship, Barzilai's reading of "Snow
White" provides a significant corrective to Gilbert and Gubar's broader
feminist reading which pits two generically oppositional types of women
against each other. However, Barzilai focuses prevalently on the Grimms'
version ignoring many other texts in which the protagonist's rivals are her
sisters. I also find Gilbert and Gubar's framework necessary to understand
the mother's behavior as not simply individual pathology but as the re-
production of a patriarchal definition of mothering.

16. Most versions feature the motif of the magic mirror (D1323.1), but
in several Italian ones the (step)mother simply questions men, and in an
African tale, the mother questions passers-by (Jones 100–104).

17. There are also a few versions that feature old women helping Snow
White's antagonist (for instance, "La locandiera di Parigi," published by
Pitrè in *Novelle popolari toscane*, where the jealous mother promises an old
woman "il pane a vita" [bread for life] if she poisons the beautiful girl). In

"La bella Ostessina" (Nerucci) it is a woman astrologer (Strolaga) who fulfills the role of the magic mirror. In that same story, however, Ostessina's helper is also an old woman or fairy so that the perspective or ideology of these characters seems to matter more than simply their sex.

18. Gilbert and Gubar argue this position cogently in the first chapter of *The Madwoman in the Attic,* when they analyze the Grimms' "Snow White" as a primary example of "the essential but equivocal relationship between the angel-woman and the monster-woman" (36). For them the male voice of the mirror is also a metaphor of textual paternity since it authors and authorizes these archetypical women characters as well as their relationship of rivalry. Within this rather grim textual scenario, the angel-woman (the "good" mother and Snow White) and the monster-woman share the same fate, as their biting into the same apple exemplifies.

19. Women are the ones to tell "Snow White," note Philip, Holbek, and Pitrè in their studies. See Luce Irigaray's work for a general discussion of ventriloquism and its gender implications.

20. I refer readers to Mieke Bal's book *On Story-Telling: Essays in Narratology* for a more developed argument which draws on the important work of Gérard Genette, especially "Frontiers of Narrative" translated in *Figures of Literary Discourse,* but also *Narrative Discourse Revisited.*

21. As a British narrator makes explicit, the mirror "awlus towld the truth," ("Snow White" in Philip 102, as printed from T.W. Thompson's early twentieth-century manuscript).

22. This is what Genette called a plausible or *vraisemblable* narrative, in which actions correspond to a set of received maxims or mental attitudes, on the basis of which the audience tacitly agrees that those actions are "true" or at least possible. See Genette's *Figures II* and Nancy K. Miller's "Emphasis Added."

23. See Pitrè's version as translated in Crane's collection.

24. See Bottigheimer's excellent linguistic analysis of the relationship between direct/indirect speech patterns and gender production in the Grimms' collection (*Grimms' Bad Girls & Bold Boys*).

25. In the already cited Bolte and Polívka (450), we find a summary of this beginning. Jones also cites this summary in his monograph (98), and so does Bettelheim. Otherwise, this is a scarcely known version. Sophie Geoffroy-Menoux refers to it as "the laconic primitive narrative the Grimm brothers themselves had used" in her perceptive study of Carter's collection *The Bloody Chamber.* Of interest in this "Snow White" summary is the use of the German *mädchen* to define the object of the man's desire as both "girl," or maiden, and "child."

In his "Confessions of a Fairy-Tale Lover," Jacques Barchilon activates another important association with "The Snow Child"'s beginning: "Anyone with even a minimal knowledge of the folktale recognizes at once a variation of the beginning of the fairly widespread Tale-type 408, *The Three Oranges,* telling of an amorous or erotic fixation in a man looking for a woman "red, white and black" (220). Barchilon notes that Angela Carter's story reminds him of several versions of "The Three Oranges" (from Basile's to Prokoviev's), but "with some crucial modifications"

(220). He adds that in "The Snow Child" the wife/"child" displacement and the Count's rape represent an "erotic wish" that "belongs artistically in a fairy tale," in addition to displaying Carter's "peculiar brand of humour" (222). I would add that Carter's unflinching and parodic narrative exposes the violence of that "erotic wish" on women.

26. As Angela Carter notes in *The Sadeian Woman* (76–77):

> To be the *object* of desire is to be defined in the passive case.
> To exist in the passive case is to die in the passive case—that is, to be killed.
> This is the moral of the fairy tale about the perfect woman.

27. The relationship between Snow White and her mother, or the Snow Child and the Countess, reproduces that of Justine and Juliette in de Sade's work. The two sisters "mutually reflect and complement one another, like a pair of mirrors" and both "are women whose identities have been defined exclusively by men"(*The Sadeian Woman* 78 and 77). See Margaret Atwood's "Running with the Tigers" in *The Flesh and the Mirror*, 117–35, for a joint discussion of Carter's *The Sadeian Woman* and *The Bloody Chamber*.

28. Coover's story was published in 1973 and then reprinted in *Spells of Enchantment* (704–11). I will be quoting from the 1973 text.

29. ". . . anthropomorphism is not just a trope but an identification on the level of substance. . . . Anthropomorphism freezes the infinite chain of tropological transformations and propositions into one single assertion or essence which as such excludes all others. It is no longer a proposition, but a proper name, as when the metamorphosis in Ovid's stories culminates and halts in the singleness of a proper name, Narcissus or Daphne or whatever" (de Man 242).

30. See Tenèze, "Du conte merveilleux comme genre" for a narratologically perceptive contrast between the wonder tale and the detective story.

31. For Wilde, one of the Barthelme's projects is to disenchant "cultural imperatives (scientific, religious, psychological, governmental, and aesthetic) of the present and the past: of everything from Batman to the American dream," and this disenchantment of the aesthetic makes "of it something no less special but less extraordinary" (57). The etymology of "marvelous" suggests both "wonder" (*mirari*) and "visible" (*mir* as root of "to see"): the water falling on her body is something wonderful but visibly ordinary.

32. We must remember that if Barthelme's concern in the novel is "language with and without the force of the imagination" (Klinkowitz 68), through most of *Snow White the* imagination is really one concept of imagination, the one associated with the well-made fiction of the fairy tale and with Romanticism.

33. The novel *Briar Rose*, forthcoming in book form as I write this, confirms Coover's serious effort to explore the ironies of masculine participation in the production of fairy tale romance.

CHAPTER THREE

1. I do not mean to suggest that this more positive reading pertains to postmodern texts exclusively. For instance, when, in the poem "Rapunzel," Anne Sexton laments Mother Gothel's emotional loss (*Transformations* 42), a woman-centered dynamics emerges which the common oedipal and marriage-centered reading of the story (AT310) otherwise silences; along with it comes a grimmer understanding of the Grimms' text, which is Sexton's main focus, but also a sense of wonder, as the rampion transforms into what Olga Broumas suggestively calls "our lush perennial" (*Beginning with O* 59). See Ellen Cronan Rose's pioneer reading of these texts.

2. While Duncker sees no sign of a woman-centered desire in Carter's tales, Clark accuses her of "narcissism, a self-pleasing concern with textual style as a commodity that is saleable because it constitutes a brand image" (159). In one case, Carter does not indulge herself enough; in the other, she does so too much. I would not say, however, that these two claims contradict each other in that women's narcissism within a masculine economy is not generally woman-centered or oriented. In both these arguments and Avis's, I appreciate the attention paid to narrative and women's desire as "commodities."

3. Duncker does provide a brief history of the transformation of folktale into fairy tale and suggests that Carter's re-imagining may have been bolder "had she studied the ambivalent sexual language that there is in the original tales" (12). However, Duncker's historical overview is scattered (excluding women's extensive fairy tale writing from the eighteenth century on, for instance, or less "woman-hating" tales written by writers such as George MacDonald) and shaped to stress that the inevitable and primary function of fairy tales is to reinforce rigid gendered behavior at the expense of women. In addition to this, having acknowledged a "radical current" in early (what she calls "original") tales, she goes on to damn the whole genre of the fairy tale by restricting her working definition to "children's literature," thus separating the folk and literary traditions. Her seemingly historicizing argument, thus, produces an equivocating, fixed vision of the fairy tale as a "closed system."

For an alternative approach to the fairy tale as framed by questions of genre and gender, I recommend Stephen Benson's 1996 essay on the "fairy tale romance." It develops a constructivist reading of generic "continuities and discontinuities" (104) in formulaic narratives, specifically in relation to women's rereading and rewriting of fairy tales as "romance."

4. I am referring here to Carter's "Afterword" to *Fireworks*, where she discusses the potentiality of the "short narrative," against the background of her own material conditions, living in a small room in Japan where (as we know from her essays in *Nothing Sacred*) the sado-masochism of heterosexuality appeared to her in a clearer, ritual and visual form. In her own argument, Duncker takes up this suggestive conflation of narrative, spa-

tial, and social dynamics only to expound the limitations of the tale as "tiny" fictional "room." What I find missing from her analysis is a more socially grounded and generous understanding of Carter's metaphor, which is clearly also in dialogue with Virginia Woolf's "A Room of One's Own."

5. The collection *Contes de ma Mère l'Oye; histoires ou contes du temps passé; avec des moralités* was published under the name of Pierre Perrault Darmancour, but there is general agreement that Charles Perrault and not his son is responsible for it. It contained seven more fairy tales: "Bluebeard," "Cinderella," "Little Thumbling," "Ricky of the Tuft," "Puss in Boots," and "The Fairies."

6. Carter's translation of the moral is in prose and ends with the more explicit: "Unfortunately, these smooth-tongued, smooth-pelted wolves are the most dangerous beasts of all" (*Sleeping Beauty* 25).

7. For Samber's 1729 text and an informative brief introduction to the history of "Little Red Riding Hood," see Opie, *The Classic Fairy Tales*.

Paul Delarue's research, presented in the *Bulletin Folklorique d'Ile-de-France* (1951) and in *The Borzoi Book of French Folk Tales* (1956), works with thirty-five oral versions of the tale—some deriving from Perrault, some mixed, and others "independent." Most of the studies that follow, extend, modify or attack Delarue's and Marianne Rumpf's hypotheses.

Among these studies, I would recommend Darnton, "Peasants Tell Tales: The Meaning of Mother Goose"; Johnson; Jones, "On Analyzing Fairy Tales: 'Little Red Riding Hood' Revisited"; Mieder, "Survival Forms of 'Little Red Riding Hood'"; Oring; Röhrich; Soriano, "Le petit chaperon rouge"; and Verdier, "Grand-mères."

Two recent and easily accessible studies in English collect extensive information on the tale and the history of its interpretation: *Little Red Riding Hood: A Casebook*, edited by Dundes, and *The Trials & Tribulations of Little Red Riding Hood*, edited by Zipes. Dundes's "casebook" provides a range of critical readings but foregrounds a comparative and psychoanalytic approach as the editor argues for the significance of the Asian cognate "The Wolf and the Kids" (AT123) to the interpretation of the European texts, and presents "Red Riding Hood" as an infantile fantasy of regression and wishful thinking. Zipes's book collects a large number of printed versions of "Red Riding Hood" from Perrault's to the present in Europe and the U.S.; the argument that structures this most important "social history" is that Perrault's revision of oral tales as well as male scholarship have done "narrative and sexual violence" to the tale and its protagonist; Zipes writes: "It is from Perrault's version that we can look backward and forward in history" (7). While disagreeing on the genealogy and function of the tale, both Dundes's and Zipes's volumes offer significant contextual and bibliographical information.

8. Zipes presents in full the text I am quoting from (*Trials and Tribulations*, 21–23); it was originally recorded in Nièvre, around 1885, and published by Paul Delarue in the 1950s. Darnton published a most similar

version but with an unhappy ending in *The Great Cat Massacre*, which he also translated from Delarue's *Le conte populaire français* (373–81).

9. Of thirty-five tales, eleven end with the death of the girl. Even if they were influenced by Perrault's text, they contain other "independent" folkloric episodes such as the striptease or the cannibalism; this hybridity shows that, while perhaps not an originally folk element, the tragic ending was accepted and functioned meaningfully in certain oral contexts.

10. For a more detailed synthesis of historical accounts, see Zipes, *Trials and Tribulations* 19–20 and 23 as well as Otten's *A Lycanthropy Reader*. In England, where the authorities claimed to have eliminated wolves by 1500 and (even though King James I wrote about "Men-Woolfes," 1597) there were almost no werewolf cases, the story of Red Riding Hood was not part of the folktale tradition until after Samber's 1729 translation of Perrault's text. (It seems, however, that the last wolf in Scotland was killed in 1743 [Summers 183] and that in Ireland, the Wolfland, wolves still abounded in the eighteenth century.) While nowadays there seems to be no connection between the presence of wolves (an endangered species) and the popularity of stories about werewolves, the earlier history of "Little Red Riding Hood" would seem to point to a connection between everyday fears and storytelling. See Faye R. Johnson, for a psycho-social interpretation of the tale's function nowadays.

11. In some oral versions, the sexual ambivalence of the protagonist's name is played out. The French "le petit chaperon rouge" is masculine and, Charles Joisten comments in a note to a French version collected in 1957, it will identify a girl or a boy "selon l'enfant à qui l'on dit le conte," depending on the child one is telling the tale to (289). In a tale collected in Touraine in the late nineteenth century, "la petite Jeanette" is also called "Fillon-Fillette, comme qui dirait moitié fille, moitié garçon," half girl and half boy; however, because the feminine is consistently used in reference to Jeanette, the ambivalence seems more a function of age—pre-puberty?—than gender (*Mélusine* 9 [1898/99]: 90–91). There is also a handful of versions in which a boy is the protagonist (see "Boudin-Boudine," in Massignon 73–76) or both a girl and a boy meet the wolf (see the version from Missouri, cited by Delarue and published by J.M. Carrière in 1937, 117–19).

12. I am thinking of stories where a young maiden goes to the woods, meets a stranger, is seduced into a kiss, and when she returns home is told by the horrified villagers that her face has blackened, her beauty is gone, her soul has been taken.

13. It is also possible, however, to say that during Perrault's time the "old neighbor wolf" ("compère le Loup") would have been implicitly associated with the werewolf. In any case, as Marina Warner notes in *From the Beast to the Blonde*, "Perrault's retelling continues an important aspect: the possibility of confusing wolf and granny" (181).

14. Earlier initiatory interpretations of "Red Riding Hood" range from P. Saintyves' reading of the heroine as the May Queen bringing spring

and fertility back after the winter, to Propp's hypothesis of primitive puberty rites for young women to Calvetti's ritualistic reading of the cannibalistic episode. See Dundes's casebook for excerpts and commentary.

15. In many oral versions, when the girl is surprised at the grandmother/wolf's hairiness, the explanation is old age: the post-menopausal woman is, thus, masculinized.

Some of Verdier's ethnographic evidence is less convincing, but still plausible: she reads the "pins" or "needles" choice as part of a sartorial discourse which was (still) socially meaningful in nineteenth-century French peasant society when girls were apprenticed for the winter to a seamstress and learned not only sewing but dancing and other "feminine" skills which would help them to develop into wives and mothers.

16. In ritualistic fashion the girl often eats the old woman's breasts or internal organs and always drinks her blood: for the girl's blood to flow, the grandmother's life and power must flow into the girl's. The presence of the animal—often a cat—reprimanding the girl for eating underlines the involuntary nature of this cannibalistic assimilation: it is in "the nature of things" for the young to replace the old. Equally significantly, in terms of cultural knowledge, the grandmother's flesh is often made into localized specialties (*tortellini* in Romagna; blood-sausage or *boudins* in the French Alps) the preparation of which requires specific skills.

Occasionally, the girl rejects this cannibalistic meal and, none the weaker, tricks the wolf in the end (e.g., "La petite fille et le loup," Millien and Delarue 67–70).

17. When Verdier suggests that Perrault's wolf stands in contrast with the Prince Charming figure of other fairy tales, I am reminded of the Prince in Disney's *Sleeping Beauty* trying to convince the young woman he came upon in the woods that *he* (unlike the wolf) is not a stranger: "We met once upon a dream!"

"All French and German writers of the eighteenth century knew that Little Red Riding Hood had been punished for her 'crime' of speaking to the devil and of laying the grounds for her seduction and rape" (Zipes in Dundes, *Little Red Riding Hood: A Casebook* 123). In Perrault's tale, the girl's exceptional prettiness and her red hood single her out as potentially "witch-like." Jack Zipes has argued most forcefully that, first through Perrault's revisions of the oral tales and then through primarily male scholarship, the "hopeful oral tale about the initiation of a young girl" was transformed into "a tragic one of violence in which the girl is blamed for her own violation" (*Trials and Tribulations* 7).

18. Paul Delarue first pointed out that Perrault's text deleted "puerile," cruel, and improper elements. If we take Verdier's explanation to heart, the "path of pins" and the "path of needles" are not simply "puerile" phrases but metaphors for courting and marrying—all the omitted elements are, thus, related to the flesh and sexuality.

19. Apparently, this new character was introduced by Ludwig Tieck in his verse drama *The Life and Death of Little Red Riding Hood: A Tragedy*

(1800) with which the Grimms were familiar and which is reprinted in Zipes, *Trials and Tribulations*. In Tieck's play, the hunter kills the wolf, but only after he has eaten Red Riding Hood. This ending was still too cruel for the Grimms.

20. Psychoanalytical studies in which the emergence of the girl and the grandmother from the wolf's belly is read as "birth" or rebirth simply confirm this text's unnatural perspective on the body. This masculine Cesarean performed on an unfeeling body is presented as an instrument of deliverance. In contrast with the Grimms' almost metaphysical representation of the body, several French oral versions stress the concrete violence of the wolf's action: he devours, gobbles up or munches on his prey; "il l'avala" (*Mélusine* 3 [1886/87]: 398); "le loup . . . se mit a la croquer" (Sebillot 235); "[il] la dévora, sans en réserver qu'un verre de sang" (Sebillot 189); "le loup la dévora" (*Mélusine* 3 [1886/87]: 272). As Zipes states: "Clearly, what had formerly been a frank oral tale about sexuality and actual dangers in the woods became, by the time the Grimms finished civilizing and refining *Little Red Cap*, a coded message about rationalizing bodies and sex" (*Trials and Tribulations* 34).

21. Zipes elaborates on the widespread influence of both texts in his monograph (*Trials and Tribulations* especially 32, 41–43, 49) and then surveys Western "radical" post-1945 versions.

22. It is not unusual for werewolves to "be" women. Here Carter is possibly playing off of a well-known account from a 1588 village in the highlands of Auvergne. A huntsman is attacked by a large wolf and cuts off one of its paws; later, wishing to give the wolf's paw to a gentleman who had witnessed the fight, the huntsman draws a hand from his pouch. On one of the fingers is a golden ring which the gentleman recognizes as his wife's. He looks for her and finds that her hand has been cut off. She is burned (Henri Boguet in Otten 80). (In Carter's story too there is a wedding ring on one of the fingers, but it is the wart that gives the old woman away because it can be readily re-interpreted as devilish.) As Montague Summers states in *The Werewolf*, this story was well known and repeated with variations in seventeenth-century British plays (228, 240). Summers also retells a similar story from 1604: after a peasant slices off the front leg of a fierce wolf, a woman was found "bleeding profusely with her arm severed. She was brought to justice and burned" (235). In Carter's story also, there is no explicit talk of transformation: rather two separate events are "logically" linked, one providing an explanation for the other. Since "very few accounts of werewolfism in England and Scotland have survived" (189) and so much wolf-lore comes from France, it is plausible that Carter knew of these "cutting off of the hand" stories, either from research or from hearsay.

23. This ideological struggle is anticipated in "The Werewolf" by the mention of "Walpurgisnacht," the night before May 1. Within the story, the belief of the "upland woodsmen" is that at midnight "the Devil holds picnics in the graveyards and invites the witches; then they dig up fresh

corpses, and eat them" (108). Historically, May Eve or "Walpurgisnacht" is an example of a pagan springtime festivity which was christianized— through the association with an eighth-century English nun, St. Walpurga—but never fully so that it is still associated with "witches."

24. While "the ecclesiastical and Scriptural werewolves are to be feared because of the wily stratagems with the Devil" and, before that in ancient mythologies, werewolves represented "generalized moral evil" warning "humans to abstain from indulging bestial appetites," the werewolf "in the medieval narratives evokes pity and sympathy for the werewolf, who, banished by fellow humans, was barbarized by his shape and excluded from human fellowship and love" (Otten 8). In Ovid, Lycaon's story is an example of bestial appetites leading to punishment in the form of physical transformation. In medieval narratives, not only was werewolfism perceived as a curse for which the victim was not responsible, but the curse was often the doing of a treacherous wife (see the Celtic tale of "Arthur and Gorlagon" in Otten). The werewolf is seen then as the victim of domestic crime; one of Carter's preludes complicates this scenario by figuring the perpetrator of domestic violence as the wolfman who cannot listen to reason.

25. Here, Carter seems, tongue-in-cheek, to be playing off of early medical diagnoses which ascribed lycanthropy (*insania lupina*) to an excess of melancholy or, within a theory of humors, black bile.

26. The narrator brings in three stories to support beliefs and statements about the werewolf. When a ferocious man-killing wolf is trapped, his death is a relief for the community but also a pitiful event, as "he" dies the death of a man. In another exemplum, a girl puts a spell on a wedding party because the groom has chosen another; she turns them all into wolves who must serenade her at night; their "misery" evokes sympathy, but who is the villain? In the third and most developed story, a young woman marries and loses her husband to the "call of nature" on her wedding night; he has become a wolf, but she believes he is dead; when he returns after years, unchanged but for his matted hair, he becomes angry because she has remarried; "to teach this whore a lesson" he changes into a wolf and attacks her children before being "chopped up with a hatchet" (112). This story—which is also retold in the movie *The Company of Wolves*—well represents the ambiguous game of domestic violence: the man holds the woman responsible for making him behave like a wolf; in spite of his violence, she only sees her sweetheart when he turns back into a man ("But when the wolf lay bleeding and gasping its last, the pelt peeled off again and he was just as he had been, years ago, when he ran away from his marriage bed, so that she wept and her second husband beat her" 112–13). This story is an interesting take on the "Arthur and Gorlagon"-like tales, in which the hero is condemned to being a wolf because of his wife's treachery.

27. When the narrator overdetermines the symbolism of the young girl in red, Carter is clearly alluding to psychoanalytical readings of "Little

Red Riding Hood," like Fromm's and Bettelheim's: "She is an unbroken
egg; she is a sealed vessel; she has inside her a magic space the entrance to
which is shut tight with a plug of membrane; she is a closed system; she
does not know how to shiver. She has her knife and she is afraid of nothing" (114). See Dundes's casebook for more on psychoanalytical interpretations of "Red Riding Hood."

28. Richard Henry Stoddard dresses his huntsman in green and has
him shoot an arrow to kill the wolf. In this 1864 American poetic version
of "Red Riding Hood," the green huntsman is also announced to the
heroine by a helpful old woman/fairy (in Zipes, *Trials and Tribulations*).
Perhaps here, as in Carter's story, the green outfit is reminiscent of the
"Green Knight." Note how in "The Company of Wolves" the huntsman
and (were)wolf are playfully represented as one, while in "The Werewolf"
there is no humor in the identification of the wolf with granny.

29. When she sheds her shawl "as red as the blood she must spill"
(117), the emphasis shifts from what the girl is expected to do (must do)
to what she chooses to do: "She will lay his fearful head on her lap and she
will pick out the lice from his pelt" (118). I do not mean to suggest that
her choice is absolutely free; it is not, for it is framed by censoring social
relations. But at the same time, I do not agree with critics who read the
ending of this story as an enjoyment or passive acceptance of rape: the girl
"sees that rape is inevitable . . . and decides to strip off, lie back and enjoy
it. She wants it really. They all do" (Duncker 7); "The point again is the acceptance of animal sexuality, but with a choice between rape and death
such acceptance might seem merely logical rather than natural"
(Lewallen 154); "These positive aspects [enjoying sexuality and tenderiz-
ing the wolf], however, are achieved at the cost of accepting patriarchal
limits to women's power: the woman is pursued, surrounded, implicitly
threatened. The wolf is agent, she is responsive object" (Clark 149). These
readings seem to be inexorably tied to the lack of options in Perrault's
version; and within such a framework it is unthinkable that Carter's "wise"
and "strong-minded" heroine would be confidently and "successfully expressing her desire" (Anwell 77–85).

30. The editorializing prelude of "The Company of Wolves" already
provides a shifting and contradictory definition of (were)wolves through
their howl and their eyes. You can tell a werewolf by the eyes, "those phos-
phorescent eyes" that remain "unchanged by metamorphosis" (113); and
yet, these eyes can "catch the light from your lantern to flash it back to
you—red, for danger" or, if they "reflect only moonlight, then they gleam
a cold and unnatural green, a mineral, a piercing colour" (110). Projection seems to have a lot to do with what those eyes signify: sex, sin, violence (red), or an inscrutable "unnatural" nature (green)? Similarly, the
wolves' howl is "the sound of the rending you will suffer, in itself a mur-
dering" (110), but there is also "a vast melancholy in the canticles of the
wolves" (112) and if their howl is "an aria of fear made audible" (110),
whose fear is it and is there something different to listen for?

Grandmother's death, in this story, can be read as the result of her unquestioned beliefs based on the "othering" of nature: she sees what she expects to see (the "beast"'s eyes, his genitals as huge as the Devil's) and she throws her Bible at him. But "the last thing the old lady saw in all this world was a young man, eyes like cinders, naked as stone, approaching her bed" (116). Where is the wolf? Is the young man a perpetrator of violence and cannibalism or is he the one who is threatening to take the old woman's little girl away from her and the church? Both, since granny is reduced to a pile of bones wrapped up in a napkin and, the narrator critically comments on the pious woman's comfortable domesticity, "we keep the wolves out by living well" (115).

Read Carter's radio play "The Company of Wolves" for further insight into the grandmother's ideological function (*Come unto These Yellow Sands*); Guido Almansi provides an exuberant reading of these little-known works in "In the Alchemist's Cave: Radio Plays" (Sage 216–29).

31. Etymologically, "carnivore incarnate" suggests the apparent paradox of personifying or embodying (*in* + *caro* = in the flesh) the voracity for meat and flesh (*caro* + *vorare*).

32. "The Angli, according to Bede, observed December 25 as their New Year's festival; the eve, modranecht or mother night, seems to have been a vigil connected with fertility rites" (Funk & Wagnall 229). Connected also with the Saturnalia, other solstice-related festivities, and the darker rituals of the return of the dead, this is—in different traditions—a time of transformation during which natural and social relations are overturned. Furthermore, the first month of the Saxon calendar was Wolf Month, in honor of the wolf god.

33. The narrative seems to support the belief that, when werewolves die, they become vampires or, at least, to capitalize on the widespread confusion of these two cannibalizing legendary beings. Typical marks of the lycanthrope in the representation of the Duke are the "old scars" on his legs "where thorns scored his pelt" (120); his "fictive pelt" (125); his "paw-prints . . . when he runs howling round the graves at night in his lupine fiestas" (121). Also, like Ferdinand, the werewolf Duke in Webster's *The Duchess of Malfi*, Carter's Duke carries "the leg of a man over his shoulder" (123; for Webster, Act V, 2). Like a vampire, however, he was born with all his teeth (122); he "sees, nowhere, a reflection of himself" (120); he "is white as leprosy" (121), and he sleeps during the day. His association with the moon works whether he is a werewolf or a vampire, and a silver bullet "protects against giants, ghosts, and witches" (motif D1385.4), i.e., creatures under a spell or curse.

34. In the name of a subjectivity that does not rely on visualization and language to the exclusion of the body, this story also resonates as a clever and moving critique of the Lacanian "mirror stage" and its implications for women ("mutilation is her lot" 121).

35. In this eleventh-century Latin poem edited by Egbert of Liège, a five-year-old girl goes to the forest "heedless of her peril"; a wolf snatches

her to its cave as meat for her cubs, but the red tunic of her baptism protects her: the wolf cubs "caress her head" for "God, their creator, soothes untame souls" (559). The tale is cited by Delarue and Bettelheim, but most "English-speaking scholarship on 'Little Red Riding Hood' over the past half century" has ignored it, Jan M. Ziolkowski complains, in part because "literary" texts have been discredited by many modern folklorists (556). Ziolkowski makes a case for the Latin poem as a "Red Riding Hood" story: it is a warning tale; it features a girl with a red hood and a wolf; the girl escapes and the red hood is symbolically important to her salvation. Furthermore, Egbert—as in many other passages of his *Fecunda ratis*—probably draws on the oral tradition for this pedagogic tale, adding a Christian message to it: baptism will protect you from the old sinner.

36. The powerful she-wolf of classic mythology was associated with Diana, the goddess of the moon, hunting, and wildlife.

37. By licking "without disgust, with quick, tender gravity" the Duke's wound which "does not smell like her wound," Wolf Alice returns his image to the Duke and grants herself a voice (she croons). Thus the scene transforms the work of death into "writing *thanks* to death, against death, alongside with death" (Cixous, "Difficult Joys" 19). When Wolf-Alice's performance is recorded by the mirror, their transformation is recognized as possibly reflecting back and changing existing social arrangements.

38. See Cardigos for a suggestive woman-centered reading of blood symbolism in fairy tales.

39. See Collick, "Wolves Through the Window" for an analysis of the movie's symbolism and treatment of the unconscious.

40. Laura Mulvey, "Cinema Magic and the Old Monsters: Angela Carter's Cinema" (Sage 230–42) focuses on how the cinematic apparatus works to represent various kinds of transformation in this movie. Mulvey also notes: "Through its series of transitions, . . . the film reproduces the story of the folk tale itself" (239).

41. Donald P. Haase argues convincingly that the movie deconstructs "proverbial language" by using proverbs against themselves.

42. Like Collick, Maggie Anwell has argued that the movie fails from a feminist perspective. I certainly agree that the frame seeks to contain the transformative energy of both the girl and her dream by turning the "beast" against her, thus punishing her. In a personal communication, Jack Zipes also confirmed that Angela Carter was angry about the last scene, which had not been part of her screenplay. My objective here, nevertheless, is not to provide a full-length interpretation of the movie, but to foreground its intertextuality and the polyvalency of the "girl meets wolf" scenario, even beyond the tellers' (in this case both the girl and Carter) intentions or expectations.

43. Part of Carter's translation of Perrault's moral reads: "Now, there are real wolves, with hairy pelts and enormous teeth; but also wolves who seem perfectly charming, sweet-natured and obliging, who pursue young

girls in the street and pay them the most flattering attentions" (*Sleeping Beauty* 25).

CHAPTER FOUR

1. Jan-Öjvind Swahn's 1955 monograph *The Tale of Cupid and Psyche* documents over one thousand versions of the AT425 tale and Donald Ward updates the number to "nearly 1500." Other studies providing extensive information on folk and literary versions of this tale are W.R.S. Ralston, "Beauty and the Beast"; Betsy Hearne, *Beauty and the Beast*; Iona and Peter Opie, *The Classic Fairy Tales*; two special issues, *Midwestern Folklore* 15, 2 (1989), edited by W.F.H. Nicolaisen, and *Merveilles et contes* 3, 1 (May 1989); Marina Warner, *From the Beast to the Blonde*, especially chapters 17 and 18; and Zipes's numerous discussions, the most recent of which is in *Fairy Tale as Myth*, 23–48. See Goldberg for an important discussion of the relationship of AT425 to other tale types.

2. The English translation of Madame Le Prince de Beaumont's text was published in 1761 as *The Young Misses Magazine Containing Dialogues between a Governess and Several Young Ladies of Quality, Her Scholars*. Hearne's beautiful book *Beauty and the Beast: Visions and Revisions of an Old Tale* offers the facsimile of the English text in its fourth edition (1783) and the Opies publish the same text in their *Classic Fairy Tales* (Hearne 189–203; Opie and Opie 182–95). The didactic and gendered nature of the tale is obvious when we read it in its immediate context: dialogues between the governess, Mrs. Affable, and her young "lady" pupils, ages five to thirteen. Like Zipes, Hearne comments on the influence of earlier literary versions on de Beaumont, especially Madame d'Aulnoy's "Le Mouton" ("The Ram" 1697) and "Serpentin Vert" ("The Green Serpent" 1697), Charles Perrault's "Riquet à la Houppe" ("Ricky of the Tuft" 1697), and Madame Gabrielle de Villeneuve's "Belle et la Bête" in *La jeune Américaine et les contes marins* (1740). These tales are translated in Zipes, *Beauties, Beasts*.

3. "King Crin" appears in Calvino's *Italian Folktales* (57–60). The supernatural husband as "swine" is a traditional motif "in Italy and the Balkan peninsula" (Swahn 229); ten of the one hundred and six Italian tales that Swahn classifies feature a pig or *porco*. "King Crin" presents some unusual features: the pig-prince actually behaves like a swine, grunting and wallowing in mud; quite uniquely, he remains a swine even after the wedding night. For a lively folk version which employs the local phrases used to shoo away or call pigs, see de Nino, "Il Porchetto" (218–21); in this tale the happy ending simply consists of the third bride's survival. In contrast, Pitrè's "Il re porco" develops the quest for the lost husband (*Novelle Popolari Toscane* 129–40).

The most common animal forms that the husband takes in AT425 are the bear (in many Norwegian tales, but also in the Italian "Il principe orso" from Siena and the Irish "The Brown Bear of Norway"), the dog, the snake (as in "The Serpent and the Grape-Grower's Daughter," Delarue, *Borzoi* 177–81), the wolf (see "La femme du loup gris" in Luzel 318–40), the bird. The bull is dominant in Celtic and English versions of AT425B (see "The Black Bull of Norroway" in Briggs 155–58), while the horse is dominant in Breton versions. Other animals, including the lion, the crab, the rat, the cat, and the porcupine appear; Swahn's study seeks to document the distribution of these variations as well as their occurrence.

"Snakes, frogs, cats, donkeys," Marina Warner reminds us, "are traditional witches' familiars as well as the ingredients of their potions, their love potions at that. They are guises of the Devil" and also of other supernatural beings, like the fairies. "In Mme de Villeneuve's 'Beauty and the Beast,' she even devises an aetiology for their connection: a fairy who is less than a thousand years old has the option of submitting 'to a change of shape . . . as a snake or bear' if she wishes to 'dispute the orders of her elders'" (*From the Beast to the Blonde* 291).

4. Hearne compares "Cupid and Psyche" to "Beauty and the Beast" in her book (15–17). Ruth B. Bottigheimer not only discusses the similarities and differences between the two tales, but foregrounds the importance of their publishing history. While "Cupid and Psyche" has folk analogues in the Indian tradition (as noted by Ralston), it became known throughout Europe in vernacular printed versions following the 1469 *Editio princeps;* similarly, Madame de Beaumont's "Beauty and the Beast" circulated in nineteenth-century Europe primarily through national editions. These tales' existence primarily as printed texts in the modern world facilitated their assumption under one "universal," normative and romantic, plot.

In "Literary Beauties and Folk Beasts: Folktale Issues in 'Beauty and the Beast,'" Larry DeVries draws some connections between AT425 and AT400, "The Man on a Quest for His Lost Wife," best known as "The Swan Maiden." Based on the motifs they share (the gossip taboo—also noticed by Swahn [306] and the formula of the "old key" [see Lüthi, *The Fairy Tale* 70–71], DeVries suggests it is helpful to treat these tale types as one, characterized by a Union-Separation-Union pattern and independent of the sex of the hero. His critique of the existing classification accurately points to the marriage of human and non-human as central to both tales, but ignores questions of gender (which are not reducible to the hero's sex): among other things, Beauty's "lack" of a husband is a matter of interpretation, while the soldier's lack of a wife is stated in AT400. Maria Tatar's discussion of gender in AT400 and AT425 brings into sharp focus the contrast between the "physical and emotional stoicism" that the men must display and the passionate and "bold expressiveness" which allows the women to be successful (*Off with Their Heads!* 160).

5. In his monograph, Jan-Öjvind Swahn discusses the "Zeus and Semele" episode in Ovid's *Metamorphoses* as an early variant of AT425 (380–84), and Eglal Henein also suggests that "The Beast's monstrosity is a reminder of Jupiter's fascinating and powerful animal shapes" (54). Henein concludes his extended discussion of the tales' treatment of ugli-

ness in connection with gender: "When attributing monstrosity to a man, the storyteller assigns to the woman the passive role of spectator and teaches her to accept a situation. . . . Women understand that *deformitas* conceals *monstrum*" (54–55).

To understand the wondrous dimension of *monstrum* we must focus on the husband as "not human," either because he is invisible (and thus possibly divine), unusual (alien to that specific culture, for instance, the way a "negro" might be in a Southern European tale [Swahn 231] or the soldier who wears a bearskin and does not wash, comb his hair, or cut his nails for seven years is in the Grimms' "Bearskin"), animal, or object-like (as in the Grimms' "The Iron Stove"). There is a mystery to be solved, a wonder to be appreciated even if the husband is a *bête* which, in French, is both "beast" and "stupid": the animal-husband is either more understanding than an average human or the human-husband is more stupid than an animal.

6. Ralston comments: "Closely connected with 'Cupid and Psyche' and 'Beauty and the Beast' stories, are the numerous tales about serpent-spouses. The oracle, in obedience to which Psyche is exposed on the mountain, attributes a 'viperous' malignity to her destined husband, whom it describes as a kind of fiery dragon. And as a terrible serpent do her sisters depict him, a monster unto those to which the Andromedas of popular tales are frequently exposed, and from which they are always saved by a hero of the Perseus or St. George class" (1008). The Opies also support the hypothesis that in antecedents of "Cupid and Psyche" the girl married a "snake-shape monster" whom Apuleius made into a "philosophical allegory" (181). And Donald Ward, relying on Nelly Naumann's study "Amor und Psyche und der Gott vom Miwa" (*Fabula* 28 [1987]: 1–33), states that in "many of the animal bridegroom stories of the Far East, and especially those recorded in China and Japan, the animal bridegroom is a divinity whose normal form is that of the serpent" (121).

7. Marina Warner further comments on the changing perceptions of Beast in the modern age: "One dominant curve can be discovered in the retellings from the seventeenth century to the present day: at first, the Beast is identified with male sexuality which must be controlled or changed or domesticated through *civilité*, a code chiefly established by women, but later the Beast is perceived as a principle of nature within every human being, male and female, young and old, and the stories affirm beastliness's intrinsic goodness and necessity to holistic survival. The variations in the ways of telling 'Beauty and the Beast' offer us a text where this fundamental change of *mentalité* can be deciphered; the representations of the Beast, circulating in other forms, in films and toys for instance, especially teddy bears, also illuminate one aspect of what the historian Keith Thomas in *Man and the Natural World* has termed one of the most profound changes in human sensibility in modern time: the reevaluation of animals" (*From the Beast to the Blonde* 280).

8. Warner thus comments on "Cupid and Psyche": "The beast stood for

the crucial choice in a growing woman's life: to leave family (as the word implies, the familiar) for the unknown and unfamiliar. The question of exogamy, or marrying out, and its accompanying dangers lies at the heart of the romance" (*From the Beast to the Blonde* 276).

9. Bottigheimer notes that "Psyche stands isolated" among humans, within her family, and then among the immortals to whom she represents a threat ("Cupid and Psyche" 5).

10. In his chapter on "The Animal-Groom Cycle of Fairy Tales," Bruno Bettelheim traces Beauty's emotional itinerary as she transfers her Oedipal attachment from the father to the husband (*The Uses of Enchantment* 277–310); he concludes that the "marriage of Beauty and the Beast is the humanization and socialization of the id by the superego" (309). While this interpretation could explain the seemingly excessive effusions Beauty exchanges with her father when she returns to his house ("He held her fast locked in his arms above a quarter of an hour" Opie 191), Bottigheimer and Zipes offer particularly convincing critiques of this Freudian approach as "unhistorical" (see Bottigheimer's "Beauty and the Beast"; and Zipes's discussion in *Fairy Tales and the Art of Subversion*).

Jacques Barchilon pursues a more plausible and interesting analysis than Bettelheim's in "Beauty and the Beast: From Myth to Fairy Tale." Barchilon's focus is not Beauty's oedipal attachment; rather he points to the parodic tone of Madame de Beaumont's presentation of Beast as both paternal (he "speaks to the transgressor as a father to a child" 8) and infantile (he says "childish things" 9). When we first encounter Beast, in other words, he has the potential for becoming a father figure, "the husband provider of the daughter" but he is also in need of growing up. Barchilon observes that "the Beast may be frightening because it is a symbol announcing sexual conquest, but this conquest must be made acceptable to a cultured and civilized audience" (10); thus, de Beaumont's version where Beast asks Beauty to marry him every night works better than de Villeneuve's text where Beast's proposition is explicitly sexual.

11. As for the mother-in-law in "Cupid and Psyche" and in de Villeneuve's "Beauty and the Beast," she functions as an antagonist: Venus sets impossible tasks for Psyche, and the queen mother in the 1740 text protests her son's marriage to a merchant's daughter. Thanks to Cupid's help, Psyche accomplishes her final task, but Venus truly accepts her as rightful daughter-in-law only when, in consideration of her beauty, Psyche is made immortal by Zeus. Similarly, Beast's mother takes Beauty into the family only when she is revealed to be of noble blood. The behavior of these mothers-in-law shows that powerful older women are not necessarily good fairies in "Beauty and the Beast" stories; it also suggests that Elizabeth Panttaja's argument connecting maternal power and class struggle in "Cinderella" could be extended to other tales.

12. Zipes argues that de Villeneuve's and de Beaumont's "Beauty and the Beast" tales take on the perspective of the aristocracy, while Fine and Ford read them as middle-class tales, concerned with education, wealth,

and success. However, Fine and Ford admit that their disagreement with Zipes depends on the misleading use of terms like "aristocracy" and "middle class" which are "too broad" to describe the class struggle and factions of eighteenth-century France (99, note 25). For instance, Fine and Ford's vision of Beast's palace as "a middle-class dreamhouse . . . filled with books, musical instruments, and magnificent gardens" also pertains to the gentry's fantasies (96). In the spirit of a more nuanced approach, Zipes has more recently stressed the contrast between de Villeneuve's allegiance to the aristocracy and de Beaumont's approval of the alliance of nobility and bourgeoisie (*Fairy Tale as Myth* 39–40).

13. Andrew Lang's much shorter version of Madame de Villeneuve's story appears in the *Blue Fairy Book* and features a weak father whose "personality defect" is presented for the first time as reason for his handing over Beauty to the Beast (Hearne 51).

14. Psyche's or Beauty's arranged marriage stands here for all marriages as institution, but should also be understood as historically specific. Maria Tatar notes that the motives for the heroine's wedding to a beast ("desire to increase wealth," "wish to preserve the honor of the family," and "jealousy") "are consonant with the circumstances of arranged marriages and point to the possibility that this tale type dramatizes the actual twists and turns of such alliances" (*Off with Their Heads!* 141).

15. Tatar observes that many versions of AT425 "highlight the importance of obedience, self-sacrifice, and self-denial, even as they downplay the courage it takes to put these virtues into practice," and that "it is extraordinary to see how easily a tale about heroic defiance can slide into a story about the virtues of obedience to the law of the father" (*Off with Their Heads!* 143, 147). In contrast "Il Principe Granchino," a Venetian AT425 version, highlights the initiative of the girl who selects herself as the one who will free the prince from his crab-shape and bravely swims out into the ocean to do so. Her father knows nothing about this: his only role in the story is to buy the crab when she asks him to and to consent to her marriage with the prince in the end (Calvino 116–20).

16. Tatar highlights the contrast between Beauty's and Psyche's task: the former must show compassion to transform Beast; the latter must resist the temptation "to be moved by pity" (*Off with Their Heads!* 151–52).

17. For Hearne, Psyche's virtue is compliance and Beauty's is active decision-making, while for Bottigheimer Psyche is an active heroine and Beauty is inert. These opposite interpretations of Beauty's personality are symptomatic of the paradox which constitutes her: she "*always chooses* to fulfill her obligations" (my emphasis) because of her "*willingness* to be dominated and to serve" (Zipes, *Fairy Tale as Myth* 30, 37).

18. Steve Swann Jones notes that the Grimms' versions of AT425 are "conformist in that they do not advocate rebellious rejection of or even individualistic alternatives to the traditional marriage contract. As a matter of fact, they even link the marriage to supernatural powers, in that it is the goal of those powers to foster marriage, thereby implicitly sanctioning

it as a cosmically endorsed phenomenon. The worldview of these tales is quite narrow: marriage is the only appropriate option available to the heroine" (*The Fairy Tale* 82). The Grimms present three versions of "The Search for the Lost Husband" tale: "The Singing, Springing Lark" (AT425B), "Bearskin" (AT425C), and "The Iron Stove" (AT425B).

19. Contemporary popular romances exploit "Beauty and the Beast"'s tremendous appeal to the female psyche. As Mary Ellen Hains argues, in these novels Beauty is a "fantasy super-being," who affirms the traditional values of self-sacrifice and family, and those of the career-oriented "new woman" whose marriage is based on respect and trust. This "super-woman" makes one contribution to the world: "the transformed Beast" (81).

20. A particularly compact case in point is the commercial shown in England in 1994–1995 for an Australian beer. A naive-looking maiden kisses a frog, which turns into a hunk; in turn, he kisses her and she transforms into what he desires, a can of beer. Having quenched his thirst, he asks the empty can: "You wouldn't have a sister, would you?" (I thank Craig Howes for bringing this example to my attention.)

See Martha Weigle's *Spiders and Spinsters: Women and Mythology* for a different "frog-husband" story: in a Tlingit tale recorded in Alaska (1904), a woman marries a frog who first appeared to her as a man. She lives with him, and eventually dies when she has to give up the black mud she had eaten during her stay with the frogs (215–16).

21. Pedro Almadovar's movie "Tie Me Up, Tie Me Down" thematizes to an extreme the attractiveness of humanizing a "beast" and, at the same time, dramatizes in its "happy" ending the social legitimation of this project for women.

22. Following Teresa de Lauretis's insight into the status of women as "literary topos" in the myth of Oedipus, Sylvia Bryant notes that Beauty is "both object of barter and plot device" but never the subject of the story (443). Bryant illustrates this point especially well when focusing on Cocteau's "voyeuristic perspective," which reproduces the Oedipal vision and plot.

23. Angela Carter's irony foregrounds this paradox when she comments on de Beaumont's narrative style: "We live inside the story until we, too, like Beauty, are almost sad to find, when we have learned to love the dear, ugly, irreplaceable Beast, that, after all, he is no more than a common or garden enchanted prince" (*Sleeping Beauty*, "About the Stories" 128).

In some folk versions Beauty's disappointment is even more explicit. When Bellinda declares her willingness to marry the monster, he vanishes, and in his place "a handsome knight" thanks her for freeing him. "Bellinda was dumbfounded. 'But I want the monster,' she said" ("Bellinda and the Monster," Calvino 202). In his *Diary of a Film*, Jean Cocteau notes that Beauty "seems to miss the kind Beast a little, and to be a little afraid of this unexpected Avenant" (3).

24. See Jacques Barchilon's discussion of "L'amour magot" (published anonymously in 1738) in *Le conte merveilleux français* (109–110). The translated tale is in Zipes, *Beauties, Beasts.*

25. At the end of Jean Cocteau's movie, Beauty exclaims: "I was the monster, my Beast" (quoted in Hearne 82). In Mlle. Catherine Bernard's version of "Riquet à la Houppe" ("Riquet with the Tuft" in Zipes, *Beauties, Beasts* 95–100), who is the *bête* in the end? The heroine has intelligence at night but is stupid during the day; her husband is a monstrous gnome; and her handsome lover has been transformed to be identical to her husband.

26. I thank Peter Moss for his comment that fear or insecurity might be motivating the question, especially in the framework of colonial othering.

27. J.P. Williams's essay and Zipes's comments in *Fairy Tale as Myth/Myth as Fairy Tale* (45–46) are the most extensive discussions of this 1987–1990 TV series. J.P. Williams does not deal with "Beauty and the Beast" analogues and echoes, but she does work with the feminization of Vincent and the paradoxes of Catherine's role to critique the gender politics of the series along lines similar to mine.

Another popular contemporary version of "Beauty and the Beast," Disney's 1990 film emerges from a similar pseudo-feminist stand and is "packaged" as a commodity—with its accompanying video-tapes, Halloween costumes, posters, clips and cups—which reinforces an unhistorical romantic myth for all young consumers across the globe (Zipes, *Fairy Tale as Myth* 46). See also Marina Warner's comments (313); Rieder's essay on the Disney and Cocteau films; and Kathleen Manley's unpublished paper "Disney's 'Beauty and the Beast.'" Cynthia Erb's recent spatial and filmic study discusses the different "AIDS allegories enacted in the 'B and B'/TV" series and Disney production (70).

28. Flash-backs in this episode also show how Vincent resolved his first struggle by choosing "Father" Jacob over the evil father figure, Paracelsus.

29. J.P. Williams utilizes Nancy Chodorow's woman-centered psychology to understand the appeal of the "Beauty and the Beast" series for women. Williams focuses on the tortured ambivalence of Vincent's body and psyche as he struggles between "maternal" and bestial impulses, and on the emotional significance of the bond between Catherine and Vincent for women viewers. She concludes, however, that within the social order Vincent and Father value—a benevolent form of patriarchy—the only role available to a woman is that of daughter. "Catherine's inability to express herself as a completely mature, autonomous woman represents the limits of the program's vision of male/female relationships" (67). After Catherine died (and Linda Hamilton left the show) and Diana replaced her as a silent "extra," women fans felt betrayed, ratings dropped dramatically, and several women fan writers have published alternative rewritings of the ending for other fans. See Henry Jenkins.

30. Zipes has pointed out the conservative political intent of this plot which entails "a reconciliation of class struggle" ("Changing Function"

27). More recently, drawing on Jessica Benjamin's *The Bonds of Love: Psychoanalysis, Feminism, and the Problem of Domination* to understand the dynamics of women's collusion in a framework of male authority and domination, Zipes writes that "despite the 'feminist' touch-up of Beauty in this TV series, the basic plot of submission/domination is merely reformed to make the contemporary beautiful working woman less aware of her bonds" (*Fairy Tale as Myth* 45–46).

31. Tanith Lee's collection *Red as Blood* historicizes the representation of women in fairy tales: by ordering her tales chronologically from the "Last Century B.C." to "The Future," she portrays fairy tale heroines like Cinderella or Little Red Riding Hood to parallel the way women were treated in a certain period. "Beauty" is the last tale in the collection and its futuristic setting assumes a utopian dimension when read in contrast to the earlier tales.

32. I agree with Zipes that "Carter's work should not be viewed as an isolated or exceptional achievement" (*Fairy Tales as Myth* 42) since many poems and fictions have questioned the magic of Beast's transformation. Actually I would add that the explosion of twentieth-century versions is reminiscent of the variety of performances that eighteenth-century French tales offered of "Beauty and the Beast"'s wonder tale: didactic, licentious, witty, and parodic. Carter's interest in "Beauty and the Beast" was sustained over the years and her review of Hearne's book confirms her knowledge of the tale's many intertexts, especially in the literary tradition.

33. I am referring to "focalization" here as understood within Mieke Bal's narratological analysis. An aspect of the "story" level (how are the events presented?), focalization deals with seeing. Who sees whom and what? Who never sees? Is the focalized (what is seen) perceptible or not? Bal links focalization with ideology and outlook but resists the psychologizing of "point of view."

34. The panting spaniel is a tongue-in-cheek reminder of the British "Small-Tooth Dog" (Briggs and Tongue, 3–5). Overall, Carter's "The Courtship of Mr. Lyon" is a parodic performance which thrives on the playfully ironic tradition of so many "Beauty and the Beast" literary texts: see Zipes, *Beauties and Beasts* and Hearne for illustrations of earlier humorous versions.

35. Swahn cites "A man loses his daughter by playing cards" as one of the possibilities for the AT425 introductory motif (25).

36. Stephen Canham suggests that the Native American "Raven" mask provides an analogy for the representation of Beast: "a human face exists at the center of his reality" (15).

37. Larry DeVries articulates the narrative logic in "Beauty and the Beast" whereby Beauty's humility demands her sisters' humiliation; he also contrasts her humility to the humiliation—the forced abasement—of the princess in "King Thrushbeard" (AT900) (Hearne 160).

38. "'The Tiger's Bride,' like the original 'Beauty and the Beast,' is a

narrative which is inherently voyeuristic; the terms of looking, however, are significantly altered, for the girl is subject of the [her] gaze as well as object of the [his, the tiger's] gaze," comments Bryant (448).

39. Beauty's tear turns into a diamond in Cocteau's movie.

40. This final scene echoes Andrew Lang's comment "that human beings may assume and lay aside the characteristics and the powers of beasts and birds as they assume and lay aside the skins of those creatures" (from his Introduction to "Cupid and Psyche," quoted by Swahn 233).

41. Marina Warner rightly notes that "Angela Carter returned to the theme of Beauty and the Beast again and again, turning it inside out and upside down; in a spirit of mischief she was seizing the chance to mawl governessy moralizers" (*From the Beast to the Blonde* 308). Carter admired "East of the Sun and West of the Moon" as "one of the most lyrically beautiful and mysterious of all Northern European fairy tales" (*Virago Book of Fairy Tales* 238; also quoted by Warner 310) and her writing in "The Tiger's Bride," for instance, invokes that wonder, but her heroines boldly "choose to play with the Beast" (Warner 308). What Carter calls her "demythologizing" vision is at the heart of her "resistant, cross-grain re-writing" (Bryant 441): "To tell a different story, to imagine and construct otherness as positive not negative difference, and to offer positive positionalities for identification within that otherness, to disrupt the ideological status quo enough to disturb the heretofore complacent acceptance it has met among readers and viewers; such is precisely the work of Carter's fairy tales narratives" (Bryant 452). Without underestimating its iconoclastic force, it is the *double* movement of this "work" that I seek to emphasize.

CHAPTER FIVE

1. While Zipes uses the spelling "Blue Beard" in his translation, I will use the more common "Bluebeard" in my text.

2. The French tale was published in English by Robert Samber in 1729 in *Histories, or Tales of Past Times*. For that translation and a concise introduction to the history of "Bluebeard" see Iona and Peter Opie 133–41. The Perrault version received wide distribution in Europe through its publication in translated volumes of Perrault's fairy tales as well as individual chapbooks and collections like Friedrich Justin Bertuch's *Blauen Bibliothek aller Nationen*. Perrault's text also clearly influenced Ludwig Tieck's play *Ritter Blaubart* (1797) and Ludwig Bechstein's 1845 *Das Märchen vom Ritter Blaubart* (70). We have no text which predates Perrault's fairy tale, but given its many folk analogues collected since the nineteenth century and its relation to folk ballads, certainly in France and in Germany, it does not seem likely for Perrault's tale to be an original; however, scholarly opinions vary on this point. For further information see Scherf 21–25; related discussions, 124–27 and 303–5; and Uther

35–54. Catherine Velay-Vallantin's analysis of French folk analogues in *L'Histoire des contes* (43–93) is particularly useful.

3. The first translation by A. E. Johnson (43) is less accurate than the one I present later (Zipes in *Beauties, Beasts* 35); see the French: "La curiosité, malgré ses attraits, / Couste souvent bien des regrets;" and "Il n'est plus d'époux si terrible, / Ny qui demande l'impossible, / . . . / Et, de quelque couleur que sa Barbe puisse estre, / On a peine à juger qui des deux est le maistre." Here is Angela Carter's tongue-in-cheek prose translation (*Sleeping Beauty* 40):

MORAL

Curiosity is a charming passion but may only be satisfied at the price of a thousand regrets; one sees around one a thousand examples of this sad truth every day. Curiosity is the most fleeting of pleasures; the moment it is satisfied, it ceases to exist and it always proves very, very expensive.

ANOTHER MORAL

It is easy to see that the events described in this story took place many years ago. No modern husband would dare to be half so terrible, nor to demand of his wife such an impossible thing as to stifle her curiosity. Be he never so quarrelsome or jealous, he'll toe the line as soon as she tells him to. And whatever colour his beard may be, it's easy to see which of the two is the master.

4. Maria Tatar, *The Hard Facts*, see chapter 7. Tatar also notes that illustrators such as Gustave Doré and Walter Crane depicted scenes that magnify the temptation-curiosity-disobedience sequence and, in the case of Crane, explicitly made the analogy with Eve.

5. Tatar criticizes both Alan Dundes and Bruno Bettelheim for turning "a tale depicting the most brutal serial murders into a story about idle female curiosity and duplicity" (*The Hard Facts* 161).

6. Hartland identifies seven types of tales which include the "Forbidden Chamber" motif. Four of these feature women, while the others have male protagonists; when the focus is on male curiosity ("Marya Morevna"; "The Teacher and His Scholar"; "The Third Royal Mendicant"), the outcome is usually positive, and if a maiden is in the forbidden chamber she becomes his helper and even his teacher. While the case of "The Faithless Sister" clearly involves malice as well as curiosity, the other female-centered tales do not straightforwardly present curiosity in a negative light. I am not focusing on all these tales, but only on the types that Hartland identifies as "Bluebeard" and "The Dead Hand" (with its "sub-genus" "The Robber Chief") because they clearly involve masculine/feminine conflict and are closely related.

7. In *Les Contes de Perrault* (161–70), Marc Soriano discusses folkloric intertexts of Perrault's tale "La Barbe-Bleue" to point out that Perrault excludes details consistently present in other versions. The ritual sugges-

tiveness of such details—the heroine's dressing like a bride for her death; the animal helpers; and the presence of threes—seems no longer relevant or even understandable within the framework of Perrault's christianized and rational logic. Because Soriano's work builds on French and French-Canadian versions of "Bluebeard" published by Delarue in 1952 and 1953, and because the oral tradition has itself been so much affected by the homogenizing influence of Perrault's literary text (which might at the time of its publication simply have been one of many circulating versions) it is important to credit Soriano's project not as a misguided effort towards the historical reconstruction of pre-seventeenth-century folkloric versions, but as a thematic comparison which recognizes the confluence of two universes, two systems of signification in Perrault's text.

Soriano suggests that the plot of initiation which sustains itself on the "Forbidden Chamber" taboo and other ritualized exchanges is re-inscribed within and obscured by Perrault's moralizing plot of transgression. For other discussions of "Bluebeard" in the context of initiation and ritual, see Saintyves 301–331; and Velay-Vallantin. Soriano clearly states: "Mais le concept de 'curiosité' affaiblit le thème singulièrement plus ample de la chambre interdite" (165). Paul Delarue comes to related but distinctly different conclusions from the versions he collected.

8. Paul Delarue actually argues that the Aarne-Thompson distinction between AT312 and AT311 is incorrect. In "Les contes merveilleux de Perrault et la tradition populaire (suite). II. Barbe-Bleue," along with several French and French-Canadian analogues, he presents the following structure of episodes which would accommodate both types: The murderer and his victims; The interdiction and its violation; Rescue by the third girl; Rescue by the heroine's brothers or relatives; Murderer's punishment.

9. Another tale, "The Castle of Murder," appeared as *KHM* 73 in the 1812 edition and was omitted from the 1819 edition "due to its Dutch origins and similarity to 'Bluebeard'" (Zipes 726). The tale is interesting because it conflates episodes from AT312 and AT955. A shoemaker's daughter marries "a well-dressed nobleman" with "a splendid carriage and servants" who seems quite rich. His castle is very beautiful, and when she is given all the keys the bride explores the castle in her husband's absence. There is no interdiction. In the cellar she finds an old woman "sitting and scraping intestines," who warns "the maiden": "Tomorrow I'll be scraping yours too!" At this point we also find out that the girl's two sisters have been killed there. Terrified, the girl drops the key in the basin of blood and the blood will not come off when the key is washed. Since no one but the master and the old woman are allowed in the cellar alive, the maiden's destiny seems sealed, but the old woman decides to help her by suggesting that she hide in the hay wagon that is about to leave the castle. The girl leaves and the old woman tells the man upon his return that she has already killed the girl and is scraping her intestines; he is satisfied. The girl goes to a nearby castle and tells her story. The lord of this castle

invites "all the gentry of the surrounding region to a great feast" and the girl, having "changed her features and clothes so she would not be recognized," tells her story. When the lord of the castle of Murder tries to force his way out, the authorities are ready to take him to prison. The maiden marries "the lord's son in the house where she had been so well received" (Zipes, *Brothers Grimm* 670–71).

10. As we have seen, in the Perrault version, the girl is attracted to her bridegroom's riches but terrified of his beard. But in "The White Dove," the 1950 version published by Delarue, the girl "systematically refused all marriage proposals, having sworn that she would marry no one save a prince who had a blue beard" (*Borzoi Book* 36); in a Breton version, "Le prince turc Frimelgus," she is a bourgeois girl who refuses to marry anyone but a prince, and a Turkish one at that (Luzel 25–39); and in the British "Mr. Fox," "No one knew who Mr. Fox was; but he was certainly brave, and surely rich, and of all lovers, Lady Mary cared for him alone" (Briggs, *DBF* Part A, vol II, 446; Carter, *Virago* 8); Elsie in the Ozark "Mister Fox," feels similarly: "Elsie had a good time, and she believed everything he said. She thought Mister Fox hung the moon" (Randolph 95). In several versions, her relatives (father or brothers) agree to the girl's marriage for economic reasons: she has no say (e.g., "Il marito aguzzino," a Sicilian tale summarized in Lo Nigro 30); in the Italian "Silver Nose," she marries against her mother's will, seeking to escape her family's poverty (Calvino 26). In "Fichter's Bird," the sorcerer abducts the girls one after the other; in a 1923 version of AT955 collected in North Carolina, "they use to be an old man, he lived way over in the forest by himself, and all he lived on was he caught women and boiled 'em in front of the fire and eat 'em" ("Old Foster," Dorson 193). In a Kentucky version, the girls follow a blue ball to the giant's den (Roberts 27); in an Italian AT955 version, "La colonna d'oro," a princess believes she is marrying a prince, but finds herself with a robber and assassin (Comparetti 76).

11. In "The White Dove," he is a giant with a blue beard "who was reputed to be a great hunter" (Delarue 36). In "Le prince turc Frimelgus" he is the son of the Emperor of Turkey, in an Orientalist move that many illustrations of Bluebeard confirm, perhaps relying on the common knowledge of Muslim marriage traditions, where a man can have several wives. In the second part of this story, after Frimelgus's death, Marguerite marries a dead man who takes her to paradise, and again her brother must intervene to solve the mystery (the tale ends abruptly with no resolution). In the British versions of "Mr. Fox," Bluebeard's foreignness is called attention to in a variety of ways. He may be "a red-headed hosebird" ("Mr. Fox's Courtship," Briggs and Tongue 93). In "The Oxford Student" "the greatest fight between Town and Gown" follows the murder of the brewer's daughter at the hands of her false lover, the student (AT955C in Briggs, *DBF* Part B vol. 2, 103). Even when he is one of "the young men of the neighborhood" or a regular customer at her parents' hotel, the girl does not know the way to his house ("The Cellar of Blood" and "Doctor Forster," Briggs, *DBF* Part A vol. 2, 390 and Part A vol. 2,

214–15). In a Native American AT311 version, the girl marries a ghost (Cole 699–704). In Italian versions, the Bluebeard figure most commonly is not human: a dragon in "The Three Chicory Gatherers" (Calvino 500–503); the Devil in several versions ("How the Devil Married Three Sisters," Crane 24–26; "The Devil" in Visentini 181–84; "Silver Nose," Calvino 26–30), an ogre ("L'orco," Imbriani 7–10). If he is human, he is a robber pretending to be a well-to-do gentleman ("I cinque ladri," Nerucci 386–95). As we have seen in the Grimms' "The Robber Bridegroom," Bluebeard can be a cannibal and in several cases he demands that the heroine partake of human flesh. This cannibalistic motif could add to Jean-Louis G. Picherit's hypothesis that Bluebeard was originally a werewolf, a thematically interesting idea though not supported by textual evidence (375). While I have not come across any versions in which he is a vampire, blood is clearly a central theme and Catherine Velay-Vallantin in *L'Histoire des contes* suggests that there is a parallel between the song "Maumariée," in which the husband feeds on his victims' blood, and "Bluebeard" (63).

12. In other words, the heroine must confront death and survive. While in AT312 versions she finds dead bodies and a pool of blood, in AT955 versions she also witnesses a murder and is directly implicated by the finger that falls onto her lap. The victims are not necessarily all women, as we can see even from the Grimms' "Fichter's Bird," where the room is "filled with dead people" (Zipes, *Brothers Grimm* 168). In other versions, especially of AT311, the forbidden chamber is Hell and its hot air makes the flower which the girls must wear in their hair or on their bosom wither ("Silver Nose," Calvino; "How the Devil Married Three Sisters," Crane); the clever girl puts the flower aside before entering the room. In other versions yet, the encounter with death occurs through the injunction of cannibalism: in "La manetta di morto" the three sisters are successively asked to eat the "little hand of the dead"; the first two chop it to pieces and bury it, but the hand answers the husband's call and reappears intact; the third girl Caterina boils it until it disintegrates and thus "passes the test" (Nerucci XLIX 406–14). In a similar tale, the clever Mariuzza grinds the human foot, puts the powder in a stocking, and hides it under her clothes on her stomach; when the dragon calls out to the foot, it replies that it is "[o]n Mariuzza's stomach" ("The Three Chicory Gatherers," Calvino 500–503). In AT955 versions, the girl keeps her wits when confronted either with another girl's murder or her own grave being dug; then she speaks up at the right time and proves him to be a criminal (most clearly in "Mr. Fox" but also in "The Girl Who Got Up the Tree" Briggs, *DBF*, Part A vol. 2, 405–6).

13. In most AT311 versions, the heroine rescues others from death or near death. In most cases it is her sisters (see "Fichter's Bird," but also "How the Devil Married Three Sisters"; "Silver Nose"; "Le gros Cheval blanc" Delarue 349–50; "The Beggar with the Baskets," Campbell 200–201); in others it is a prince or a young man who escapes with her (in the Italian "Perdeneroso" from Abruzzi, she revives the handsome man

she finds in the attic with the magic ointment that her husband gave her, de Nino 329–36; in several cases, when the heroine marries the man she saved, the Bluebeard figure seeks revenge and the tale is not over until he is killed: see "I cinque ladri," Nerucci XLVII 386–95). In AT955 versions, she does not rescue the butchered women, but she avenges them and avoids marriage with the Bluebeard figure altogether. The British AT311 "Captain Murderer," as retold by Charles Dickens, is an interesting case because there is no prohibition, simply a Captain Murderer whose "mission was matrimony, and the gratification of a cannibal appetite with tender brides." The last bride is suspicious and manages to end his career but not to save herself. She takes an awful poison just before he puts her in a pie; having "picked her last bone," Captain Murderer swells up and finally blows up "with a loud explosion" (Briggs, *DBF*, Part A vol. 1, 175–77).

14. In Perrault's "Blue Beard," she shares his money with her sister and brothers; in the Ozark "How Toodie Fixed Old Grunt," she shares her farm and money with her folks and her future husband Jack (Randolph 63–65). As Mieke Bal notes in "Real Rape: The Importance of Telling Stories," in "The Robber Bridegroom" the heroine identifies with the murdered girl and her solidarity is evident when she accuses the criminal "in the name of the murdered woman," by pointing *her* finger (*Reading Rembrandt* 88–89). In several tales that feature the Forbidden Chamber, kindness or generosity is part of the test which the heroine or hero must undergo so that we are reminded of "The Kind and the Unkind Girls" (AT480): see, e.g., the British AT311 "Perifool" (Briggs, *DBF*, Part A vol. 1, 446–47) and the related Kentucky tale "The Bloody House," which features two brothers, Stingy and Clever (Roberts 28–30).

15. As Soriano and others have remarked, Perrault's tale has little of the initiatory power of folk "Bluebeard" versions. Hartland notes: "In Perrault's version the lady's cleverness has disappeared, leaving as its only relic the constant excuses and delays wherewith she puts off her husband's vengeance until her brothers are able to rescue her" (204). Perrault's passive lady certainly does not exemplify the typical "Bluebeard" heroine. In several AT311 tales, she rescues her prince as well as herself (see previous note) and in AT955 versions she succeeds in unmasking the Bluebeard figure without marrying him.

16. The girl's distinctive treatment of the egg, ball or flower in AT311 versions is significant. Her sisters submit to the Bluebeard figure's orders as much as they possibly can by carrying the test gift with them even when they are going into the forbidden room. Thus these women symbolically submit their life-giving potential to his death-project. The girl who leaves her egg outside the bloody chamber recognizes the primacy of self-preservation.

17. In the Breton "La fille qui naquit avec une couleuvre autour du cou," the girl sends her little dog with a letter to her parents both of whom, with all their people or servants, come to her rescue; the serpent actually bites the husband to death just as he is about to strike Lévéne,

and the serpent is then identified as her sister (Luzel 341–48). In a French tale, the girl's father gives her three doves as a means of communicating with the family; when she sends the black one to him, he comes to her rescue ("The White Dove," Delarue 36–41).

18. In the Breton legend "Comorre," another Bluebeard story, the evil giant's four dead wives step out of their graves in the chapel where Triphyna prays and warn her: Comorre will try to kill her. They give the girl gifts that will help her escape (Soupault 165–74). In the Italian "Il diavolo" from Sardinia, the girl opens the door to Hell and the souls of condemned women therein tell her how to get rid of her husband, the Devil: she must go to her mother's, get a rooster from her, and—halfway back to her husband's home—she must squeeze its wings together. The husband will disappear (Mango 67–70 and 131–34). Hartland also cites a Portuguese story in which her sisters reward the girl for having saved them with directions "for wiping the key clean" (197). In a Gaelic tale also mentioned by Hartland and published by Campbell in *Tales of the West Highlands,* an enchanted cat—who is really a woman—cleans the protagonist's blood-stained foot in exchange for some milk and is, in one version, disenchanted after drinking the milk (story No. 41, 265 and 274 as cited in Hartland 197–98). And let's not forget the old woman in the cellar who helps the protagonist of the Grimms' "The Robber Bridegroom" and "The Castle of Murder," though her case is undoubtedly more complex in that she has been doing 'the dirty work' for the cannibalistic robber or gentleman.

19. When we view the heroine in a larger social context and within an initiatory framework, James McGlathery's reading of "Blue Beard" stories as "the indirect or symbolic portrayal of maidenly ambivalence about marrying" (67), and of the Grimms' "Bluebeard" (AT312) in particular as a "brother and sister type" story (69) seems quite narrow. What makes the husband's crimes simply a projection of "maidenly resistance to the thought of marrying" rather than "a portrayal...of bachelor misogyny" (71)? And why is her attachment to her brothers a "passionate dependence," something that disables the girl from healthily marrying, when this same brother-sister devotion saves her from death?

20. See Dorson 193–95 for the lynching. In a British "Doctor Forster" the guilty man is almost shot on the spot, but "the detectives" take him away "to be hanged" (Briggs, *DBF*, Part A vol. 1, 214–16). In "Mr. Fox": "At once her brothers and friends drew their swords and cut Mr. Fox into a thousand pieces" (Briggs). In "The Oxford Student," where the girl dies, the town avenges her "and Brewer's Lane ran with blood" (Briggs).

21. Hartland cites an Estonian tale, "The Wife-Murderer," in which a gooseherd warns the heroine against her bridegroom and eventually marries her (198). In the Ozark "How Toodie Fixed Old Grunt," Toodie marries Grunt against her will; her boyfriend Jack finds the remains of her two sisters in Grunt's house and warns her. She throws pepper in Old Grunt's eyes when he tries to kill her, and she and Jack cut the old man's head off: "It served him right, too." Toodie and Jack eventually get mar-

ried and share their wealth with her family (Randolph 63–65).

22. The Ozark "Mr. Fox" ends with Elsie not wanting to marry at all: she "just stayed around with the kinfolks. They was glad to have her, of course" (Randolph 95–97). In the Italian "Il diavolo," thanks to the youngest girl's cleverness all twenty-four daughters are returned to the family with riches as well (Visentini 181–84).

23. Walter Scherf notes the girl's transformation even in the bland Perrault text: at the end of the tale the heroine has found herself. Scherf observes that recognizing this transformation is up to the reader's or listener's sensitivity, and that an explicit comment on the part of the narrator would be inappropriate (24).

24. Uther remarks that Bluebeard is not the most important character in the tale and that, consequently, many versions are named after both the protagonist and the antagonist in keeping with the double structure of the tale (40).

25. Philip Lewis's "Bluebeard's Magic Key" focuses on the "pervasive duality and doubling" of Perrault's "La Barbe Bleue" within a post-Freudian framework which is influenced by Irigaray's ideas about blood and femininity in the economy of the same. In spite of its jargony prose, I highly recommend this essay. Because Lewis deals only with one text, and a peculiarly distinctive one as noted earlier, he sees the magic key as "the key to the story" (42) and seems to, perhaps unintentionally, foreground the "alarming resemblance" of Bluebeard and his wife as a factor that incriminates her. Nevertheless, when Lewis identifies the "structure of castrational supplementarity" at work in the tale, his insight is invaluable. His comments on blood as a double mark are also suggestive, especially since they have economic and not simply ritual value.

26. Neil Philip in his notes to "Mr. Fox" remarks that in one tale "The Oxford Student" "the girl confronts her suitor alone, and is herself killed" (*English Folktales* 160). Not just "Mr. Fox," but all Bluebeard figures are marked by "cunning, greed and cowardice": he acts under false pretense; kills compulsively; isolates his victim before attacking, and blames her for his violence.

27. See "La colonna d'oro" in Comparetti 76–80 (No. XVIII).

28. As Velay-Vallantin points out, in "Comorre" Triphyna sees a change in her husband when she announces her pregnancy; she becomes afraid of him and his murdered wives' ghosts confirm her suspicions. Comorre has been told—a well-known mythic motif—that his son will destroy him, and, of course, that is what happens in the end.

29. Sharon Rose Wilson's well-documented study *Margaret Atwood's Fairy-Tale Sexual Politics* discusses Atwood's "Bluebeard" intertexts extensively. In the chapter connecting Atwood's visual art with her writing, I find the 1970 "Fichter's Bride" watercolor particularly suggestive (Wilson, Plate 3). The untitled watercolor represents the bride-doll that the heroine tricks the sorcerer with: we see the skull, the white gown and veil, and the predominantly red flowers crowning the skull and trailing down her skirt. Wilson also describes "The Robber Bridegroom" watercolor "which pictures a man holding both an axe and a blond head. The head emits

light" (from an Atwood Telephone Call, Wilson 46). Through phone interviews with the author and plot-based analogies, Wilson establishes that
"Atwood's texts both parody and echo fairy tales" (263). She argues that
"Atwood's characters re-member their own symbolically dismembered
bodies and re-vision the discredited old stories" (314). Following Atwood's statements, Wilson names the Grimms' tales as the most
significant intertexts—especially "Fichter's Bird" (AT311), "The Robber
Bridegroom" (AT955), "The Girl Without Hands" (AT706), "The Juniper
Tree" (AT720), "The White Snake" (AT673), and "Red Cap. The Glutton" (AT333)—along with some French-Canadian tales. Wilson provides
an analysis of Atwood's use of "Fichter's Bird," clearly the most pervasive
fairy-tale intertext in Atwood's work, in a variety of texts from 1971 to
1992, including unpublished papers and the core-text, "Bluebeard's Egg"
in the homonymous collection (1983).

In the Preface, Wilson describes her ambitious project: "this book examines what fairy tale patterns . . . mean within Atwood's texts; how these
patterns change throughout Atwood's career (e.g., becoming more political); and how her handling of these intertexts varies from Gothic to
tragic to tragicomic, comic, satiric, and parodic" (xi–xii). Wilson's book is
significant methodologically in that it combines folklore and literature
analysis. She appends a list of Aarne-Thompson tale types and Thompson
motifs; she also states that her study "is the first to apply the folklore
classifications to the tales and motifs Atwood uses" (xvii). Critics like Barbara Godard and Sherrill E. Grace have also done their folklore home-
work, but they do not foreground tale classification or folk motifs as
much. The great advantage of Wilson's procedure is to make some basic
folklore studies tools more widely available; the danger is to make intertextuality into a detective game of the old "folklore in literature" type.
Wilson transcends that danger when she focuses on how Atwood twists
the fairy tale in a gothic or comic mode, but often the identification of
clues overburdens her analysis. By focusing, like Atwood, on the Grimms,
Wilson also narrows, but justifiably so, the scope of her folklore and literature analysis.

For a useful introduction to Atwood's "attraction" to fairy tales, the
Grimms' especially, see also Elizabeth R. Baer's essay. For a methodologically and pedagogically important reading of "Atwood's Reconstruction
of Folktales," see Kathleen E. B. Manley.

My discussion of Atwood's "Bluebeard" performances is limited to
"Bluebeard's Egg" and "Alien Territory" in *Good Bones*.

30. Barbara Godard also highlights "doubling" in Atwood's "self-reflexive narrative," which tells "tales within tales": "Such specular fiction, as
Lucien Dällenbach terms it, involves a process of fiction doubling back on
itself, mirroring itself, and offering a metaphor of its own origins" (61). In
analyzing this narrative strategy, Godard focuses on how Atwood embeds
"oral anecdotes of local experience" as well as written narratives (like
"Fichter's Bird") from other cultures (82). Godard's discussion of folk
narratives, then, emphasizes Atwood's attention to performative contexts
and telling/listening dynamics.

31. Sally misunderstands the heroine's goal which is not to be the true bride: that is her reward in her husband-to-be's plot; in her own, it is simply a ploy, a way to gain power over him. Sally reduces female cleverness to knowing how to catch a man and keep him.

Along these lines, what Sally, at the end of "Bluebeard's Egg," believes the tale omits ("This is something the story left out, Sally thinks: the egg is alive, and one day it will hatch" 182) is certainly related to what she omits herself from her retelling of the story.

32. I agree with Wilson's analysis of Sally as "Fichter's bride and Fichter" as well as "false bride," though I believe the motif of "The False Bride" could be an echo of Bluebeard stories as well as other Grimms' tales.

Wilson reads doubling in "Fichter's Bird" in a decidedly positive way: "Contrary to most interpretations, 'Fichter's Bird' actually critiques rather than perpetuating suppression of women. . . . [T]he third sister actually passes the test by violating patriarchal strictures: . . . Ultimately, he [the wizard] becomes his own victim" (261). But in my view, the value of doubling is ambivalent: it also works to implicate the heroine in Bluebeard's plot.

33. Godard, like many other critics, also remarks that Atwood's self-reflexive texts "refuse an ending" that would involve the "final transformation" of death or marriage for female protagonists (68).

34. Wilson points to the Grimms' "The Crystal Ball" (AT302) to "suggest the external soul (Motif E711.1) in the egg, which helps to explain Sally's association of the egg with the heart in Atwood's story" (269). But this common motif can also be found in Bluebeard stories such as "The Three Chicory Gatherers." In it, the dragon, who has come to trust the third sister, gets drunk and confesses: "If you cut off the dove's head, you'll find an egg in its brain . . . and if you break the egg over my forehead . . . I'm done for" (Calvino 503). The third sister cracks the egg on the dragon's forehead, he dies; she escapes with her reborn sisters and the dragon's treasure. I am not suggesting that Atwood knew this story, but that the motif of the egg or "external soul" is not alien to the Bluebeard folk tradition.

It is also significant to the inner self-within-inner-self structure of Sally's relationship to Ed that the "external soul" motif usually has a Chinese box structure itself: the egg is in the brain of the dove in the cage, for instance. See a discussion of the "external soul enclosed in a succession of wrappings" in the notes by Joseph Jacobs to *Indian Fairy Tales* (239).

35. Wilson states: "Whether or not she will flee Fichter's castle like a bird is unclear, but the egg of possibility is alive, pulsing and likely to hatch" (268–69). As she develops her analysis though, "the egg of possibility" becomes more narrowly a "fertility symbol" that applies to primarily Sally: "her search for a point of view in the Bluebeard story and her encounter with her own inner world promise, if not magic transformation, a new world of vision, possibly a reborn self" (269). It is true that "Ed gives no indication of dropping disguise" (269) or of changing his collector's

approach to women; while I certainly do not want to redeem him, it is also true that prior to her "revelation" Sally shows no sign of respecting him or other women.

In contrast to Wilson's affirming reading of "Bluebeard's Egg," Sherrill Grace argues that Sally, "like the other women in the collection, is shattered by knowledge yet helpless to change or improve anything" (261). However, Grace's article on the "Modern Treatment of the Bluebeard Theme" focuses primarily on *Lady Oracle* by Atwood and *The Collector* by Fowles, and its point is to show the influence of Béla Bartók's opera on twentieth-century fictions. Bartók's *Duke Bluebeard's Castle* has no happy ending and shows the darkness of death taking over.

Realizing that her perception is not the only significant one is an important step in Sally's potential transformation, for she becomes "capable of perceiving the story of the other, the egg" ("Tales Within Tales" 72).

I am using Victor Turner's terminology here in referring to the phases of initiation (*The Forest of Symbols*).

36. Sherrill Grace remarks that in Bartók's opera "the 'happy ending' of the fairy tale, on any level, has gone; knowing and having are equally destructive; male and female, man and nature are doomed. By using the Bluebeard story, but radically altering its structure, Bartók presents his vision of human self-destruction. Fowles and Atwood [in *Lady Oracle*] follow his lead" (254).

37. One could say this symbolic system simply maps out the inevitable "battle of the sexes," but Atwood provides sufficient socio-cultural parameters within which to recognize this, indeed, compulsive pattern as unnatural. The claim in "The Female Body" that male and female brains work differently need not be read as biological destiny. References to marketing and commodification alert us to the economic structure sustaining these warped sexual politics. Furthermore, not all men and women need fall prey to this plot, and, though the alternative may be a question mark, the socio-economic pattern in this gender scenario (section seven of "Alien Territory") stands in marked contrast to the "Bluebeard" rewards of money and comfort. As the ensuing discussion of Carter and Campion will show, I believe it is fair to say that Atwood's sexual politics highlight the symbolic rather than the economic dynamics governing "Bluebeard."

38. Here Atwood is also rewriting T.S. Eliot's "The Hollow Men." See the first two stanzas of the last section especially; significantly, she replaces the shadow of death with the beginnings of compassion.

39. Patricia Duncker observes that, in the *Jane Eyre* tradition, the piano-tuner must be "damaged," for "the power balance inherent in all heterosexual relationships [to be] levelled off" (11). Elaine Jordan responds: "The blindness of the piano-tuner . . . is produced by the needs of the story's argument. The bride has already been too much seduced by seeing herself as the object of an erotic gaze, so that any other lover must be marked as 'not like that,' one who knows her in his heart, and can appreciate her skill as a musician. He must be disabled in some respect, so that

it is the bride's mother not he who rescues her" ("Dangers" 122). I would add that if the blind piano-tuner as alternative to Bluebeard indicates a "lack," it is symptomatic of the problematic resolution of this narrative. Can the solution to viewing oneself in the mirror of the masculine gaze simply be shutting off that gaze altogether? If the mirror remains unchanged, how can one's self-image really change? I believe Carter addresses this question throughout *The Bloody Chamber* and that the homonymous story is certainly not accidentally placed as the first story in the volume, that is, in the beginning of this exploration.

40. "The Bloody Chamber" also calls on a variety of texts, from "Genesis" to Colette's novels, from Baudelaire to the gothic, from opera to Redon's charcoal drawings. For an analysis of two more intertexts—Carter's own published essays on sexual exploitation in Japan to the hagiographic story of St. Cecilia—see Bacchilega, "Sex Slaves and Saints?" For a detailed analysis of Carter's "active reading of Sade both in her *The Sadeian Woman* and in "The Bloody Chamber," see Robin Ann Sheets, "Pornography, Fairy Tales, and Feminism."

This "excess of intertexts" (Jordan, Enthralment 40) is not simply a display of erudition, but an explosive charge which will go off at different points for different readers upon one or more readings. Carter's stated object for setting the charge is to crack or shatter imprisoning social fictions (see "Notes from the Front Line"). Clearly, the Breton versions of "Bluebeard" and other intertexts are not as widely accessible or known as Perrault's; few readers will recognize them. However, as I argue in my discussion of Carter's "Little Red Riding Hood" retellings, the effect of more obscure intertexts is not lost or trivial. First, these details have a life of their own in Carter's text, so that readers can feel their impact, or some of it, without knowing the original intertexts. Second, Carter's recovery of these intertexts is necessary to her "metafolkloric" archeological, historicizing project, which unveils the ideological workings of fairy tales. Third, as Jordan boldly asks, "So all this demands special knowledge? Yes, why not? Curiosity, as Charles Perrault said, is a charming passion. It is not essential for a feminist writer to assume naive readers, or for every reader to see all possible readings. In my mother's tenements there are many apartments, and that's not the only house there is" (Dangers 122). My reading is set in a specific apartment with many "Bluebeard" rooms.

41. Danielle Roemer explores Carter's text as "the space of confrontation and contemplation" in which the past is not simply repeated, but "subjected to scrutiny and re-evaluation." Roemer's fine analysis, which draws on Victor Turner's and Bakhtin's ideas, combines narrative and historical or political concerns. While I like Roemer's distinction between "repetition" and "reflection" based on their different approaches to the authority of the past, I have not adopted it in my discussion.

42. While Patricia Duncker has equated this introspective exposition to the endorsement of "the classic pornographic model of sexuality" (11) and Avis Lewallen has expressed her "unease at being manipulated by the

narrative to sympathize with masochism" (151), Kari Lokke in an analysis of "The Grotesque of Self-Parody and Self-Assertion" in modern "Blue-beard" retellings celebrates the "emancipatory function" of the ironic and parodic repetition of grotesque sexuality in Carter's "The Bloody Chamber." See also the comments Brooks makes (150–52).

43. Clearly the heroine of "Fichter's Bird" (who serves Atwood so well in her exploration of the trickster role) or of "The Robber Bridegroom" would not lend herself readily to Carter's project. Carter, nevertheless, does allude to them. The third dead wife's representation eerily resembles the surrogate doll-bride with which the heroine tricks the wizard: "this skull . . . had been crowned with a wreath of white roses, and a veil of lace, the final image of his bride" (TBC 29). The best known text of "Mr. Fox" has the murderer dragging one of his victims "up the stairs into the Bloody Chamber" (Jacobs, *English Fairy Tales* 150; Briggs, *DBF* Part A, vol II, 447; Carter, *Virago* 9), a phrase that might be the source for Carter's title. I cannot say for sure that Carter knew "Mr. Fox" at the time that she was writing *The Bloody Chamber*; however, given her knowledge of folk and fairy tales, it is not unlikely, and she did select "Mr. Fox" for her 1990 *Virago Book of Fairy Tales*, offering extensive notes on it as well. For *Strange Things Sometimes Still Happen*, published posthumously, she selected a North Carolina version of "Old Foster," another AT955 version. Based on the plausibility of Carter's knowledge of these "Bluebeard" analogues, I would argue that *not* using them is symptomatic of Carter's strategic focus on the victim role, pointing to a "lack" in the resolution of "The Bloody Chamber" itself.

44. Avis Lewallen remarks: "The heroine's corruption is three-fold: material, as she is seduced by wealth; sexual, as she discovers her own sexual appetite; and moral, in the sense that 'like Eve'. . . she disobeys her master-husband's command" (150).

A later description of the ruby choker as "coiled like a snake about to strike" (TBC 37) could possibly refer to a Breton "Bluebeard" version, "La fille qui naquit avec une couleuvre autour du cou," in which the snake is the female protagonist's twin sister. In that tale, the sisterly serpent leaves "un collier rouge, imitant parfaitement une couleuvre" around the girl's neck; erases the mark when the girl marries; and quickly comes to her rescue, when her husband is about to decapitate her, by poisoning him with her bite (Luzel 341–48).

45. Duncker, Clark, and Lewallen have chastised Carter for manipulating her readers into sympathizing with female masochism, endorsing a regressive model of sexuality, and reinforcing violent eroticism.

46. See note 7 and later discussion of initiation in this chapter.

47. In "Sex Slaves and Saints?" I suggest how Carter's commentary on gendered relations in Japan can set the stage for such a recognition of masochism, in its relation to sexual and economic exploitation, as well as its ambiguous effects.

48. The protagonist of "The Bloody Chamber" is like Saint Cecilia (so

much so that her husband believes she will make a perfect martyr and she herself aspires to some saintly, superior status), but ultimately the analogy falls apart because most of the allusions to Saint Cecilia's features (lily-like innocence, way unto the blind, diligence, and wisdom) are highly ambivalent (Bacchilega, "Sex Slaves and Saints?").

In Huysmans' *Down There* (*La Bas*), both the story of Gilles de Rais (presumed by many to be Bluebeard) and the legend of Comor (Comorre) are told as Durtal and Chantelouve debate "Bluebeard" in relation to satanism (167–77 and 183).

49. Elaine Jordan cogently asserts that Carter, throughout her work, questions "the subject position of the virtuous victim," as well as "its adequacy as a position from which to resist oppression" because this "sentimental" position implies the belief in a reward for suffering and a "benign authority that can make it all better" ("Dangers" 120).

50. Mirroring this nurse is the Marquis' "foster mother...bound to his family in the utmost feudal complicity"; by running Bluebeard's castle smoothly, she enacts her allegiance to him and not to his many wives; however, she also steals from him when she can (TBC 14, 36).

51. While I do not know of any "Bluebeard" version in which the mother alone comes to the heroine's rescue, it is clear that in the folk tradition various possibilities are available and they are not gender-exclusive. In the following discussion I suggest that having a mother rather than a sister as the rescuer, for instance, could point to the importance of looking "back" into the value of "blood ties."

Patricia Duncker finds the indomitable mother to be "The Bloody Chamber"'s one redeeming feature: "Here Carter is transforming the sexual politics of the fairy tales in significant ways. . . . Carter's tale, perhaps unwittingly, carries an uncompromisingly feminist message; for the women's revolution would seal up the door of the bloody chamber forever" (12).

52. Significantly the newly formed community (mother, woman, and lover) has three members, like the Freudian nuclear family and the "families" the heroine has belonged to in the past, including the nurse-mother-daughter trio. However, clearly, it is socially marginal and suspect.

53. I cannot prove that Carter knew this story, but it is widely available in British fairy tale and literary traditions. While retelling "Captain Murderer," a story his nurse would tell him, Dickens comments on the blood stain: "(To this terrific point I am indebted for my first personal experience of a shudder and cold beads on the forehead.)" The quoted passages can be found in Briggs (*DBF*, Part A, vol. 1, 175) and Philip (187–89).

Working intertextually with Colette's works and her "mother-daughter" relationship with Carter, Elaine Jordan suggests that "The Bloody Chamber" is "a strong answer to an existing representation, Colette's/Claudine's desire to be ravaged by the other, saying 'I can see the fascination, but just look where it gets you—... to a place in the series of defunct and mutilated brides.' Better the man who's a friend and ally, the blind piano tuner" ("Dangers" 129). Her interpretation is similar to mine though we work with different intertexts and in this article she stresses more what is "constructive" than what is reflective in Carter's writing.

54. Citations are from Jane Campion's *The Piano* (New York: Hyperion/Miramax, 1993), which includes the script as well as notes and commentary of the making of the movie. Jane Campion and Kate Pullinger also published a novelization of the movie (1994), to which I will refer occasionally. Both written texts offer more information than the movie itself—the script, because of its descriptive and emotionally suggestive stage directions; the novel, because it fills in narrative gaps, such as the trauma leading to Ada's "elective mutism" and the relationship out of which Flora is born. Though I quote from the script, I focus primarily on the movie itself for analysis, using the written texts as before- or after-the-fact interpretations of the movie. Harvey Greenberg uses the clinical term "elective mutism" in his review, specifying that this "rare, puzzling condition" which "occurs rather more frequently in girls than boys...is thought by some to represent a strategy of active manipulation and control, rather than being a symptom of autistic withdrawal" (46).

55. Andrew McAlpine, *The Piano*'s production designer, specifies in the notes to the script how the "dank darkness" of Stewart's landscape was constructed in contrast to "this green cathedral of *nikau* and *punga* that is Baines's life: a very gothic landscape, surrounded by this cool green light" (140). In more general terms, one could argue that New Zealand itself is a liminal space where the "white" Victorians encounter their repressed "dark" selves. The movie's photography encourages this ideologically problematic vision by foregrounding the underwater quality of the bush, associating the landscape with the unconscious. Lynda Dyson provides a strong critique of the film's "signifying chain New Zealand/sheep/land" which "transforms history into nature" (121). Unfortunately, when it comes to colonialism, Campion's awareness seems limited in this film.

56. Greenberg notes that "Ada's muteness can be interpreted as a limit case of patriarchal domination, both symptom *and* countercoup" (48). Pat Dowell states: "This mute woman's relation to her piano and her music is plumbed with endless variations. Her art is her voice, her accomplished self, and her salvation. It conducts her to physical passion, but also serves as her surrogate life" (33).

57. The notes to the script state: "She starts [playing] with whole-hearted feeling, her eyes closed, but before long she is surprised by a moving reflection across the piano and she starts, glancing over her shoulder. She stops and begins again. But once more a reflex has her glance across her left shoulder and she pauses in her playing. Disquieted, she starts again and again she looks away. She stops, confused, unable to go on, unable to get up, one hand on the lid and one on the piano keys" (80). The relationship between Ada and George, of which I am illuminating

the positive aspects, could also be explored as yet another sado-masochistic heterosexual relationship which debases Ada rather than validates her strength and integrity. I choose to follow, in this case, the lead of the camera which in its close-ups invites us to collude with Ada's actions and reactions, though it does not focalize exclusively through her. Therefore, I am argumentatively supporting Ada's own interpretation of her initiation as successful transformation and rebirth. See Bruzzi and Gillett for positive readings of Campion's film: one analyzes how the film undoes the norm of male scopophilia by working with the languages of costume, touch, and music; the other argues "*The Piano* interrogates the conventional expectations of femininity, masculinity and heterosexuality" (282).

However, as I take it, this "romantic" endorsement of passion (see reviews cited as well as the Notes to *The Piano* with Campion's comments on Emily Brontë's influence on her work) and risk-taking curiosity is to be understood in response to the specifically Victorian power play and repression represented here, not to be celebrated per se as a timeless "solution" to the problems of gender interaction. And, needless to say, this romantic plot has its cost.

58. See Greenberg's comments on "Baines's defensive brutishness yielding to an amazing, grave sweetness" (50).

59. The script makes explicit the role of curiosity in this scene: "[Stewart] reels back, angry, and just as we might expect him to burst through, he steps up to look again; the fatal second look, the look for curiosity" (83).

60. Ada and Flora constitute a parallel pair to Baines and Stewart, enacting opposite Victorian feminine roles: Ada, the whore; Flora, the angel. Unlike Ada, Flora internalizes guilt and tells on her mother twice in reaction to her mother's exclusive passion for Baines and the possibility of familial safety that Stewart offers. However, Flora's closeness to her mother, her strong will, and her curiosity also point to her as Ada's double. An exploration of this mother-daughter relationship would take me too far from the "Bluebeard" focus of my discussion, but it certainly merits attention.

61. Talking to Mary Colbert, the production designer Andrew McAlpine said, "The Bluebeard concert provided us with wonderful imaginative license. Jane [Campion] was intrigued by a form of drama from her (?) [sic] childhood in New Zealand, that of the shadow play, which is still very popular in parts of Asia, especially Indonesia. The inspiration came from a small Victorian photograph of women's heads peeping through a hole in a curtain, which led Jane to look for some bit of theatre as relief" (*Sight and Sound* 9). Campion mentions this image as a source of inspiration in two interviews (*Positif* 6 and *Cahiers du cinéma* 20). She also states she read "Bluebeard" only when she was about to finish the screenplay and that while she found strong affinities with her project she did not wish to burden the film with more metaphors (*Cahiers du cinéma* 20).

62. The director of photography and lighting designer for the movie, Stuart Dryburgh, remarks that without this *mise en scène* and the Aunt

Morag/Nessie episodes, *The Piano* "would have been so hard-driven as to be unwatchable" (*Sight and Sound* 9). McAlpine's comments are consistent with this interpretation (see note 61). While most reviewers have ignored the episode, a few have commented on it briefly: Bluebeard's violence prefigures Stewart's use of the axe (Halprin 35); and, while the Maoris are "indeed untutored in Western drama, . . . Bluebeard's sadistic intention toward his wives is deeply offensive to them" (Greenberg 49).

63. "Nearly every nineteenth-century printed version of 'Bluebeard' singles out the heroine's curiosity as an especially undesirable trait," writes Maria Tatar (*The Hard Facts* 158), who adds that a "nineteenth-century Scottish version summarizes in its title the nearly collective critical wisdom of the past three centuries on this tale: "'The Story of Bluebeard, or, the effects of female curiosity'" (160). We do not know if audiences and readers took this message to heart, but writers and critics seemed to. From my limited research on nineteenth-century dramatic retellings of "Bluebeard," I gather that the theme of female curiosity was approached either tragically or comically. For instance, see Francis Egerton Ellesmere's tragedy *Bluebeard, or, Dangerous curiosity & justifiable homicide* (1841) and H. J. Tully's "burlesque burletta" *Blue Beard, or Hints to the curious* (185?). "Bluebeard" was clearly a popular "script" for the stage in England, even as a Christmas pantomime, and in Germany following Ludwig Tieck's play.

64. The novelization of *The Piano* refers to "Bluebeard" as "a parable the European audience found fearsome though familiar" (Campion and Pullinger 130).

For Pat Dowell, the Maoris "function as the return of the repressed," a stereotypical "post-'60s version of the noble savage" (33). Dyson identifies it as "primitivism" (128). Harvey Greenberg's comment is more positive. The novelization, which refers to the intervening Maoris as "offended warriors" (Campion and Pullinger 133), would seem to confirm Greenberg's observation. My analysis privileges a fairy-tale and Western-centered intertextuality and, in that context, reads the role of the Maoris as heroic and wise. Dowell and Dyson also have a point when the scene is read in the context of the cultural representation of the Maoris in the film. While Campion's statements in interviews and in the notes accompanying the script highlight the issues of colonization, the representation of the Maoris in the movie appears predictable.

65. Pamela Banting's ideas in "The body as pictogram" are active in my reading of the body and its language in *The Piano*. As Banting writes "Cixous's recourse to the body is *not* a return to a natural, speechless or prelinguistic body but rather to a signifying body continually networking with its own flesh and the surfaces and particularities of the world" (229). For an important study of the body in relation to sexuality and narrative, see Brooks, *Body Work*.

WORKS CITED

PRIMARY SOURCES

Apuleius. *The Golden Ass.* Trans. Robert Graves. New York: Farrar, Straus & Giroux, 1951.

Atwood, Margaret. "Bluebeard's Egg." 1983. Zipes, *Don't Bet on the Prince.* 161–82.

——. *Good Bones.* Toronto: Couch House, 1992.

Bartók, Béla. "Bluebeard's Castle." *Kekszakallu herceg vara.* German and English. Vienna: Universal Edition, 1925.

Barthelme, Donald. *Snow White.* New York: Atheneum, 1967.

Basile, Giambattista. *The Pentamerone.* Trans. and ed. N.M. Penzer. New York: Dutton, 1932.

Beauty and the Beast. Dir. Ron Koslow. CBS, 1987–1990.

Beauty and the Beast. Dir. Gary Trousdale and Kirk Wise. Walt Disney Co., 1991.

Bechstein, Ludwig. "Die hoffärtige Braut." *Märchen.* 1845. Stuttgart: Parkland, 1985.

Bernstein, Charles. *Rough Trades.* Los Angeles: Sun & Moon Press, 1991.

Bolte, Johannes and Georg Polívka. *Anmerkungen zu den Kinder-und Hausmärchen der Brüder Grimm 1913–32.* Hildesheim: Georg Olms Verlagsbuchhandlung, 1963.

Briggs, Katharine M. *A Dictionary of British Folk-Tales in the English Language.* pt. A, 2 vols. London: Routledge, 1970.

Briggs, Katharine M. and Ruth L. Tongue. *Folktales of England.* Chicago: University of Chicago Press, 1965.

Broumas, Olga. *Beginning with O.* New Haven, Conn.: Yale University Press, 1977.

Calvino, Italo. *Italian Folktales.* Trans. George Martin. New York: Pantheon, 1980. Trans. of *Fiabe italiane.* Torino: Einaudi, 1956.

Campbell, Marie. *Tales from the Cloud Walking Country.* Bloomington: Indiana University Press, 1958.

Campion, Jane. *The Piano.* New York: Hyperion/Miramax, 1993.

Campion, Jane and Kate Pullinger. *The Piano: A Novel.* New York: Hyperion/Miramax, 1994.

Carrière, Joseph M. *Tales from the French Folk-Lore of Missouri.* Evanston, Ill.: Northwestern University Studies in the Humanities 1. 1937. Rpt. New York: AMS Press, 1970.

Carter, Angela. *Fireworks: Nine Profane Pieces.* 1974. New York: Harper & Row, 1981.

——, trans. *The Fairy Tales of Charles Perrault.* London: Gollancz, 1977.

——. *The Bloody Chamber and Other Stories.* 1979. Harmondsworth: Penguin, 1981.

——. *Come unto These Yellow Sands.* Newcastle upon Tyne: Bloodaxe-Books, 1985

——, ed. *The Virago Book of Fairy Tales.* London: Virago, 1990. Rpt. *Old Wives' Fairy Tale Book.* New York: David McKay, 1990.

——, ed. and trans. *Sleeping Beauty & Other Favourite Fairy Tales.* Ill. Michael Foreman. 1982. Boston: Otter Books, 1991.

——, ed. *The Second Virago Book of Fairy Tales. Strange Things Sometimes Still Happen. Fairy Tales from Around the World.* Boston: Faber and Faber, 1993.

——. *American Ghosts & Old World Wonders.* London: Vintage, 1994.

Cole, Joanna, ed. *Best-Loved Folktales of the World.* New York: Doubleday, 1982.

The Company of Wolves. Dir. Neil Jordan. Screenplay by Angela Carter and Neil Jordan. ITC Entertainment/Palace Production, 1984.

Comparetti, Domenico. *Novelline popolari italiane.* Torino, 1875.

Coover, Robert. *Pricksongs & Descants, Fictions.* New York: Dutton, 1969.

——. "The Dead Queen." *Quarterly Review of Literature* 8 (1973): 304–13.

——. "Briar Rose." *Conjunctions* 26 (1996): 87–125.

Coronedi-Berti, Carolina. "Giricoccola." *Al sgurgiol di ragazú* Bologna, 2 (1883): 212–15.

Crane, Thomas Frederick. *Italian Popular Tales.* Boston and New York: Houghton Mifflin, 1885.

de Beaumont, Madame LePrince. "Beauty and the Beast." Opie and Opie, *Classic Fairy Tales.* 182–95.

——. "Beauty and the Beast." Hearne, *Beauty and the Beast.* 189–203.

De Nino, Antonio. *Usi e Costumi Abbruzzesi. Vol. III: Fiabe descritte da —.* Firenze, 1883. Rpt. Avezzano: Studio Bibliografico A. Polla, 1981.

Delarue, Paul. "Les contes merveilleux de Perrault et la tradition populaire: I. Le petit chaperon rouge." *Bulletin Folklorique d'Ile de France* 13 (1951): 221–28; 251–60; 283–91.

——. "Les contes merveilleux de Perrault et la tradition populaire (suite). II. Barbe-Bleue." *Bulletin folklorique d'Ile-de-France* 14 (1952): 348–57.

——. "Compléments et rectifications aux articles précédents." *Bulletin Folklorique d'Ile-de-France* 15 (1953): 511–17.

——, ed. *The Borzoi Book of French Folk Tales.* Trans. Austin E. Fife. Ill. Warren Chappell. New York: Knopf, 1956.

——. *Le conte populaire français.* Paris: Edition Erasme, 1957.

Dorson, Richard. *Buying the Wind: Regional Folklore in the United States.* Chicago: University of Chicago Press, 1964.

Edwards, Carol L. "The Fairy Tale 'Snow White.'" *Making Connections*

Across the Curriculum: Reading for Analysis. Ed. Patricia Chittenden and Malcolm Kiniry. New York: Bedford, St. Martins, 1983. 579–646.

Egbert of Liège. "De Puella a lupellis seruata." *Fecunda ratis,* ed. Ernst Voigt. Halle a.S 1889. 232–33. (See Ziolkowski 558–59.)

Eliot, T.S. *Collected Poems, 1909–1962.* New York: Harcourt, Brace & World, 1970.

Ellesmere, Francis Egerton. *Bluebeard, or, Dangerous Curiosity &Justifiable Homicide.* London: Printed by T. Brettell, 1841.

Huysmans, J. K. *Down There (La Bas): A Study in Satanism.* Trans. Keene Wallis. New York: University Books, 1958.

Imbriani, Vittorio. *La novellaja fiorentina.* Livorno: F. Vigo, 1877. Rpt. Palermo: Edikronos, 1981.

Jacobs, Joseph, ed. *English Fairy Tales.* 1898. New York: Dover, 1967.

———. *Indian Fairy Tales.* New York: Dover, 1969.

Joisten, Charles. *Contes populaires du Dauphiné.* Vol I. Grenoble: Musée dauphinois, 1971.

Lang, Andrew, ed. *The Blue Fairy Book.* 1889. New York: Dover, 1965.

Lee, Tanith. *Red as Blood or Tales from the Sisters Grimmer.* New York: Daws Books, 1983.

Lo Nigro, Sebastiano. *Racconti popolari siciliani.* Firenze: Leo O. Olschki, 1957.

Luzel, F. M. *Contes populaires de Basse-Bretagne.* Paris: Maissoneuve & Larose, 1887. Rpt. 1967.

Mango, Francesco, comp. *Novelline popolari sarde.* Palermo, 1890.

Massignon, Geneviève, ed. *Folktales of France.* Trans. Jacqueline Hyland. Chicago: University of Chicago Press, 1968.

Mélusine. Paris, 3 (1886/87); 6 (1892/93); 9 (1898/99).

Millien, Achille and Paul Delarue. *Contes du Nivernais et du Morvan.* Paris, 1953.

Molinaro, Ursule. *A Full Moon of Women: 29 Word Portraits of Notable Women from Different Times and Places + 1 Void of Course.* New York: Dutton, 1990.

Nerucci, Gherardo. *Sessanta novelle popolari montalesi.* 2nd ed. Firenze, 1891.

Opie, Iona and Peter Opie. *The Classic Fairy Tales.* New York: Oxford University Press, 1974.

Perrault, Charles. *Contes de ma Mère L'Oye; Histoires ou contes du temps passé; avec des moralités.* Paris: Fleuron, 1697.

———. *Contes de ma Mère L'Oye.* Ed. André Coeuroy. Paris, 1948.

———. *Perrault's Complete Fairy Tales.* Trans. A.E. Johnson. New York: Dover, 1969.

Philip, Neil. *The Penguin Book of English Folktales.* London: Penguin, 1992.

Pitrè, Giuseppe. *Novelle popolari toscane.* Vol. XXX, *Opere complete di Giuseppe Pitrè,* edizione nazionale, 1885. Roma, 1941.

Randolph, Vance. *The Devil's Pretty Daughter and Other Ozark Folk Tales.* New York: Columbia University Press, 1955.

Roberts, Leonard W. *South from Hell-fer-Sartin: Kentucky Mountain Folk Tales.* Lexington: University of Kentucky Press, 1955.

Sebillot, Paul. *Littérature orale de la Haute-Bretagne.* Paris, 1881.

Sexton, Anne. *Transformations.* Boston: Houghton Mifflin, 1971.

Soupault, Re. *Breton Folktales.* Trans. Ruth E.K. Meuss. London: G. Bell & Sons, 1971.

Tie Me Up, Tie Me Down. Dir. Pedro Almadovar. Miramax Films and Eldeseo S.A., 1990.

Tully, J.H. *Blue Beard, or Hints to the curious.* London: W.W. Barth, 185–?.

Visentini, Isaia, comp. *Fiabe mantovane.* Torino, 1879.

Webster, John. *The Duchess of Malfi. John Webster and Cyril Tourner (Four Plays).* New York: Hill and Wang, 1956.

Weigle, Martha. *Spiders and Spinsters: Women and Mythology.* Albuquerque: University of New Mexico Press, 1982.

Zipes, Jack, ed. *Don't Bet on the Prince: Contemporary Feminist Fairy Tales in North America.* New York: Methuen, 1986.

———, ed. and trans. *The Complete Fairy Tales of the Brothers Grimm.* New York: Bantam, 1987.

———, ed. and trans. *Beauties, Beasts and Enchantment: Classic French Fairy Tales.* New York: New American Library, 1989.

———, ed. *Spells of Enchantment: The Wondrous Fairy Tales of Western Culture.* New York: Viking, 1991.

SECONDARY SOURCES

Aarne, Antti and Stith Thompson. *The Types of the Folktale: A Classification and Bibliography.* FF Communications 184. Helsinki: Academia Scientiarum Fennica, 1961.

Almansi, Guido. "In the Alchemist's Cave: Radio Plays." Sage, *The Flesh and the Mirror.* 216–29.

Antonnen, Pertti J. "Folklore, Modernity, and Postmodernity: A Theoretical Overview." *Nordic Frontiers. Recent Issues in the Study of Modern Traditional Culture in the Nordic Countries.* Ed. Pertti J. Antonnen and Reimund Kvideland. Turku: Nordic Institute of Folklore, 1993. 17–27.

Anwell, Maggie. "Lolita Meets the Werewolf: *The Company of Wolves.*" *The Female Gaze: Women as Viewers of Popular Culture.* Ed. Lorraine Gamman and Margaret Marshment. Seattle: Real Comet Press, 1989. 76–85.

Apo, Satu. *The Narrative World of Finnish Fairy Tales. Structure, Agency, and Evaluation in Southwest Finnish Folktales.* Helsinki: Academia Scientiarum Fennica, 1995.

Babcock, Barbara. "Feminisms/Pretexts: Fragments, Questions, and Reflections." *Anthropological Quarterly* 66 (1993): 59–66.

Bacchilega, Cristina. "Folk and Literary Narrative in a Postmodern Context: The Case of the *Märchen.*" *Fabula* 29 (1988): 302–16.

———. "Adapting the Fairy Tale for Hawaii's Children." *The Lion and the Unicorn* 12, 2 (1988): 121–34.

———. "The Fruit of the Womb: Creative Uses of a Naturalizing Tradition in Folktales." Bronner, *Creativity and Tradition in Folklore.* 153–66.

———. "Introduction: The Innocent Persecuted Heroine Fairy Tale."*Western Folklore* 52, 1 (1993): 1–12.

———. "'Writing' and 'Voice': The Articulations of Gender in Folklore and Literature." Preston, *Folklore, Literature, and Cultural Theory*. 83–101.

———. "Sex Slaves and Saints? Resisting Masochism in 'The Bloody Chamber.'" *Across the Oceans: Studies from East to West in Honor of Richard Seymour*. Ed. Irmengard Rauch and Cornelia Moore. Honolulu: University of Hawaii Press, 1995. 77–86.

Baer, Elizabeth R. "Pilgrimage Inward. Quest and Fairy Tale Motifs in *Surfacing*." *Margaret Atwood: Vision and Forms*. Ed. Kathryn VanSpanckeren and Jan Garden Castro. Carbondale: Southern Illinois Press, 1988. 24–34.

Bal, Mieke. *On Story-Telling: Essays in Narratology*. Sonoma, Calif.: Polebridge Press, 1991.

———. *Reading Rembrandt. Beyond the Word-Image Opposition*. New York: Cambridge University Press, 1991.

Banting, Pamela. "The Body as Pictogram: Rethinking Hélène Cixous's Ecriture Féminine." *Textual Practice* 6, 2 (1992): 225–46.

Barchilon, Jacques. "Beauty and the Beast: From Myth to Fairy Tale." *Psychoanalysis and the Psychoanalytic Review* 46, 4 (1960): 2–12.

———. *Le conte merveilleux français de 1690 à 1790*. Paris: Champion, 1975.

———. "Confessions of a Fairy-Tale Lover." *The Lion and the Unicorn* 12, 2 (1988): 208–23.

Barthes, Roland. *Mythologies*. Trans. Annette Lavers. London: Granada, 1973.

Barzilai, Shuli. "Reading 'Snow White': the Mother's Story." *Signs* 15 (1990): 515–34.

Bauman, Richard. "Conceptions of Folklore in the Development of Literary Semiotics." *Semiotica* 39, 1/2 (1982): 1–20.

———. *Story, Performance, and Event: Contextual Studies of Oral Narrative*. New York: Cambridge University Press, 1986.

Benhabib, Seyla, Judith Butler, and Nancy Frazer. "An Exchange on Feminism and Postmodernism." *Praxis International* 11, 2 (1991): 137–94.

Benjamin, Walter. "The Storyteller." *Illuminations*. Trans. Harry Zohn. New York: Harcourt, Brace and World, 1968.

Benson, Stephen. "Stories of Love and Death: Reading and Writing the Fairy Tale Romance." *Image and Power: Women in Fiction in the Twentieth Century*. Ed. Sarah Sceats and Gail Cunningham. New York: Longman, 1996. 103–13.

Bettelheim, Bruno. *The Uses of Enchantment: The Meaning and Importance of Fairy Tales*. New York: Random House, 1977.

Böklen, Ernst. *Sneewittchenstudien*. Liepzig, 1910.

Bottigheimer, Ruth B., ed. *Fairy Tales and Society. Illusion, Allusion and Paradigm*. Philadelphia: University of Pennsylvania Press, 1986.

———. *Grimms' Bad Girls & Bold Boys: The Moral and Social Vision of the Tales*. New Haven, Conn.: Yale University Press, 1987.

———. "Cupid and Psyche vs. Beauty and the Beast: The Milesian and the

Modern." *Merveilles et contes* 3, 1 (1989): 4–14.

———. "'Beauty and the Beast'": Marriage and Money—Motif and Motivation." *Midwestern Folklore* 15, 2 (1989): 79–88.

Briggs, Charles and Amy Shuman, eds. "Theorizing Folklore: Toward New Perspectives on the Politics of Culture." *Western Folklore* 52, 2–3–4 (1993).

Bronner, Simon, ed. *Creativity and Tradition in Folklore: New Directions.* Logan: Utah State University Press, 1992.

Brooks, Peter. *Body Work: Objects of Desire in Modern Narrative.* Cambridge, Mass.: Harvard University Press, 1993.

Bruzzi, Stella. "Tempestuous Petticoats: Costume and Desire in *The Piano.*" *Screen* 36, 3 (1995): 257–66.

Bryant, Sylvia. "Re-Constructing Oedipus Through 'Beauty and the Beast.'" *Criticism* 31 (1989): 439–53.

Butler, Judith. *Bodies That Matter: On the Discursive Limits of "Sex".* New York: Routledge, 1993.

———. *Gender Trouble: Feminism and the Subversion of Identity.* New York: Routledge, 1990.

Butler, Judith and Joan W. Scott, eds. *Feminists Theorize the Political.* New York: Routledge, 1992.

Calvino, Italo. "Cybernetics and Ghosts." *The Uses of Literature.* Trans. Patrick Creagh. New York: Harcourt, 1986. 3–27.

Campion, Jane. "Jane Campion: *The Piano.*" Interview by Milo Bilbrough. *Cinema Papers* (May 1, 1993): 4.

———. "*Entretien avec* Jane Campion." Interview by Thomas Bourguignon and Michel Ciment. *Positif* (June 1993): 6–11.

———. "*Entretien avec* Jane Campion." *Cahiers du Cinéma* 467/8 (1993): 17–20.

Canham, Stephen. "What Manner of Beast? Illustrations of 'Beauty and the Beast.'" *Image and Maker* (1984): 12–25.

Cardigos, Isabel. *In and Out of Enchantment: Blood Symbolism and Gender in Portuguese Fairytales.* Diss. University of London, King's College, 1993.

Carter, Angela. *The Sadeian Woman and the Ideology of Pornography.* New York: Pantheon, 1979.

———. *Nothing Sacred: Selected Writings.* Rev. ed. London: Virago, 1992.

———. "Notes from the Front Line." *On Gender and Writing.* Ed. Michelene Wandor. London: Pandora Press, 1983. 69–77.

———. Review of Hearne, *Beauty and the Beast: Visions and Revisions of an Old Tale. Folklore* 102, 1 (1991): 123–124.

Cixous, Hélène. "Castration or Decapitation?" Trans. Annette Kuhn. *Signs: Journal of Women in Culture and Society* 7, 1 (1981): 41–55.

———. "Difficult Joys." Wilcox et al., *The Body and the Text.* 5–30.

Cixous, Hélène and Catherine Clément. *The Newly Born Woman.* Trans. Betsy Wing. Minneapolis: University of Minnesota Press, 1986.

Clark, Robert. "Angela Carter's Desire Machine." *Women's Studies* 14 (1987): 147–61.

Collick, John. "Wolves Through the Window: Writing Dreams/Dreaming

Films/Filming Dreams." *Critical Survey* 3 (1991): 283–89.

Cocteau, Jean. *"Beauty and the Beast": Diary of a Film.* New York: Dover, 1972.

Culler, Jonathan. *Structuralist Poetics: Structuralism, Linguistics, and the Study of Literature.* Ithaca, N.Y.: Cornell University Press, 1975.

———. *On Deconstruction: Theory and Criticism after Structuralism.* Ithaca, N.Y.: Cornell University Press, 1982.

———. *Framing the Sign: Criticism and Its Institutions.* New York: Blackwell, 1988.

Darnton, Robert. "Peasants Tell Tales: The Meaning of Mother Goose." *The Great Cat Massacre and Other Episodes in French Cultural History.* New York: Vintage Books, 1985. 9–72.

de Beauvoir, Simone. *The Second Sex.* Trans. E.M. Parshley. London: Penguin, 1972.

de Lauretis, Teresa. *Alice Doesn't: Feminism, Semiotics, and Cinema.* Bloomington: Indiana University Press, 1984.

———. *Technologies of Gender: Essays on Theory, Film, and Fiction.* Bloomington: Indiana University Press, 1987.

de Man, Paul. *The Rhetoric of Romanticism.* New York: Columbia University Press, 1984.

DeVries, Larry. "Literary Beauties and Folk Beasts: Folktale Issues in 'Beauty and the Beast.'" Hearne, *Beauty and the Beast.* 156–86.

Dorst, John D. "Postmodernism vs. Postmodernity: Implications for Folklore Studies." *Folklore Forum* 21 (1988): 216–20.

———. "'Sidebar Excursions to Nowhere': The Vernacular Storytelling of Errol Morris and Spalding Gray." Preston, *Folklore, Literature, and Cultural Theory.* 119–34.

Dowell, Pat. Review of *The Piano. In These Times* 18, 1 (Nov. 29, 1993): 32.

Duncker, Patricia. "Re-Imagining the Fairy Tale: Angela Carter's Bloody Chambers." *Literature and History* 10, 1 (1984): 3–12.

Dundes, Alan. "Texture, Text, and Context." *Interpreting Folklore.* Bloomington: Indiana University Press, 1980. 20–32.

———. *Little Red Riding Hood: A Casebook.* Madison: University of Wisconsin Press, 1989.

Dyson, Lynda. "Post-Colonial Anxieties and the Representation of Nature and Culture in *The Piano.*" *Sites* 30 (Autumn 1995): 119–30.

Eliade, Mircea. "Les savants et les contes de fées." *Nouvelle Revue Française* 4 (1956): 884–91.

———. *Rites and Symbols of Initiation. The Mysteries of Birth and Rebirth.* Trans. Willard R. Trask. New York: Harper & Row, 1958.

Erb, Cynthia. "Another World or the World of an Other? The Space of Romance in Recent Versions of 'Beauty and the Beast.'" *Cinema Journal* 34, 4 (1995): 50–70.

Ferguson, Margaret and Jennifer Wicke, eds. "Feminism and Postmodernism." *boundary 2* (Summer 1992).

Fine, Gary Alan and Julie Ford. "Magic Settings: The Reflection of Middle-Class Life in 'Beauty and the Beast.'" *Midwestern Folklore* 15, 2

(1989): 89–100.

"Folklore and Literature: A Symposium." *Journal of American Folklore* 70 (1957).

Fowl, Melinda G. "Angela Carter's *The Bloody Chamber* Revisited." *Critical Survey* 3, 1 (1991): 71–79.

Genette, Gérard. *Figures II*. Paris: Seuil, 1969.

———. *Figures of Literary Discourse*. New York: Columbia University Press, 1982.

———. *Narrative Discourse Revisited*. Ithaca, N.Y.: Cornell University Press, 1988.

Geoffroy-Menoux, Sophie. "Angela Carter's *The Bloody Chamber*: Twice Harnessed Folk-Tales." *Paradoxa* 2 (1996): 249–62.

Gilbert, Sandra and Susan Gubar. *The Madwoman in the Attic: The Woman Writer and the Nineteenth-Century Literary Imagination*. New Haven, Conn.: Yale University Press, 1979.

Gillett, Sue. "Lips and Fingers: Jane Campion's *The Piano*." *Screen* 36, 3 (1995): 277–87.

Girardot, N.J. "Initiation and Meaning in the Tale of Snow White and the Seven Dwarfs." *Journal of American Folklore* 90 (1977): 274–300.

Godard, Barbara. "Tales Within Tales: Margaret Atwood's Folk Narratives." *Canadian Literature* 109 (Summer 1986): 57–84.

Goldberg, Christine. "The Forgotten Bride (AaTh 313 C)." *Fabula* 33 (1992): 39–54.

Goldsworthy, Kerryn. "Angela Carter." *Meanjin* 44, 1 (1985): 4–13.

Grace, Sherrill. "Courting Bluebeard with Bartók, Atwood, and Fowles: Modern Treatment of the Bluebeard Theme." *Journal of Modern Literature* 11, 2 (1984): 245–62.

Greenberg, Harvey. Review of *The Piano*. *Film Quarterly* 47, 3 (Spring 1994): 48.

Grosz, Elizabeth. "The Subject." *Feminism and Psychoanalysis: A Critical Dictionary*. Ed. Elizabeth Wright. London: Blackwell, 1992.

Haase, Donald. "Is Seeing Believing? Proverbs and the Film Adaptation of a Fairy Tale." *Proverbium* 7 (1990): 89–104.

———. "Response and Responsibility in Reading Grimms' Fairy Tales." *The Reception of Grimms' Fairy Tales: Responses, Reactions, Revisions*. Ed. Donald Haase. Detroit: Wayne State University Press, 1993.

Hains, Maryellen. "Beauty and the Beast: 20th Century Romance?" *Merveilles et contes* 3.1 (1989): 75–83.

Halprin, Sara. "A Key to *The Piano*." Review of *The Piano*. *Women's Review of Books* 11, 10–11 (July 1994): 35–36.

Haring, Lee. "Pieces for a Shabby Hut." Preston, *Folklore, Literature, and Cultural Theory*. 187–203.

Hartland, E. Sidney. "The Forbidden Chamber." *Folk-Lore Journal* 3 (1885): 193–242.

Hearne, Betsy. *Beauty and the Beast: Visions and Revisions of an Old Tale*. Chicago: University of Chicago Press, 1989.

Henein, Eglal. "Male and Female Ugliness Through the Ages." *Merveilles et*

Contes 3, 1 (1989): 45–56.

Holbek, Bengt. *Interpretation of Fairy Tales: Danish Folklore in a European Perspective.* Helsinki: Academia Scientiarum Fennica, 1987.

Hutcheon, Linda. "Beginning to Theorize Postmodernism." *Textual Practice* 1, 1 (1987): 10–31.

———. *A Poetics of Postmodernism: History, Theory, Fiction.* New York: Routledge, 1988.

Irigaray, Luce. *Speculum of the Other Woman.* 1974. Ithaca, N.Y.: Cornell University Press, 1985.

Jameson, Fredric. "Magical Narratives: On the Dialectical Use of Genre Criticism." *The Political Unconscious. Narrative as a Socially Symbolic Act.* Ithaca, N.Y.: Cornell University Press, 1981. 103–50.

Jenkins, Henry. "'It's Not a Fairy Tale Anymore': Gender, Genre and *Beauty and the Beast.*" *Journal of Film and Video* 43 (Spring-Summer 1991): 90–110.

Johnson, Faye R. "'Little Red Riding Hood' Then and Now." *Studies in Popular Culture* 14 (1992): 71–84.

Jones, Steven Swann. "On Analyzing Fairy Tales: 'Little Red Riding Hood' Revisited." *Western Folklore* 46 (April 1987): 97–106.

———. *The New Comparative Method: Structural and Symbolic Analysis of the Allomotifs of "Snow White."* Helsinki: Academia Scientiarum Fennica, 1990.

———. "The Innocent Persecuted Heroine Genre: An Analysis of Its Structures and Themes." *Western Folklore* 52, 1 (1993): 13–41.

———. *The Fairy Tale: The Magic Mirror of the Imagination.* New York: Twayne, 1995.

Jordan, Elaine. "Enthralment: Angela Carter's Speculative Fictions." *Plotting Change: Contemporary Women's Fiction.* Ed. Linda Anderson. London: Edward Arnold, 1990. 18–40.

———. "The Dangers of Angela Carter." *New Feminist Discourses. Critical Essays on Theories and Texts.* Ed. Isobel Armstrong. New York: Routledge, 1992. 119–31.

Klinkowitz, Jerome. *Literary Disruptions/The Making of Post-Contemporary Fiction,* Urbana: University of Illinois Press, 1975.

Leach, Maria and Jerome Fried, eds. *Funk & Wagnalls Standard Dictionary of Folklore, Mythology, and Legend.* 1949. Rev. ed. New York: Harper & Row, 1972.

Lerner, Gerda. *The Creation of Patriarchy.* Oxford: Oxford University Press, 1986.

Lewallen, Avis. "Wayward Girls But Wicked Women? Female Sexuality in Angela Carter's *The Bloody Chamber.*" *Perspectives on Pornography: Sexuality in Film and Literature.* Ed. Gary Day and Clive Bloom. New York: St. Martin's Press, 1988. 144–57.

Lewis, Mary Ellen B. "The Study of Folklore and Literature: An Expanded View." *Southern Folklore Quarterly* 40 (1976): 343–51.

Lewis, Philip. "Bluebeard's Magic Key." *Les contes de Perrault, la contestation et ses limites, Furetière.* Ed. Michel Bareau, Jacques Barchilon et al. Paris:

Papers on French Seventeenth-Century Literature, 1987. 41–51.

Lindhal, Carl. "On the Borders of Oral and Written Art." *Folklore Forum* 11 (1978): 94–123.

Lokke, Kari E. "*Bluebeard* and *The Bloody Chamber*: The Grotesque of Self-Parody and Self-Assertion." *Frontiers* 10, 1 (1988): 7–12.

Lüthi, Max. *The European Folktale: Form and Nature*. 1974. Trans. John D. Niles. Bloomington: Indiana University Press, 1986.

———. *The Fairytale as Art Form and Portrait of Man*. 1975. Trans. Jon Erickson. Bloomington: Indiana University Press, 1987.

McGlathery, James M. *Fairy Tale Romance. The Grimms, Basile, and Perrault*. Urbana: University of Illinois Press, 1991.

Manley, Kathleen E. B. "Disney's 'Beauty and the Beast': Perpetuating Some American Beliefs About Gender Relationships." American Folklore Society Meeting. Jacksonville, Florida, 1992.

———. "Atwood's Reconstruction of Folktales: *The Handmaid's Tale* and 'Bluebeard's Egg.'" *Approaches to Teaching Atwood's "The Handmaid's Tale" and Other Works*. Ed. Sharon R. Wilson, Thomas B. Friedman, and Shannon Henger. New York: Modern Language Association, 1996.

Mieder, Wolfgang. "Survival Forms of 'Little Red Riding Hood' in Modern Society." *International Folklore Review* 2 (1982): 23–40.

———. *Tradition and Innovation in Folk Literature*. Hanover, N.H.: University Press of New England, 1987.

Miller, Nancy K. "Emphasis Added: Plots and Plausibilities in Women's Fictions." *The New Feminist Criticism: Essays on Women, Literature, and Theory*. Ed. Elaine Showalter. New York: Pantheon, 1985. 339–60.

Mills, Margaret. "Critical Theory and the Folklorists: Performance, Interpretive Authority, and Gender." *Southern Folklore* 47 (1990): 5–16.

———. "Feminist Theory and the Study of Folklore: A Twenty Year Trajectory." *Western Folklore* 52, 2–3–4 (1993): 173–92.

Mulvey, Laura. "Cinema Magic and the Old Monsters: Angela Carter's Cinema." Sage, *The Flesh and the Mirror*. 230–42.

Narvaez, Peter. "Chuck Berry as Postmodern Composer-Performer." Preston, *Folklore, Literature, and Cultural Theory*. 169–86.

Nenola, Aili. "Folklore and the Genderized World: Or Twelve Points from a Feminist Perspective." *Nordic Frontiers. Recent Issues in the Study of Modern Traditional Culture in the Nordic Countries*. Ed. Pertti J. Antonnen and Reimund Kvideland. Turku: Nordic Institute of Folklore, 1993. 49–62.

Nicholson, Linda, ed. *Feminism/Postmodernism*. New York: Routledge, 1990.

Nicolaisen, W.F.H. "Why Tell Stories?" *Fabula* 31 (1991): 5–10.

———. "Why Tell Stories About Innocent Persecuted Heroines?" *Western Folklore* 52, 1 (1993): 61–71.

Nutt, Alfred. "The Lai of Eliduc and the *Märchen* of Little Snow White." *Folk-Lore* 3 (1892): 26–28.

Oring, Elliott. "On the Meanings of Mother Goose." *Western Folklore* 46

(1987): 106–11.

Otten, Charlotte. *A Lycanthropy Reader.* New York: Dorset Press, 1986.

Panttaja, Elizabeth. "Going Up in the World: Class in 'Cinderella.'" *Western Folklore* 52, 1 (1993): 85–104.

Perco, Daniela. "Female Initiation in Northern Italian Versions of 'Cinderella.'" Trans. Cristina Bacchilega. *Western Folklore* 52, 1 (1993): 73–74.

Picherit, Jean-Louis G. "Qui était Barbe Bleue?" *Neuphilologische Mitteilungen: Bulletin de la Societé Neophilologique/Bulletin of the Modern Language Society* 89, 3 (1988): 374–77.

Preston, Cathy Lynn. "'Cinderella' as a Dirty Joke: Gender, Multivocality, and the Polysemic Text." *Western Folklore* 53, 1 (1994): 27–49.

———, ed. *Folklore, Literature, and Cultural Theory: Collected Essays.* New York: Garland, 1995.

Radner, Joan N., ed. *Feminist Messages: Coding in Women's Folk Culture.* Urbana and Chicago: University of Illinois Press, 1993.

Ralston, W.R.S. "Beauty and the Beast." *Nineteenth Century* 4 (July 1878): 990–1012.

Rieder, John. "Two Adaptations of 'Beauty and the Beast.'" *1992 Proceedings. Literature and Hawaii's Children. Stories as Bridges to Many Realms.* Ed. Judith Kellogg and Jesse Crisler, Honolulu: Literature and Hawaii's Children, 1995. 236–41.

Roemer, Danielle M. "Angela Carter's 'The Bloody Chamber': Liminality and Reflexivity." American Folklore Society Meeting, Jacksonville, Florida. October 1992.

———. "Graffiti as Story and Act." Preston, *Folklore, Literature, and Cultural Theory.* 22–28.

Röhrich, Lutz. *Folktales and Reality.* Trans. Peter Tokofsky. Bloomington: Indiana University Press, 1991.

Rose, Ellen Cronan. "Through the Looking Glass: When Women Tell Fairy Tales." *The Voyage In: Fictions of Female Development.* Ed. Elizabeth Abel, Marianne Hirsch, and Elizabeth Langland. Hanover, N.H.: University Press of New England for Dartmouth, 1983. 209–27.

Rosenberg, Bruce A. *Folklore and Literature. Rival Siblings.* Knoxville: University of Tennessee Press, 1991.

Ruf, Theodor. *Die Schöne aus dem Glassarg.* Würzburg: Königshausen Neumann, 1995.

Rumpf, Marianne. "Rotkäppchen: Eine vergleichende Märchenuntersuchung." Ph.D. dissertation, Göttingen 1951.

Saintyves, Pierre. *Les contes de Perrault et les récits parallèles.* Ed. Francis Lacassin. Paris: Robert Laffont, 1987.

Sage, Lorna, ed. *The Flesh and the Mirror: Essays on the Art of Angela Carter.* London: Virago, 1994.

Sautman, Francesca, "Le conte 425B: Rites de mariage et parcours magique." *Merveilles et Contes* 3, 1 (1989): 28–44.

Scherf, Walter. *Lexikon der Zaubermärchen.* Stuttgart: Kröner, 1982.

Sheets, Robin Ann. "Pornography, Fairy Tales, and Feminism: Angela

Carter's 'The Bloody Chamber.'" *Journal of the History of Sexuality* 1 (1991): 633–57.

Sight & Sound. Review of *The Piano.* 3, 10 (1993): 6.

Soriano, Marc. *Les contes de Perrault: Culture savante et traditions populaires.* Paris: Gallimard, 1968.

———. "Le petit chaperon rouge." *Nouvelle Revue Française* 16(1968): 429–43.

Stahl, Sandra Dolby. *Literary Folkloristics and the Personal Narrative.* Bloomington: Indiana University Press, 1989.

Stewart, Susan. *Nonsense. Aspects of Intertextuality in Folklore and Literature.* Baltimore: The Johns Hopkins Press, 1978.

Stone, Kay. "Feminist Approaches to the Interpretation of Fairy Tales." Bottigheimer, *Fairy Tales and Society.* 229–36.

Summers, Montague. *The Werewolf.* London: Kegan Paul, Trench, Trubner & Co., 1933.

Swahn, Jan-Öjvind. *The Tale of Cupid and Psyche.* Lund: CWK Gleerup, 1955.

Tatar, Maria. *The Hard Facts of the Grimms' Fairy Tales.* Princeton, N.J.: Princeton University Press, 1987.

———. *Off with Their Heads! Fairy Tales and the Culture of Childhood.* Princeton: Princeton University Press, 1992.

Tenèze, Marie Louise. "Du conte merveilleux comme genre." *Arts et Traditions Populaires* 18 (1978): 11–65.

Turner, Victor. *The Forest of Symbols: Aspects of Ndembu Ritual.* Ithaca, N.Y.: Cornell University Press, 1967.

Uther, Hans-Jörg. "Der Frauenmörder Blaubart und seine Artverwandten." *Schweizerisches Archiv für Volkskunde.* 84.1–2 (1988): 35–54.

Velay-Vallantin, Catherine. *L'histoire des contes.* Paris: Fayard (CNL), 1992.

Verdier, Yvonne. "Grand-mères, si vous saviez . . . Le petit chaperon rouge dans la tradition orale." *Cahiers de Littérature Orale* 4 (1978): 17–55.

Walker, Nancy A. *The Disobedient Writer: Women and Narrative Tradition.* Austin: University of Texas Press, 1995.

Ward, Donald. "'Beauty and the Beast': Fact and Fancy, Past and Present." *Midwestern Folklore* 15, 2 (1989): 119–25.

Warner, Marina. "Mother Goose Tales: Female Fiction, Female Fact?" *Folklore* 101 (1990): 3–25.

———. *From the Beast to the Blonde: On Fairy Tales and Their Tellers.* London: Chatto & Windus, 1994.

Wicke, Jennifer and Margaret Ferguson. "Introduction: Feminism and Postmodernism." *boundary* 2 19, 2 (1992): 1–9.

Wilcox, Helen, Keith McWatters, Ann Thompson, and Linda R. Williams, eds. *The Body and the Text: Hélène Cixous, Reading and Teaching.* New York: St. Martin's Press, 1990.

Wilde, Alan. "Barthelme Unfair to Kierkegaard: Some Thoughts on Modern and Post-Modern Irony," *boundary* 2 5 (Fall 1976): 45–70.

Williams, J. P. "'A Bond Stronger Than Friendship or Love': Female Psychological Development and *Beauty and the Beast.*" *NWSA Journal* 4, 1

(1992): 59–72.

Wilson, Sharon Rose. "Bluebeard's Forbidden Room: Gender Images in Margaret Atwood's Visual and Literary Art." *American Review of Canadian Studies* 16 (1986): 385–97.

———. *Margaret Atwood's Fairy-Tale Sexual Politics.* Jackson: University Press of Mississippi, 1993.

Workman, Mark. "The Serious Consequences of Ethnic Humor in *Portnoy's Complaint.*" *Midwestern Folklore* 13 (1987): 16–26.

———. "Folklore in the Wilderness: Folklore and Postmodernism." *Midwestern Folklore* 15 (1989): 5–14.

———. "Narratable and Unnarratable Lives." *Western Folklore* 51, 1 (1992): 97–107.

———. "Tropes, Hopes, and Dopes." *Journal of American Folklore* 106 (1993): 171–83.

———. "Folklore and the Literature of Exile." Preston, *Folklore, Literature, and Cultural Theory.* 29–42.

Young, Katherine and Barbara Babcock, eds. "Bodylore." *Journal of American Folklore* 107 (1994).

Ziolkowski, Jan M. "A Fairy Tale from Before Fairy Tales: Egbert of Liège's 'De puella a lupellis seruata' and the Medieval Background of 'Little Red Riding Hood.'" *Speculum* 67 (1992): 549–75.

Zipes, Jack. *Breaking the Magic Spell: Radical Theories of Folk and Fairy Tales.* Austin: University of Texas Press, 1979.

———. *Fairy Tales and the Art of Subversion.* London: Wildman, 1983.

———. *The Brothers Grimm: From Enchanted Forests to the Modern World.* New York: Routledge, Chapman and Hall, 1988.

———. "The Changing Function of the Fairy Tale." *The Lion and the Unicorn* 12, 2 (1988): 7–31.

———. *The Trials and Tribulations of Little Red Riding Hood.* New York: Routledge, 1993 (rev. ed.).

———. *Fairy Tale as Myth/Myth as Fairy Tale.* Lexington: University Press of Kentucky, 1994.

INDEX

LaVergne, TN USA
15 April 2010
179373LV00002B/118/A